This book is designed to provide students of phonology with an accessible introduction to the phonological architecture of words. It offers a thorough discussion of the basic building blocks of phonology – in particular features, sounds, syllables and feet – and deals with a range of different theories about these units. Colin Ewen and Harry van der Hulst present their study within a non-linear framework, discussing the contributions of autosegmental phonology, dependency phonology, government phonology and metrical phonology, among others. Their coherent, integrated approach reveals that the differences between these models are not as great as is sometimes believed. The book provides a more detailed analysis of this subject than previously available in introductory textbooks and is an invaluable and indispensable first step towards understanding the major theoretical issues in modern phonology at the word level.

D1056545

CAMBRIDGE TEXTBOOKS IN LINGUISTICS

General editors: S. R. ANDERSON, J. BRESNAN, B. COMRIE,
W. DRESSLER, C. J. EWEN, R. HUDDLESTON, R. LASS,
D. LIGHTFOOT, J. LYONS, P. H. MATTHEWS, R. POSNER,
S. ROMAINE, N. V. SMITH, N. VINCENT

THE PHONOLOGICAL STRUCTURE OF WORDS

THE PHONOLOGICAL STRUCTURE OF WORDS

AN INTRODUCTION

COLIN J. EWEN

UNIVERSITY OF LEIDEN

HARRY VAN DER HULST

UNIVERSITY OF CONNECTICUT

CAMBRIDGE
UNIVERSITY PRESS

PUBLISHED BY THE PRESS SYNDICATE OF THE UNIVERSITY OF CAMBRIDGE
The Pitt Building, Trumpington Street, Cambridge, United Kingdom

CAMBRIDGE UNIVERSITY PRESS
The Edinburgh Building, Cambridge CB2 2RU, UK   www.cup.cam.ac.uk
40 West 20th Street, New York, NY 10011–4211, USA   www.cup.org
10 Stamford Road, Oakleigh, Melbourne 3166, Australia
Ruiz de Alarcón 13, 28014 Madrid, Spain

First published 2001

Printed in the United Kingdom at the University Press, Cambridge

Typeface 9.5/13 pt Times NR   [GT]

A catalogue record for this book is available from the British Library

Library of Congress Cataloguing in Publication data
Ewen, Colin J.
    The phonological structure of words: an introduction / Colin J. Ewen, Harry van
der Hulst.
    p. cm. – (Cambridge textbooks in linguistics)
    Includes bibliographical references and index.
    ISBN 0 521 35019 0 (hardback) – ISBN 0 521 35914 7 (paperback)
    1. Grammar, Comparative and general – Phonology. I. Hulst, Harry van der. II.
Title. III. Series.
    P217.E94   2000
    414 – dc21   00-025958

ISBN 0 521 350190 hardback
ISBN 0 521 359147 paperback

CONTENTS

PREFACE

Our aim in writing this book has been to introduce the reader to some of the issues in the representation of the structure of the basic units of phonology. We have approached this by first, in Chapters 1 and 2, considering the ways in which the smallest phonological units, features, characterise the structure of sounds, or, more technically, segments. Chapters 3 and 4 are concerned with larger phonological units, in particular syllables and feet. As the title of the book suggests, we do not consider the representation of phonological units larger than the word, and therefore pay little attention to topics such as intonation.

Most of our analyses are formulated in terms of what has come to be referred to as **non-linear phonology**, as opposed to the 'linear' theories of phonological representation manifested in work in the tradition of Chomsky and Halle (1968). The term 'non-linear phonology' does not refer to a single coherent theory of the representation of phonological structure – whether segment-internal or suprasegmental – rather, since the early 1980s, work in phonology which has been concerned with enriching the structural properties of linear models has dealt with different aspects of these models, so that various apparently distinct theories have grown up. Two of the most familiar of these are **metrical phonology**, originating in the work of Liberman (1975) and Liberman and Prince (1977), and **autosegmental phonology**, which finds its first exposition in Goldsmith (1976). However, in recent years it has become apparent that many of the claims made in the various models are not in fact independent of each other, and that claims made within the framework of one approach are often restatements of those made elsewhere. In this book, therefore, we shall attempt to avoid a strict delineation between different 'sub-theories', and we shall concentrate on presenting what we consider to be the most characteristic aspects of non-linear phonology in general. It has therefore not been our intention to present any of these sub-theories in detail; rather, it has been our concern to show the reader how elements from various approaches might coexist in the characterisation of phonological structure.

The number of issues which might be dealt with in a book on phonological representation is substantial. Here, however, we are concerned with presenting the most important aspects of the subject to the student who is approaching it with little previous knowledge, and we have concentrated on presenting the material in such a way that it is reasonably self-contained, and, we hope, indicates the areas in which the theory makes interesting claims. However, we assume a basic knowledge of phonetic theory and terminology. In addition, some familiarity with basic phonological concepts which do not form an essential part of a specifically non-linear approach to phonology, such as traditional phoneme theory, is also desirable. Where appropriate, we refer to other sources for discussion of topics of a more general phonological nature.

Representation is only one aspect of a fully fledged phonological theory. Such a theory combines a specific view on phonological representations with a view on the relationship between various levels of structure, sometimes referred to as underlying (or lexical) structure and surface structure. More generally, what is the relationship between the most abstract level of representation, the input, and the least abstract, the output? Current views on the relationship between input and output are that the amount of computation required to get from one to the other must be minimal. In some theories, in fact, input and output are non-distinct. More often, however, they are distinct, and are related by a system that either derives the output via a set of (transformational) rules or by a procedure of selecting the correct output from a pool of possible candidates (as in Optimality Theory; see Kager 1999 for an introduction to Optimality Theory). In this book we take no principled stand with respect to these matters. As a matter of convenience we formulate most of the processes we consider in terms of derivational rules, but we are not concerned with the status of these rules in the phonology of the language under consideration; they should be viewed primarily as descriptive devices.

The material used for exemplification has been drawn as far as possible from languages which are likely to be reasonably familiar to many readers, in particular from English. This is in keeping with our aim of making the book accessible to as wide a readership as possible, rather than representing any prejudice on our part. Where evidence from these sources for a particular point does not exist, however, we have drawn our data from less familiar languages.

We hope that this book can be used as a first step towards an understanding of some of the major theoretical issues in modern phonology. As such, it is of interest (and accessible) to students and researchers who either intend to specialise further in phonology or need a thorough grounding in the issues of representation in phonology.

This book has been a long time in the making. The fact that it has been completed is due primarily to the encouragement and patience of the editorial staff – past and present – at Cambridge University Press. We are sincerely grateful to, among others, Judith Ayling, Kate Brett, Penny Carter and Andrew Winnard; we appreciate how lucky we have been. We have been equally fortunate to have Neil Smith as our series editor. Apart from the fact that he has saved us from getting some of our more spectacular errors into print, he has been a fund of useful and relevant advice on content and presentation. Many generations of students have been confronted with earlier versions of parts of this book. We are grateful to all of them, particularly those whose comments have helped us to improve it, and we are equally appreciative of other people who have taken the trouble to comment on the manuscript. Among others, those who have helped us in the latter stages of the book's writing include Véronique van Gelderen, Martina Noteboom, Nancy Ritter, Erik Jan van der Torre and Jeroen van de Weijer. None of them – nor anyone else – is responsible for what we have done with their advice.

I
Segments

1.1 Introduction

The fact that words, or more generally stretches of speech, can be divided up into individual segments, or speech-sounds, is familiar to speakers of languages. Thus speakers of English will generally agree that the word *bat* consists of the three sounds 'b', 'a' and 't'. They will further agree that the spelling system of English, i.e. its orthography, does not correspond in a one-to-one fashion to the 'sounds' of the language, so that a word such as *thatch*, although made up of six distinct orthographic symbols, contains only three, or perhaps four, sounds: 'th', 'a' and 'tch' (or perhaps 't' and 'ch'). This discrepancy means that phoneticians and phonologists require a system of transcription for the units of sound analogous to, but different from, that for the units of spelling. Various such systems have been proposed, and are familiar to the user of any dictionary giving the 'pronunciation' of the words of a language. In this book we will generally use the transcription system of the International Phonetic Association (IPA; see Appendix).

The transcription of the sounds of a word is not an entirely straightforward undertaking, and raises interesting theoretical questions in phonology. Thus the transcription of the English word *thatch* requires a decision (implicit or explicit) on the part of the compiler of the system as to whether the sequence *tch* represents two sounds, or **phonological segments** (specifically the two sounds found at the beginning of English *tore* /tɔː/ and *shore* /ʃɔː/),[1] or whether it is to be treated as a single sound, normally referred to as an **affricate**. In systems based on the IPA alphabet, the first option is taken, so that *chore* is represented phonemically as /tʃɔː/ and *thatch* as /θætʃ/, with *ch* or *tch* being

---

[1] In this book we will in general transcribe English words in the form in which they are realised in RP (Received Pronunciation), the prestige accent of British English. This is a matter of convenience; we are not thereby implying that RP has in any sense a privileged status in terms of its linguistic properties. We will, however, frequently consider other varieties where necessary; in particular we will have occasion to examine data from **rhotic** dialects, i.e. dialects in which postvocalic /r/ is pronounced. RP is non-rhotic, as evidenced by the realisations /tɔː/ and /ʃɔː/ for *tore* and *shore*; compare the pronunciations /toːr/ and /ʃoːr/ (or /toːɹ/ and /ʃoːɹ/) in a rhotic dialect such as Scots English.

I

represented as a sequence of /t/ and /ʃ/ (although the claim that /t/ and /ʃ/ are more closely related than a normal pair of segments can be indicated by the use of a ligature, as in /θæt͡ʃ/, or, more commonly, by combining the two symbols, as in /θætʃ/). In North American systems, however, such orthographic sequences are generally treated unambiguously as single segments, so that we find transcriptions such as /θæč/.

Notice that the concept of affricate illustrates not only that the relationship between sound and spelling is not entirely straightforward, but also, and perhaps more obviously of relevance for the phonologist, that the relationship between 'phonetic' and 'phonological' representation is also a matter of analysis. From a purely phonetic point of view, the nature of the relationship between the stop and the fricative in the final cluster of English *thatch* does not seem markedly different from that between the stop and the fricative in the final cluster of *hats*: in both cases we have a *phonetic* sequence of stop + fricative, [t̠ʃ] and [ts], respectively (we adopt the usual convention of giving phonetic representations in square brackets, and phonological ones between slant brackets; the line under [t] in [t̠ʃ] denotes retraction of the articulation, in this case to the postalveolar place of articulation of the [ʃ]). However, while the *tch* sequence is commonly treated as an affricate in phonological analysis, phonologists do not generally make a similar claim for the *ts* sequence of *hats*. On the other hand, the phonetically more or less identical cluster in German *Satz* [zats] 'sentence' *is* so treated.

The reasons for these differences (which we will not explore in any detail here) are thus phonological, rather than phonetic, although it is usually claimed that for something to be considered phonologically an affricate it must in any case have the phonetic property of **homorganicity**: i.e. the stop and the fricative must have the same place of articulation, so that [ts] (where both elements are alveolar) and [t̠ʃ] (where both elements are postalveolar) are both conceivable phonological affricates, while a sequence such as [ps] in English *cups* would not be. This claim is associated with the fact that it is just these homorganic sequences which may display a different distribution from 'normal' sequences of consonants. Affricates can generally occur *both* in syllable-initial position *and* in syllable-final position in a language, and thus violate the 'mirror-image' constraint on syllable structure.[2] This constraint states that a consonant cluster which can be syllable-initial in a language cannot be syllable-final, while the same cluster with its consonants in reverse order shows the opposite properties. English is typical in having initial /kl-/ and final /-lk/ (*class*, *sulk*), but not initial */lk-/ or final */-kl/ within a single

---

[2] We consider syllable structure in Chapter 3.

syllable. Contrast this with the distribution of affricates: /tʃ/ can be both initial and final in English (*chip* /tʃɪp/ and *pitch* /pɪtʃ/), as can /ts/ in German (*Ziel* /tsiːl/ 'goal' and *Satz*). On the other hand, the English sequence /ts/, like other stop + fricative sequences (e.g. /ps/, /ks/), occurs only in syllable-final position (and then almost exclusively as the result of morphological suffixation: e.g. *hats* = HAT + PLURAL).[3]

A full discussion of the status of affricates would take us much further. We return in §1.4 to the status of segments (or sequences) such as these, which exemplify the problem of dealing with what have been referred to as 'complex segments', and we will see that these phenomena have been the trigger for a great deal of interesting work in theories dealing with representation in phonology. Let us first, however, consider a rather more fundamental question regarding phonological representation: does the phonological segment have any internal structure? That is, is there anything which we can say about the way in which sounds behave by assuming some sort of internal structure which we could not say by having segments as the smallest phonological units?

1.2 Evidence for internal structure

It is not difficult to demonstrate that phonological segments in languages can be grouped together, in the sense that particular sets of segments may undergo what seems to be the same kind of **phonological process**. We are assuming here, fairly non-controversially, that it is reasonable to talk about phonological processes, in which a particular segment, or, more importantly here, a group of segments, is affected in some way. These may be either 'events' in the history of a language or relationships holding between the most abstract phonological representation of a segment or group of segments and its surface phonetic realisation.[4]

One such phonological process is that of **nasal place assimilation**, whereby a nasal consonant has the same place of articulation as a following obstruent (i.e. a stop, fricative or affricate). In English, for example, the effects of this process can be identified in various contexts, as in (1):[5]

---

[3] We indicate morphemes, i.e. minimal syntactic units, by the use of small capitals, as here.

[4] In the context of this book, however, we will beg the question of exactly what is meant by a surface 'phonetic' representation. For practical purposes, the 'surface' representations we consider will be fairly 'shallow' or 'concrete' *phonological* representations. Nevertheless, we will continue to refer to such representations as phonetic. More generally, as we noted in the Preface, we are assuming a model of phonology which is essentially derivational, in the tradition of Chomsky and Halle (1968). We do not adopt here the constraint-based model of Optimality Theory (see, e.g., McCarthy and Prince 1993; Prince and Smolensky 1993; Kager 1999). This is a matter of convenience, however, as we claim that much of what we have to say about the phonological representation of words is independent of whether we adopt a derivational or a constraint-based approach.

[5] The asterisks in (1c) denote that a sequence is ill formed.

3

(1) a. Edinburgh [ɛmbrə]
         handbook   [hæmbʊk]
     b. unpopular [ʌmpɒpjələ]
         unfair   [ʌɱfɛə]
     c. camber   [kæmbə]   *[kænbə]   *[kæŋbə]
         canter   [kæntə]   *[kæmtə]   *[kæŋtə]
         canker   [kæŋkə]   *[kæmkə]   *[kænkə]

(1) shows examples of agreement in place of articulation between the nasal and the following obstruent. (1a, b) involve optional assimilations, particularly associated with fast-speech situations: realisations such as /ɛdɪnbʌrə/ and /ʌnpɒpjələ/, which do not show assimilation, also occur, of course. Those in (1b) can be analysed morphologically as involving a prefix ending underlyingly in the alveolar nasal /n/; e.g. UN + FAIR /ʌn + fɛə/. This analysis is supported by the fact that in such cases there are only two possible phonetic realisations of the nasal in the prefix: either as [n] or as the nasal which is homorganic with the following consonant. In addition, if there is no question of a possible assimilation, as in (2), where the following morpheme begins with a vowel or /h/, the only possible realisation is [n]:

(2) unequal [ʌniːkwəl]
     unhappy [ʌnhæpɪ]

The forms in (1c) demonstrate a general constraint on English intervocalic clusters (at least those immediately following a stressed vowel within a single morpheme), which states that a sequence of nasal + stop must be homorganic. These differ from (1a, b), however, in that we are no longer dealing with cases in which, say, the labial nasal can be said to be *derived* from an alveolar nasal, as in [ɛmbrə] or [ʌmpɒpjələ] – there is no possibility of *camber* or *canker* occurring with /n/, as in *[kænbə] or *[kænkə], and there is no internal morphological structure which would lead us to suspect that these words have some kind of prefix CAN-.

Thus the process of nasal place assimilation is instantiated in various ways in English, and indeed in many other languages. However, our concerns here are not primarily with the status of the various different types of examples in the phonology of English; rather they focus on the characterisation of this type of process. In other words, how can we formalise the constraint represented in various ways by the data in (1)? Let us consider first (1a, b), in which we see that a cluster of /n/ followed by a stop may become homorganic in English. If the smallest available phonological units are complete segments, then we might represent the processes as in (3) (for the sake of simplicity, we ignore the case of nasals preceding /f/):

4

(3)   a.   /n/ → [m] / __ {/p/, /b/}
    b.   /n/ → [ŋ] / __ {/k/, /g/}

We use here a traditional **linear** type of notation for phonological rules:[6] the arrow denotes 'is realised as'; the underlying segment is given in slant brackets and its surface phonetic realisation in square brackets; the horizontal line denotes the environment in which the segment affected by the rule occurs, in this case preceding {/p/, /b/}; and the braces denote a set of segments. (3a), then, can be read as: 'Underlying /n/ is realised as phonetic [m] when it precedes either /p/ or /b/.'

There are various objections which can be raised with respect to the formulations of nasal place assimilation in (3). The common core of these objections is that the two parts do not look any more likely to be recurrent phonological rules than, say, any of the processes in (4), which are not likely to occur in any language:

(4)   a.   /n/ → [m] / __ {/k/, /g/}
    b.   /n/ → [ŋ] / __ {/p/, /b/}
    c.   /n/ → [m] / __ {/k/, /d/}
    d.   /n/ → [l] / __ {/t/, /d/}

Formally, the various rules in (4) are no more or less complex than those in (3), which express recurrent processes – surely an undesirable state of affairs. More particularly, the type of formulation in (3) and (4) is inadequate in two ways. In the first place, the formalism fails to relate the change characterised by a particular rule to the environment in which it occurs. Thus (4a), in which an alveolar nasal becomes labial in the environment of velar stops, is no more difficult to formulate than (3a), in which the same change takes place in the environment of labial stops. Yet (3a) is a natural process of assimilation, while (4a) is not. Secondly, the formalism does not show that the sets of consonants in the environments in (3a, b) are ones that we would expect to find triggering the same kind of change, whereas that in (4c), a set consisting of a voiceless velar stop and a voiced alveolar stop, would be most unlikely to be responsible for the change in (4c) (or, indeed, any other assimilation process). Again, though, (4c) is no more difficult to formulate than any of the other rules in (3) and (4).

This state of affairs clearly arises because we have neither isolated the phonetic properties which are shared by the set of segments involved in the process – nasality in the case of the input and the output (why should the output of (3a) be [m] rather than, say, [l]?); place of articulation in the

---

[6] See the Preface for a discussion of the difference between linear and non-linear approaches to phonological representation.

case of the output and the environment – nor incorporated them in our rule. In other words, we have failed to take account of the fact that it is the phonetic properties of segments which are responsible for their phonological behaviour, i.e. that phonological segments are not indivisible wholes, but are made up of properties, or, as they are usually referred to, **features**, which to a large extent correspond to the properties familiar from traditional phonetic description.

Furthermore, the fact that a change such as (4c) is an unlikely candidate for an assimilation rule shows that the class of segments triggering the process must share a particular property – in the case of (3a), for example, the property of labiality. A further examination of the phonologies of languages of the world would quickly show that a class of segments like this forms what is referred to as a **natural class**, i.e. a set of segments which *recurrently* participates as a class in phonological processes, such as the ones sketched above. Thus a set of segments which shares some phonetic property or combination of properties, to the exclusion of other sets of segments, forms a natural class.

Let us now identify a number of (ad hoc) phonological features which are relevant here, specifically [nasal], [labial], [alveolar] and [velar]. (Features are by convention enclosed in square brackets.)

We can use these features to write a general rule to characterise the assimilation processes illustrated by (3):

$$(5) \quad \text{a.} \begin{bmatrix} \text{nasal} \\ \text{alveolar} \end{bmatrix} \rightarrow \text{[labial]} / \_\_ \text{[labial]}$$

$$\text{b.} \begin{bmatrix} \text{nasal} \\ \text{alveolar} \end{bmatrix} \rightarrow \text{[velar]} / \_\_ \text{[velar]}$$

However, we can formulate a rather more general statement about nasal place assimilation in English, which will also incorporate the data in (1c), in which there appears to be no reason to derive [m] and [ŋ] from an underlying /n/. This general statement about the class of nasals is given in (6):

(6) a. [nasal] → [labial] / __ [labial]
    b. [nasal] → [alveolar] / __ [alveolar]
    c. [nasal] → [velar] / __ [velar]

(6) successfully shows that the rule is a statement about a particular class of segments, nasals, characterised by a single feature which serves to distinguish the class from any other segments in the language. In other words, only nasals undergo the processes characterised by the rule, and no other segments in the language. Furthermore, it shows that the outputs and environments share a feature, namely the feature characterising place of articulation, which

6

makes just these processes more likely to occur than those in (4), for example. (6) is a non-arbitrary process, then.

Examples like these, which are typical of the way in which phonological processes operate in language, provide evidence for incorporating features in phonological description. It is with the nature of these features, and more particularly the question of whether they are organised in any way in the representation of segments, that we will be largely concerned in the remainder of this chapter.

However, at this point, let us note that the particular formulation in (6) will turn out to be far from adequate on a number of grounds, which do not, however, affect the validity of the points just made. Let us consider here just two of the problems.

(6) appears to consist of three sub-processes, whereas, as we have seen, nasal place assimilation is a single process in English. In traditional linear phonology, it is usual to 'collapse' rules like those in (6), all of which share the same input, to give (7):

(7)
$$[\text{nasal}] \rightarrow \begin{cases} [\text{labial}] \,/\, \_\_ \, [\text{labial}] \\ [\text{alveolar}] \,/\, \_\_ \, [\text{alveolar}] \\ [\text{velar}] \,/\, \_\_ \, [\text{velar}] \end{cases}$$

The three expressions contained in braces are to be seen as alternatives; i.e. nasals are labial before labials, alveolar before alveolars and velar before velars. Thus the 'shared' part of the rule – the input – is mentioned only once.[7]

However, conventions such as that used in (7) still permit the collapse of unrelated rules, as well as rules which apparently belong together. Thus some languages have a rule whereby a nasal consonant becomes voiceless preceding a voiceless (aspirated) consonant. In some dialects of Icelandic, for example, *hempa* /hɛmpʰa/ 'cassock' is realised as [hɛm̥pa], with devoicing of the /m/. There seems to be no formal reason why the rule characterising this process cannot be collapsed with (7), especially as Icelandic also has nasal place assimilation processes:

(8)
$$[\text{nasal}] \rightarrow \begin{cases} [\text{labial}] \,/\, \_\_ \, [\text{labial}] \\ [\text{alveolar}] \,/\, \_\_ \, [\text{alveolar}] \\ [\text{velar}] \,/\, \_\_ \, [\text{velar}] \\ [\text{voiceless}] \,/\, \_\_ \, [\text{voiceless}] \end{cases}$$

In other words, we have still failed to show that the features involved in the nasal assimilation process, i.e. [labial], [alveolar] and [velar], are related to

---

[7] A fuller formulation of the rule in question would also involve reference to other features; we ignore this here, as before.

each other in some way, i.e. that they characterise place of articulation, whereas [voiceless] is not related to any of the other three in this way.

A second problem is that, merely by incorporating features in our rules, rather than the segments of (3) and (4), we have not removed the possibility of formulating what are sometimes referred to as 'crazy rules'. Thus (9) is as easy to formulate as (7):

$$(9) \quad [\text{nasal}] \rightarrow \begin{cases} [\text{labial}] \,/\, \_\_ [\text{alveolar}] \\ [\text{alveolar}] \,/\, \_\_ [\text{velar}] \\ [\text{velar}] \,/\, \_\_ [\text{labial}] \end{cases}$$

Underlying these criticisms of the formal conventions of linear phonology is the belief that a phonological theory should be as restrictive as possible, in the sense that an ideal system should be able to represent only phonologically natural events and states, and should not be able to characterise unnatural events such as (4) or (9). This belief underpins many **non-linear** alternatives to the formulations above, alternatives which we will begin to consider in §1.4. For the moment, however, we turn in greater detail to the nature of the features which will be required in phonology.

1.3 Phonological features

The idea that segments are made up of phonological features has a long tradition, and received its first comprehensive formalisation in Jakobson *et al.* (1951). The most widely known system is that proposed by Chomsky and Halle (1968; henceforth *SPE*), which differs from the Jakobsonian model in a number of respects, most notably in that the later features are based entirely on articulatory parameters, whereas those of Jakobson *et al.* were defined primarily in terms of acoustic properties. A second important difference involves the fact that many of the Jakobsonian features were relevant to the description and characterisation of both vowels and consonants, while the *SPE* system used largely separate sets of features. Feature theory is not unique to linear approaches to phonology; indeed, much work within non-linear phonology adopts the set of features proposed in the linear framework of *SPE*. However, non-linear phonology typically differs from linear accounts of the segment in incorporating a greater degree of internal structure than a simple list of features, as we shall demonstrate later in this chapter.

As there is a great deal of discussion of individual features available in the literature (e.g. Kenstowicz and Kisseberth 1979; Lass 1984a: chs. 5–6; Keating 1988a; Clements and Hume 1995), we shall not attempt to provide a comprehensive account of the features which would be required to characterise the segments making up the phonological system of English, for example. Rather, we shall introduce individual features as and when they become relevant, and only provide extensive discussion when necessary. Here the focus will be on how features interact in the representation of the segment, and in particular on the degree of structure required.

In the linear model of *SPE*, segments were viewed as consisting simply of an unordered list of binary features, which were established on grounds similar to those discussed above, i.e. the potential of a feature to define a natural class of segments. The features characterising a segment were organised into a **feature-matrix** in which the features were simply listed along with their value (either + or −) for the segment in question; thus the feature-matrix for the English vowel /iː/, for example, contains the following features, among others:

$$(10) \quad \begin{bmatrix} +\text{sonorant} \\ -\text{consonantal} \\ +\text{continuant} \\ +\text{voice} \\ +\text{high} \\ -\text{low} \\ -\text{back} \\ -\text{round} \end{bmatrix}$$

Within recent non-linear phonology, in which a more elaborate internal structure has been assigned to the segment, it has become customary to use a different type of formalism to represent the segment. We return in §§1.3.1 and 1.3.5 to the kind of motivation that can be adduced for suggesting a greater degree of structure than is embodied in (10); however, to facilitate comparison, we take the opportunity at this point of providing a 'non-linear' equivalent of (10), in which all of the features making up the segment are ASSOCIATED to a single segmental NODE, represented in (11) by 'o':

(11)

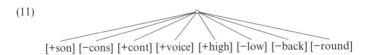

[+son] [−cons] [+cont] [+voice] [+high] [−low] [−back] [−round]

This node is generally referred to as the ROOT NODE – see §1.4.

In (11), as in (10), the features are unordered with respect to each other; any change in this ordering (vertical in the case of the feature-matrix in (10), horizontal in the case of the feature 'tree' in (11)) does not in this case yield anything different from the segment /iː/. We return in due course to the different claims made by the formalisms; in the meantime we devote a little space to the features themselves.

9

Segments

1.3.1 Major class features

The first two features in the matrix in (10) give the 'major class' to which the segment belongs, i.e. vowel; vowels are non-consonantal and, like liquids (i.e. *l* and *r* sounds) and nasals, they are sonorant. In the *SPE* model, sonorancy was defined in articulatory terms, as involving 'a vocal tract configuration in which spontaneous voicing is possible' (*SPE*: 302), but an acoustic definition is equally plausible: sonorant segments have relatively more periodic acoustic energy than non-sonorants (cf. Lass 1984a: 83). By characterising vowels, liquids and nasals as sharing the feature-value [+sonorant], of course, we are making the claim that they form a natural class (cf. §1.2), i.e. that there are phonological processes affecting just this group of segments, and no others. Equally, by assigning the value [–sonorant] to a particular group of segments (the class normally referred to as obstruents, made up of stops, fricatives and affricates), we are claiming that this group too should function as a class. It is not difficult to find processes to demonstrate this; thus the class of obstruents is typically the only class to display 'final devoicing' in many languages, as in various Scottish dialects of English, and Dutch, from which the examples in (12) are taken:

(12) *singular*   *plural*
  a. rib 'rib'   /rɪb/ [rɪp]   ribben /rɪbən/ [rɪbə]
     bed 'bed'   /bɛd/ [bɛt]   bedden /bɛdən/ [bɛdə]
  b. lip 'lip'   /lɪp/ [lɪp]   lippen /lɪpən/ [lɪpə]
     kat 'cat'   /kat/ [kat]   katten /katən/ [katə]
     nek 'neck' /nɛk/ [nɛk]   nekken /nɛkən/ [nɛkə]
  c. kam 'comb' /kam/ [kam]   kammen /kamən/ [kamə]
     man 'man'   /man/ [man]   mannen /manən/ [manə]
     ring 'ring' /rɪŋ/ [rɪŋ]   ringen /rɪŋən/ [rɪŋə]
     nar 'fool' /nar/ [nar]   narren /narən/ [narə]
     bel 'bell' /bɛl/ [bɛl]   bellen /bɛlən/ [bɛlə]

The obstruents in the singular forms of (12a, b), which are syllable-final, must be voiceless, irrespective of whether they are voiced (12a) or voiceless (12b) in other contexts, such as in the plural forms, where they occur intervocalically. Because the obstruents in (12a) are voiced in other contexts, we assume that they are phonologically, i.e. underlyingly, voiced. In other words, we ascribe their voicelessness in (12a) to the environment in which they occur, i.e. syllable-final position.[8]

[8] Notice that if we had assumed that the obstruents in (12a) were underlyingly voiceless, rather than voiced, we would not have been able to predict whether they would surface intervocalically as voiced (as in *bedden*) or voiceless (as in *katten*). However, it should not be thought that a state of affairs in which an underlying voiceless obstruent becomes voiced intervocalically in a language is impossible; indeed, intervocalic voicing is a very common process.

The liquids and nasals in (12c), however, remain voiced in all contexts. Thus the rule of final devoicing in Dutch must make reference to the natural class of non-sonorant consonants, and can be formulated as (13):

(13)   *Dutch Final Devoicing*
       [−son] → [−voice] / __]$_\sigma$

(where we use]$_\sigma$ to denote 'end of syllable').

We can also find cases in Dutch in which [+sonorant] functions as a natural class. Dutch has a process of diminutive formation in which the diminutive suffix is added to a noun. The suffix has a number of different allomorphs, illustrated in (14):

(14)   *noun* | | | | | *diminutive* |
|---|---|---|---|---|---|---|
| a. | nek | 'neck' | /nɛk/ | [nɛk] | nekje | [nɛkjə] |
| | pruik | 'wig' | /prœyk/ | [prœyk] | pruikje | [prœykjə] |
| b. | kam | 'comb' | /kɑm/ | [kɑm] | kammetje | [kɑmətjə] |
| c. | pruim | 'plum' | /prœym/ | [prœym] | pruimpje | [prœympjə] |
| | boon | 'bean' | /boːn/ | [boːn] | boontje | [boːntjə] |
| | haring | 'herring' | /haːrɪŋ/ | [haːrɪŋ] | harinkje | [haːrɪŋkjə] |
| | beer | 'bear' | /beːr/ | [beːr] | beertje | [beːrtjə] |
| | uil | 'owl' | /œyl/ | [œyl] | uiltje | [œyltjə] |
| d. | ui | 'onion' | /œy/ | [œy] | uitje | [œytjə] |

The form of the allomorph of the diminutive suffix is predictable according to the phonological form of the noun to which it is attached. Crucially for our purposes here, it takes the form [[stop] + jə] only if the preceding segment is [+sonorant] (a consonant in (14c), a vowel in (d)). (Notice that in (c) the stop assimilates in place to the preceding consonant; the difference between the forms of the suffix in (b) and (c) is due to the nature of the segments preceding the final liquid or nasal.) Thus [+sonorant], just like [−sonorant], can function to identify a natural class of segments.[9]

This phenomenon also provides evidence that natural classes can be defined by a combination of two or more features. (14b), for example, is representative of the larger class in (15):

(15) *noun*				*diminutive*	
kam	'comb'	/kɑm/	[kɑm]	kammetje	[kɑmətjə]
man	'man'	/mɑn/	[mɑn]	mannetje	[mɑnətjə]
ring	'ring'	/rɪŋ/	[rɪŋ]	ringetje	[rɪŋətjə]
nar	'fool'	/nɑr/	[nɑr]	narretje	[nɑrətjə]
bel	'bell'	/bɛl/	[bɛl]	belletje	[bɛlətjə]

[9] In this discussion we are making no assumptions about the underlying form of the diminutive suffix in Dutch, which has been an issue of some debate (see, e.g., Ewen 1978; Trommelen 1983; van der Hulst 1984; Booij 1995 for discussion of diminutive formation). The validity of the particular argument here depends on the assumption that the allomorphs [tjə], [pjə] and [kjə] are derived, rather than underlying.

The class of segments which determine the choice of the [-ətjə] suffix, i.e. the class of nasals and liquids, is defined by the feature combination [+sonorant, +consonantal], together with the nature of the preceding vowel.

Similar evidence from natural class behaviour can be cited in the justification of the various features which we identify in what follows. However, we will only consider such evidence when it is of particular interest for the point we are making.

The next two features in (10), [continuant] and [voice], are used to make further distinctions among the various major classes (vowels, liquids, nasals, obstruents). [+continuant] sounds differ from [–continuant] sounds in not having a complete closure in the oral tract. In the obstruent category ([–sonorant]), fricatives (e.g. /f v ʃ ʒ x ɣ χ/) are [+continuant], in that the stricture of close approximation does not block the airstream entirely, while stops (/p b t d k g q/, etc.) are [–continuant]. Similarly, within the [+sonorant, +consonantal] category, nasals (/m n ŋ/) are [–continuant], in that there is again a complete obstruction of the airstream in the oral cavity (although air does of course escape through the nasal cavity, so that nasal stops can be prolonged), while liquids are [+continuant].[10]

As might be expected, [+voice] sounds are those produced with vibration of the vocal cords; [–voice] are those with no such vibration.

In this discussion, we have implicitly assumed a grouping of features ([consonantal] with [sonorant], which together define 'major classes'; [voice] with [continuant], involved in characterising 'manner of articulation') which is in no way reflected in the matrix in (10). Indeed, the internal structure of the feature-matrix seems quite irrelevant – for example, as we have seen, changing the order in which the features occur in the matrix does not yield a segment which is different in any way. There is, however, a great deal of evidence that grouping of this kind is phonologically relevant: the sets of segments characterised by combinations of particular values of the features within these 'groups' are typically – and recurrently – appealed to in phonological

---

[10] Notice, though, that it has been claimed that lateral liquids are [–continuant], because, although there is a stricture of open approximation at the sides of the tongue, they also display complete *central* closure. This claim is given weight by the fact that there appear to be processes in some languages in which the lateral liquid forms a natural class with the nasals, as opposed to the non-lateral liquid. Thus Ó Dochartaigh (1978) notes that in some dialects of Scottish Gaelic short vowels diphthongise before /l n/, but lengthen before /r/. Similarly, Clements (1989) demonstrates that in some rhotic dialects of English words like *prince* and *false* may be realised with an epenthetic or inserted [t], i.e. as [prɪnˈs] and [fɔːlˈs]. However, between an /r/ and an /s/, as in *nurse* ([nʌrs]), insertion is not possible, again showing that the lateral forms a natural class with the nasal, rather than with the non-lateral liquid. Behaviour like this would support the point of view that laterals may be [–continuant]. In other processes, however, they clearly form a natural class with the non-lateral liquids (e.g. /r/), and so appear to be [+continuant]. We will not be concerned here with how our feature system should capture this apparent anomaly.

processes. Consider again the features [consonantal] and [sonorant], which, it will be recalled, divide up the 'major classes' of segments as in (16):[11]

(16)   O   N/L   V
   [son]   –   +   +
   [cons]   +   +   –

('O' is obstruent, 'N' nasal, 'L' liquid, 'V' vowel). The interaction of these two features is relevant to a number of phonological phenomena. In other words, various combinations of the two features define classes which occur frequently in phonological processes. In addition, the ordering of elements within a syllable is typically determined by these features, so that a vowel ([+sonorant, –consonantal]) forms the peak of a syllable, and an obstruent ([–sonorant, +consonantal]) the margin, with any liquids or nasals ([+sonorant, +consonantal]) being intermediate. Thus /prɪns/ is a well-formed English syllable, while */rpɪsn/ is not.

It is often claimed that the features [sonorant] and [consonantal] determine a **sonority hierarchy** (or sonority scale), and that this hierarchy is reflected in the behaviour of segments in the syllable: the higher the sonority of a segment, the closer it is to the peak of the syllable (see, e.g., Vennemann 1972; Hooper 1976; Kiparsky 1981; Clements 1990). Such hierarchies have a more widespread role, and sometimes involve the other two features already discussed, [continuant] and [voice]. Although we will not discuss this in detail at this point, [+continuant] segments are higher on the sonority hierarchy than [–continuant], and [+voice] segments are higher than [–voice]. This can be established with respect to processes such as the historical 'weakening' or lenition of stops to sonorants in intervocalic position, which involves the gradual assimilation of the features of the stop to those of the surrounding vowels, as illustrated by the development from Pre-Old English to Modern English of the word *own* (from Lass and Anderson 1975: 158):

(17)   Pre-OE *[aagan] > OE [aaɣan] > ME [ɔɔwən] > lME [ɔɔn] > MdE /oon/
       (/oʊn/, /əʊn/, etc.) 'own'[12]

Each of the changes in (17) represents a step along a lenition hierarchy, which for velars in intervocalic position involves the steps in (18):

---

[11] It will be observed that the combination [–sonorant, –consonantal] is also formally possible. Given the definition of [sonorant], it is difficult to see what class of segments might be assigned this representation; [–consonantal] segments (vowels) appear to be inherently sonorant. Chomsky and Halle (1968) in fact assign the combination to [ʔ h], but it is not clear from the phonological behaviour of this set of segments that they should be treated as non-consonantal. We consider an alternative account of [h] in §1.3.5; we will assume here that there are no [–sonorant, –consonantal] segments.

[12] OE = Old English; ME = Middle English; lME = late Middle English; MdE = Modern English.

(18) k > (x *or* g) > ɣ > w

On the basis of processes such as these, Lass and Anderson (1975: 150) establish the general lenition hierarchy in (19):[13]

(19)

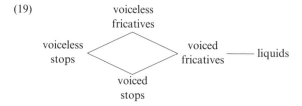

Notice that nasals typically do not participate in intervocalic lenition processes, for reasons that need not concern us at present; however, their status with respect to sonority within the class of sonorant consonants can be established on the basis of their behaviour in syllable structure: liquids ([+continuant]) are closer to the syllabic element than nasals ([−continuant]), as is evidenced by syllables such as English *kiln* and *barn* (/bɑrn/ in postvocalic *r*-pronouncing (i.e. rhotic) dialects of English), as opposed to the unacceptable syllables */kɪnl/ and */bɑnr/.

We have now shown that the four features considered so far together form a group with respect to which phonological regularities can be uncovered, as they, and they alone, distinguish the classes involved in sonority-based phenomena, as in (20):

(20)

	voiceless stops	voiced stops	voiceless frics	voiced frics	N	L	V
[son]	−	−	−	−	+	+	+
[cons]	+	+	+	+	+	+	−
[cont]	−	−	+	+	−	+	+
[voice]	−	+	−	+	+	+	+

(Here we ignore oppositions between voiced and voiceless sonorants, i.e. nasals, liquids and vowels.)

1.3.2 Vowel features

Let us now consider the remaining four features in (10), [high], [low], [back] and [round]. In *SPE*, these features, used primarily to distinguish the vowels of a language, are defined in terms of the position of the highest point of the tongue in the production of a vowel (for [high], [low] and [back]), and the

---

[13] Lass and Anderson in fact claim that lenition ultimately yields deletion, as illustrated by the development of *own* in (17), possibly via a vowel stage. For the moment, however, we confine the discussion to the consonant-types involved in such processes.

presence or absence of lip-rounding (for [round]). The definitions of the first three features refer to a 'neutral' position for the tongue (roughly the position for [ɛ]), such that [+high] sounds have their closest constriction higher than the neutral position, whereas [–high] sounds do not, and similarly for [+low] vs [–low] and [+back] vs [–back].

A system of this sort essentially treats the vowel features as interpretations of two axes, as in (21):

(21)

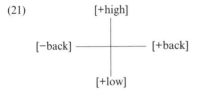

The claim inherent in the set of features given above is that languages typically make a three-way opposition on the vertical axis, but only a two-way opposition on the horizontal axis. Thus there is no separate feature [±front] beside [±back], but we do have a separate feature [±low] alongside [±high]. The only way of characterising a three-way opposition on the high–low axis within a binary feature framework is to postulate two features, giving the following possibilities:

(22)

	[–back]		[+back]	
	[–round]	[+round]	[–round]	[+round]
[+high, –low]	i	y	ɯ	u
[–high, –low]	e,ɛ	ø,œ	ɤ,ʌ	o,ɔ
[–high, +low]	a	Œ	ɑ	ɒ

(For illustration we use here the Cardinal Vowel symbols (originally proposed by Daniel Jones; see e.g. Abercrombie 1967: ch. 10), rather than the vowels of any particular language.) Notice that the definitions of the features exclude the fourth logically possible combination of the two features defining the high–low axis, i.e. [+high, +low].

It is clear that other features will be required to characterise the vowel space, seeing that those discussed so far apparently fail to distinguish between various pairs of [–high, –low] vowels, for example. This is an area which has been the subject of major rethinking since the publication of *SPE*, and we devote some space here to a discussion of the issues involved.

1.3.3 The vowel-height dimension and related issues

There have been a number of proposals for distinguishing the various pairs of [–high, –low] vowels in (22). These proposals can be divided into three major groups: (i) those which distinguish the members of each pair by means of a binary feature [tense]; (ii) those which try to reflect the difference in height 'directly'; and (iii) those which introduce a feature [advanced tongue root] to distinguish the members of the various pairs.

The first proposal is found in *SPE*, in which it is argued that the difference is one of tense vs lax, with the tense vowel of each pair being 'executed with a greater deviation from the neutral or rest position' than its lax counterpart, so that 'the greater articulatory effort in the tense vowels is further manifested by their greater distinctiveness and the markedly longer duration during which the articulatory configuration remains stationary' (*SPE*: 324–5). Such a distinction is applicable to certain pairs of vowels which we have not yet considered, such as /iː/ vs /ɪ/ in RP English (e.g. *meal* /miːl/ vs *mill* /mɪl/), or in the German pairs given by Chomsky and Halle (e.g. *ihre* [īrə] 'her' vs *irre* [irə] 'err', or the similar *Huhne* [hūnə] 'chicken' vs *Hunne* [hunə] 'Hun'; notice that Chomsky and Halle distinguish tense vowels from their lax counterparts by means of a macron over the tense vowel).

This approach is also readily applicable to the [–high, –low] vowels in a system such as RP, in which the opposition between the members of each pair is again not just one of tongue-height (quality), but also of length (quantity). Thus the distinction between the two vowels in *beat* /iː/ and *bit* /ɪ/ is one which can be interpreted as tense vs lax, as is that between *mane* /eɪ/ and *men* /ɛ/, as well as in *coat* /əʊ/ vs *cot* /ɒ/.[14] The crucial claim that is being made here, then, is that the *type* of phonological opposition between, say, the two [–high, –low] vowels ([e] and [ɛ]) is different from that holding between, say, the high vowel [i] and the higher of the two mid vowels [e], or between the lower of the two mid vowels [ɛ] and the low vowel [a].

As we have seen, this account seems appropriate for a system like RP, but it has encountered criticism from those who believe that there are vowel systems in which it is reasonable to speak of (at least) *four* distinct vowel heights. The front-vowel system in (23), for example, is that of some dialects of Scots English:

(23)   *beat*   [bit]
         bit   [bɪt]
         bait   [bet]
         bet   [bɛt]
         bat   [bat]

---

[14] We are here following Chomsky and Halle's position that the phonological distinction between these pairs is one of quality, not length. Notice too that the diphthongs of *main* and *coat* are tense, just like the monophthong of *beat*.

Here the various vowels are apparently distinguished *only* by vowel height, with no apparent difference in length, and any appeal to the notion of tense vs lax, as defined by Chomsky and Halle, seems inappropriate.

The existence of systems like this has led some phonologists to propose systems which reflect the height dimension more directly. Thus Wang (1968) replaces the feature [low] by [mid], which allows the expression of four heights, rather than the three of *SPE*:

(24) $\begin{bmatrix} +\text{high} \\ -\text{mid} \end{bmatrix}$ $\begin{bmatrix} +\text{high} \\ +\text{mid} \end{bmatrix}$ $\begin{bmatrix} -\text{high} \\ +\text{mid} \end{bmatrix}$ $\begin{bmatrix} -\text{high} \\ -\text{mid} \end{bmatrix}$

      /i/   /e/   /ɛ/   /æ/

Such a formulation certainly allows the expression of four heights, but notice that there is still a fundamental problem associated with the expression of vowel height by means of binary features: the fact that we have to use (at least) two binary features to express what appears to be a *single* phonetic dimension. That is, a sequence such as /i/–/e/–/ɛ/–/æ/ can be seen as a set of points on a single scale, and this has led some phonologists, e.g. Ladefoged (1975) and Williamson (1977), to abandon binary features for the expression of vowel height, and to introduce a **multivalued scalar** feature, as in (25):

(25) /i/   [4 high]
      /e/   [3 high]
      /ɛ/   [2 high]
      /æ/   [1 high]

We do not pursue this approach at this point (but see our discussion of features in §2.1). Rather, we now consider the third type of proposal that has been made in this area, the introduction of a feature [advanced tongue root] (henceforth [ATR]).

It has been observed that one of the articulatory correlates of the difference between a pair of vowels such as [e] and [ɛ] typically involves the position of the tongue root: for [e] the tongue root is further forward, while for [ɛ] it is further retracted. A similar relationship holds between [i] and [ɪ]. Thus the difference between the two vowels does not relate exclusively to the relative height of the *body* of the tongue, as is suggested by (25), but involves additional phonetic parameters.

Clearly, the choice amongst the three alternatives just outlined – we refer to them here as the tense/lax, height and ATR approaches – depends on whether we can show that one of them more successfully predicts what actually happens in phonological systems and processes than the others. That is, if we find processes which show that the relationship between [i] and [e] is phonologically the same as that between [e] and [ɛ], this would provide evidence in favour of a multivalued feature [high], as in (24).

In fact, we believe that all three approaches are required in phonological theory. That is to say, we believe that vowel systems may be organised along any one of the three lines suggested by the approaches just discussed, so that the nature of the phonetic parameters which play a role in a particular sound-system is reflected in the phonology of the language in question.

Let us illustrate this with a further consideration of [tense] and [ATR]. We have already seen that the feature [tense] plays a role in the phonology of RP, for example. Thus /ɪ/ in *bit* and /ʊ/ in *look* are the [−tense] counterparts of /iː/ in *beat* and /uː/ in *Luke*, with which they are otherwise identical in terms of their feature make-up. The fact that the [−tense] vowels of RP form a class (which includes, besides /ɪ ʊ/, also /ɛ æ ʌ ɒ ə/) is shown by the fact that just this set of vowels cannot occur in final position in a stressed syllable, while the set of [+tense] vowels can (cf. /biː/ *bee* and */bɪ/, for example).[15] Similarly, they can occur before /ŋ/, while the [+tense] vowels cannot (e.g. *bang* /bæŋ/, but **boong* /buːŋ/).[16] Thus a feature such as [tense] is required in the analysis of systems such as RP. Crucially, at least with respect to the oppositions between /iː/ and /ɪ/ and between /uː/ and /ʊ/, the vowel system is organised in terms of 'central' vs 'peripheral' vowels. (26) gives the representation of a ten-vowel system such as this, consisting of a peripheral ([+tense]) set /i u e o ɑ/ and a central ([−tense]) set /ɪ ʊ ɛ ɔ ə/. Notice that for the low vowels peripherality is often manifested as greater pharyngeal constriction, so that peripheral /ɑ/ is considerably retracted:

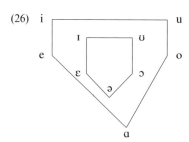

(26)

---

[15] It is also possible to deal with these restrictions in terms of vowel-length, rather than the apparently qualitative distinction of tense vs lax. We discuss vowel-length in Chapter 3.

[16] The RP vowel /ʊ/ does not in fact occur before /ŋ/ in the native vocabulary of English. However, in loanwords such as *Jung* from German, we find /ʊ/, not /uː/ (cf. Collins and Mees 1996: 97), which further demonstrates the validity of the analysis.

The status of /ə/ is more problematical. It again fails to occur before /ŋ/, and shows other phonological behaviour which suggests that it forms a set of its own in some respects. However, given that it patterns with the lax vowels in not taking stress in final position in a syllable, we feel justified in categorising it in this set.

18

Such an analysis is proposed for Classical Latin by Allen (1973: 132), who observes: 'the tenseness is . . . responsible for the long vowels occupying a larger, more "centrifugal" perimeter of articulations'. He represents the system of Latin as in (27), where the long tense vowels are represented with a macron (ˉ), the short lax vowels with a breve (˘):

(27)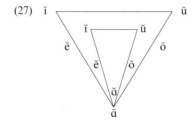

Other vowel systems, however, are organised quite differently, even though they may contain more or less the same vowels as (26). In particular, many languages divide the set of vowels not into a tense and a lax subset as in (26), but rather into two subsets according to tongue-root position, i.e. into one [+ATR] set and one [–ATR] set, as in (28):

(28)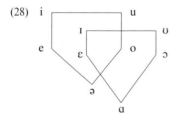

Here the vowels are grouped into /i u e o ə/ ([+ATR]) and /ɪ ʊ ɛ ɔ ɑ/ ([–ATR]).[17] The evidence that there are ten-vowel systems which are organised in this way comes from processes involving **vowel harmony**, i.e. processes in which all the vowels within a particular domain, often the word, must have the same value for a particular phonological feature. One such system is that of the Asante dialect of Akan, a language spoken in Ghana, in which all the vowels within a single word must have the same value for [ATR] (see Stewart 1967, 1983; Clements 1981). Stewart (1967: 186) gives the following examples:

---

[17] The relation between the symbols used for the non-low back vowels in (28) is to some extent arbitrary, although conventional. Thus /ʊ/ is used in (28) for a vowel which is apparently more peripheral on the front–back dimension than /u/, whereas in (26) this relationship is reversed. The opposite choice would be equally arbitrary, however, in that the same discrepancy would hold, but on the high–low dimension, rather than the front–back.

(29)	[–ATR]		[+ATR]	
	/wʊbɛnʊm?/	'you will drink it'	/wubenum?/	'you will suck it'
	/ɔːbɛtʊ?/	'it is going to lay'	/oːbetu/	'he is going to pull it out'
	/mɪkjɪrɛ/	'I show'	/mitie/	'I listen'

The forms in (29), involving the non-low vowels of Akan,[18] show the harmony process in operation: all the vowels in the left-hand column are [–ATR], while those in the right-hand column are [+ATR]. Forms with a mixture of [–ATR] and [+ATR] vowels, such as */wʊbenum?/, are ill formed.

We do not at this point pursue the question of how such harmony processes are to be analysed, an issue which we return to in some detail in §1.4.2 in relation to Turkish; however, the phenomena just outlined provide us with sufficient reason to claim that systems such as (26) and (28) are both to be found in languages of the world, and hence that the tense/lax and ATR features must *both* form part of our feature system.

We can also find evidence to support the point of view that the vowels of languages may be organised in terms of relative height, as suggested by the Scots English data in (23). Such evidence can be adduced from processes in which some or all of the vowels of a language move one 'step' up or down. For example, the effect of the English Great Vowel Shift was to move non-high long vowels up one step, giving the changes in (30) (from Lass 1987: 130), which shows various Middle English and early Modern English forms (*c.* 1600):

(30)		ME		1600
	beet	eː	>	iː
	beat	ɛː	>	eː
	mate	aː	>	ɛː
	boot	oː	>	uː
	boat	ɔː	>	oː

There are also processes which make appeal to the notion 'one step lower'. Lindau (1978: 545) observes that in Scanian, a Swedish dialect spoken in Malmö, there is a process in which the diphthongisation of a long vowel yields a first element which is one step lower than the original monophthong:

---

[18] As is typical in [ATR] harmony systems, the low vowels of Akan behave rather differently from the non-low ones, for reasons which need not concern us at this point.

(31) /iː/ → [ei]   /yː/ → [øy]   /uː/ → [eu]
      /eː/ → [ɛe]   /øː/ → [œø]   /oː/ → [ɛo]
      /ɛː/ → [æɛ]

The range of processes surveyed in this section suggests that vowel systems
can be organised along different phonetic and phonological parameters, and
hence that our feature system must be rich enough to be able to describe all
of the parameters found to play a role in the organisation of vowel systems.[19]

1.3.4 Consonantal features

The fact that the set of features we have now isolated forms an intuitively
obvious group hardly needs confirmation: there are clearly many phonological processes which make reference to particular subsets of vowels.

Much the same observation applies to the set of features defining articulatory place for consonants, which were not included in the feature-matrix
for the vowel in (10). It is particularly clear that this set forms a group, as will
be seen by a further consideration of (7). One of the respects in which (7) is
inadequate is its failure to represent the notion 'agreement in place of articulation' in any coherent way. In other words, it fails to show that the features
[labial], [alveolar] and [velar] form a group, just as the matrix in (10) fails to
identify the various groups of features we have distinguished.

There are formidable difficulties in formalising these observations, in particular with the formalisation of the notion 'nasals agree with a following
consonant in all the features forming the group characterising place of articulation', and we postpone discussion of this until §1.4. This problem is exacer-
bated by the fact that there is little agreement on what should constitute the
set of features in this group. An *SPE*-type system would characterise, say,
English /t/ by means of a matrix something like:

(32) $\begin{bmatrix} -\text{sonorant} \\ +\text{consonantal} \\ -\text{continuant} \\ -\text{voice} \\ +\text{anterior} \\ +\text{coronal} \\ -\text{high} \\ -\text{low} \\ -\text{back} \\ -\text{round} \end{bmatrix}$

---

[19] In §2.5 we consider an approach which characterises scalar processes like these in terms of dependency
relations between the features involved.

The two features [anterior] and [coronal] distinguish the major places of articulation as in (33):[20]

(33)	labial	alveolar	post-alveolar	palatal	velar	uvular	pharyngeal
	p b	t d		c ɟ	k g	q ɢ	
	ɸ β	s z	ʃ ʒ	ç ʝ	x ɣ	χ ʁ	ħ ʕ
[ant]	+	+	−	−	−	−	−
[cor]	−	+	+	−	−	−	−

[+anterior] sounds are produced with a stricture in front of the postalveolar region; [+coronal] sounds are produced with the blade of the tongue raised above the 'neutral' position. We will not consider the motivation for the definitions here, other than noting that natural classes can be defined along the expected lines.

The tongue-body and tongue-root consonants (i.e. the [−anterior, −coronal] set) can be distinguished from each other by the use of the 'vowel' features [high], [low] and [back], as shown in (34):

(34)	labial	alveolar	post-alveolar	palatal	velar	uvular	pharyngeal
	p b	t d		c ɟ	k g	q ɢ	
	ɸ β	s z	ʃ ʒ	ç ʝ	x ɣ	χ ʁ	ħ ʕ
[ant]	+	+	−	−	−	−	−
[cor]	−	+	+	−	−	−	−
[high]	−	−	+	+	+	−	−
[low]	−	−	−	−	−	−	+
[back]	−	−	−	−	+	+	+

The representation of place of articulation is an area which has given rise to a number of alternative proposals in recent years, and we shall outline one here which has gained wide currency, and which differs in various respects from the original *SPE* proposal.

McCarthy (1988: 99) characterises the *SPE* proposal as embodying 'place of articulation theory', in which the feature [anterior] is defined in terms of the passive articulator (in front of the postalveolar region). He contrasts this with 'articulator theory', in which the distinctions between the segments are made in terms of 'the active articulator making the constricting gesture rather than by place of articulation'. In articulator theory, the major places of articulation are distinguished by the features [labial], [coronal], [dorsal] and [radical], as in (35):

[20] For reference, in the following discussion we will provide symbols for representatives of each of the categories given, drawn from the stop and fricative series.

(35)	labial	alveolar	post-alveolar	palatal	velar	uvular	pharyngeal
	p b	t d		c ɟ	k g	q ɢ	
	ɸ β	s z	ʃ ʒ	ç ʝ	x ɣ	χ ʁ	ħ ʕ
[lab]	+	–	–	–	–	–	–
[cor]	–	+	+	+	–	–	–
[dors]	–	–	–	+	+	+	–
[rad]	–	–	–	–	–	+	+

In line with McCarthy's distinction between articulator and place of articulation theory, we can say that [labial] consonants are produced with the lips, [coronal] consonants with the blade of the tongue, [dorsal] consonants with the tongue body (dorsum), and [radical] consonants with the tongue root.

What advantages does (35) have over the system given in (33) and (34)? Notice first of all that [anterior] is no longer used to identify any of the major places of articulation. One reason for this is that in the *SPE* treatment, the class of labials and alveolars is predicted to form a natural class, characterised as [+anterior]. As Yip (1989: 350) points out, this is not a recurrent class in the phonologies of languages; we do not find phonological processes affecting the set of coronal and non-coronal anteriors (e.g. /p t̪ t/). Abandoning [anterior] as the characterisation of a major place of articulation means that this anomaly is removed (although, as we shall see presently, [anterior] is still required in this system to subcategorise the class of coronals).

The introduction of a feature [labial] allows the class of labial consonants to be given a 'positive' characterisation, rather than their somewhat opaque definition in *SPE*: 'consonants produced with a stricture in front of the palato-alveolar region whose production does not involve raising of the blade of the tongue', i.e. [+anterior, –coronal].

As we have already noted, tongue-body consonants are characterised as [dorsal]. However, notice that in (35) the segments characterised as being [coronal] have been extended so as to include palatals (e.g. /ç ʝ/) as well as postalveolars (e.g. /ʃ ʒ/). Whether palatals should be characterised as [coronal] or as [dorsal], or perhaps as both, is a topic of some debate. Although, as we have seen, Chomsky and Halle characterise them as [–coronal], in accordance with their definition of [+coronal] as involving raising of the blade of the tongue, Hall (1997: 6) observes that 'the vast majority of phonologists have concluded that palatal sounds are [+coronal] because they pattern in many languages with the alveolars', and notes that this causes Halle and Stevens (1979: 346) to reformulate the definition of [+coronal] as involving 'the raising of the frontal (i.e. tip, blade, and/or central) part of the tongue so as to make contact with the palate'. We will assume here that palatals are indeed [+coronal].[21]

Articulator theory, then, allows a positive characterisation of each of the major places of articulation. However, it is clear that in the coronal region, many more oppositions are required than we have considered up to now. Phonological distinctions in this region are found which involve a number of parameters which we have not yet considered in either of the theories which we have been discussing.

The feature [anterior] is generally retained in articulator theory, but is restricted to those segments which are [coronal]. That is, [coronal] segments may be [+anterior] or [−anterior], but segments which are not coronal simply have no specification for the feature [anterior].[22] The situation for coronals is shown in (36) (we add dental and retroflex consonants to the set in (35), and consider palatals to be [+coronal]):

(36)		dental	alveolar	postalveolar	retroflex	palatal
		ţ ḓ	t d		ţ ḍ	c ɟ
		θ ð	s z	ʃ ʒ	ʂ ʐ	ç ʝ
[cor]		+	+	+	+	+
[ant]		+	+	−	−	−

Thus the definition of [anterior] is retained, but now applies only to consonants produced with the tongue-blade as active articulator.

Two other features, originally proposed by Chomsky and Halle (1968), provide further distinctions amongst the various coronal segments. These are [strident] and [distributed].

The feature [strident] distinguishes various members of the class of fricatives, on the basis of the relative amount of 'high-frequency noise' involved. Thus sounds such as [s z ʃ ʒ] have a relatively large amount of high-frequency noise, and are [+strident] as opposed to their counterparts [θ ð ç ʝ]. Although this feature is not defined in terms of place, we include it here, as it serves to subcategorise consonants in the coronal area. Its phonological relevance can be seen in processes such as that illustrated in (37):

---

[21] Hall (1997: §1.2) suggests that the uncertainty surrounding the status of palatals with respect to the feature [coronal] is due to the fact that palatal fricatives such as /ç ʝ/ behave differently from non-continuants such as /c ɟ ɲ/. The fricatives behave as dorsals rather than as coronals. Hall cites a process from a dialect of German spoken near Düsseldorf, in which uvular /ʀ/ is devoiced to [χ] before coronal /t s ʃ/, but not before /p f k ç/. Thus /ç/ here patterns with the non-coronals. On the other hand, non-continuants (/c ɟ ɲ/) typically pattern with coronals, rather than with dorsals. Hall concludes that the continuants are [−coronal] and the non-continuants [+coronal], and attributes this to an articulatory difference; the 'palatal' stops are in fact alveolo-palatal, he claims.

[22] In §2.2 we consider the question of how the notion of a feature not being relevant to a segment can be formalised.

(37) a. masses MASS+PL /mæsəz/   b. moths MOTH+PL /mɒθs/
     buzzes BUZZ+PL /bʌzəz/   lathes LATHE+PL /leɪðz/
     coshes COSH+PL /kɒʃəz/
     edges EDGE+PL /ɛdʒəz/

In the formation of English plurals we find a different form of the suffix after the [+strident] fricatives in (37a) (/-əz/, or /-ɪz/, depending on dialect) than after the [–strident] fricatives in (b).

Stridency does not seem to be directly relevant to plosives;[23] in (38) we show how it further subcategorises the set of coronals:

(38)

	dental	alveolar	postalveolar	retroflex	palatal
	θ ð	s z	ʃ ʒ	ʂ ʐ	ç ʝ
[cor]	+	+	+	+	+
[ant]	+	+	–	–	–
[strid]	–	+	+	+	–

[+distributed] sounds are those in which the consonantal stricture is 'relatively long'. This feature is often used to distinguish tongue-blade (laminal) sounds, which are [+distributed], from tongue-tip (apical) sounds [–distributed], and non-retroflex [+distributed] from retroflex [–distributed].

The feature [distributed] is often seen as somewhat unsatisfactory (see e.g. Keating 1991). On the one hand, it is not clear that the phonetic definition is entirely appropriate, and on the other, evidence that [+distributed] consonants can function as a class as opposed to [–distributed] consonants is limited. However, Pulleyblank (1989: 384–5) cites processes in Australian languages which have the four coronal stops given in (39):

(39) laminal   apical   apical   laminal
      (inter)dental alveolar   postalveolar palatal alveolar
      ḏ̪   d   ḍ   ɟ

Pulleyblank, following Dixon (1980: §6.4), notes that the palatal and (inter)dental stops, which are laminal, pattern together in phonological processes in these languages, as opposed to the alveolar and postalveolar stops, which are apical. A grouping of this sort can be satisfactorily characterised by the feature [distributed]. In view of facts like these, we include [distributed] here, although we suspect that it need only be used for stops – for fricatives, [strident] is sufficient to characterise the oppositions found in languages. (40) shows how [distributed] subcategorises the coronal series of stops:[24]

---

[23] However, notice that Jakobson *et al.* (1951: 24) use the feature [strident] to distinguish affricates from plosives, irrespective of place of articulation.

[24] We distinguish apicals from laminals by means of the diacritics ˌ and ˌ, respectively.

(40)

	apical dental	laminal dental	apical alveolar	laminal alveolar	retroflex	palatal
	t̪ d̪	t̪ d̪	t d	t̪ d̪	ʈ ɖ	c ɟ
[cor]	+	+	+	+	+	+
[ant]	+	+	+	+	−	−
[distr]	−	+	−	+	−	+

Notice that the distinction between [+distributed] and [−distributed] segments is independent from that between dentals and alveolars, which can both be either laminal or apical. However, it is generally claimed that languages do not *contrast*, say, laminal dentals with laminal alveolars, so that in a language which has both /t̪/ and /t/, the two stops will be distinguished not only by place, but also by laminality vs apicality; [distributed] can then be used to characterise the difference between them.

This concludes our discussion of individual features. It is of course clear that additional features will be required in phonological descriptions (see again the references in §1.3), in particular features characterising the various airstream mechanisms (i.e. pulmonic, glottalic and velaric) utilised in the languages of the world, and those characterising different phonation types (voice, voicelessness, breathy and creaky voice and aspiration) and tonal contrasts. We introduce these in the course of our discussion, as and when they become necessary.

1.3.5 *The characterisation of grouping*

We have now identified a set of features which can be used in phonological description, and have also uncovered some evidence which suggests that these features might be organised into groups. Evidence for the grouping of features can be found in hierarchy-related processes such as weakening, for example, but also in cases where two or more features together define a class of segments which functions together in some phonological process, and thus forms a natural class. Thus we saw in (15) that [sonorant] and [consonantal] behave in this way; the conjunction of the values [+sonorant] and [+consonantal] in the last segment of a noun in Dutch, among other things, determines that a schwa will be inserted before the diminutive suffix.

Similar evidence can be found in the process of nasal place assimilation, which we discussed at some length in §1.2, but whose formulation we have not yet considered in terms of the features developed above.[25] A direct 'translation' of (7), our last attempt at a formulation of nasal assimilation, would yield (41):

---

[25] For the purposes of this discussion, we utilise the feature system proposed in *SPE* for the characterisation of place of articulation, rather than that based on articulator theory.

(41)

$$[+\text{nas}] \rightarrow \left\{ \begin{array}{l} \begin{bmatrix} +\text{ant} \\ -\text{cor} \end{bmatrix} / \underline{\hspace{1em}} \begin{bmatrix} +\text{ant} \\ -\text{cor} \end{bmatrix} \\[2ex] \begin{bmatrix} +\text{ant} \\ +\text{cor} \end{bmatrix} / \underline{\hspace{1em}} \begin{bmatrix} +\text{ant} \\ +\text{cor} \end{bmatrix} \\[2ex] \begin{bmatrix} -\text{ant} \\ -\text{cor} \end{bmatrix} / \underline{\hspace{1em}} \begin{bmatrix} -\text{ant} \\ -\text{cor} \end{bmatrix} \end{array} \right\}$$

In assimilations of place like these, then, [anterior] and [coronal] form a group, as we would expect.[26]

Examples like these could be multiplied, and we can identify other kinds of phonological behaviour which provide further evidence for feature grouping. For example, it has been argued that /h/ in many languages is a 'defective' segment, in that it lacks a particular group of features, those characterising place of articulation. In other words, /h/ has no independent place of articulation, but acquires its specification for these features from a following vowel: in English *heat* /hiːt/, for example, the articulators adopt the position of the following high vowel during the production of /h/, whereas in *harp* /hɑːp/, the articulation of /h/ is very different.

If feature grouping plays such an important role in phonology, it is clear that this must be formalised in some way. In other words, the simple list of features found in the *SPE* approach must be structured in such a way that it reflects our claims about the grouping of features.

Perhaps the most straightforward solution, originally proposed in Lass and Anderson (1975) and Lass (1976), is simply to divide the feature-matrix into submatrices, or **gestures**. Thus we might distinguish a **categorial gesture**, containing the features [sonorant], [consonantal], [continuant] and [voice], i.e. the group of features which seems to be involved in the expression of the relative sonority of segments, and a **place gesture**, containing the features characterising the vowel space and defining consonantal place of articulation. However, the categorial gesture might have to show a further subdivision, given our claim that [sonorant] and [consonantal] are more closely related to each other than to [continuant] and [voice], and vice versa. Let us call these the **major class** and **manner** gestures. The feature-matrix for English /θ/ might have the representation in (42):[27]

---

[26] The vowel features [high], [low], [back] and [round] would also be required in a full statement of the process; for simplicity, we omit these features here.

[27] Note that, for ease of exposition, we restrict ourselves to a subset of the features which we have introduced. In addition, we do not consider the incorporation into (42) and (43) of features characterising tone and phonation.

(42)

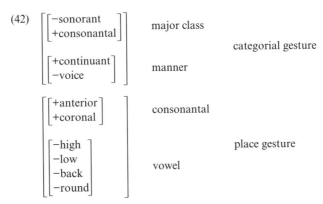

However, in recent work in phonology the notion of grouping has been presented in terms of a rather different set of notational conventions from that given in (42). Furthermore, the terminology used is different. Within the model of **autosegmental phonology**, which we introduce in §1.4, the segment has in recent years been represented in terms of a **feature geometry**, i.e. a tree-like structure similar to that which we introduced in (11):

(43)

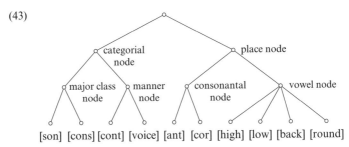

Notice that although (42) and (43) look very different, they are entirely equivalent in the claims made about the structure of the segment; a labelled bracketing like (42) and a tree structure (or feature geometry) like (43) are notational variants.

Explicit proposals for a geometrical structure of the type in (43) were first made by Clements (1985), and have been developed in a number of publications since (e.g. Sagey 1986; McCarthy 1988; Clements and Hume 1995; Pulleyblank 1995). The particular structure in (43) is merely intended to show how the gestural representation in (42) can be 'translated' into a geometrical representation. Proposals within geometrical phonology differ in various respects from (43), and we return in §1.4 to a discussion of some of the substantive issues involved. Here we consider only the general claims made about the nature of segmental structure within a geometrical approach, rather than the specific form of the geometry in (43).

In a geometry such as (43), features are seen as labels for NODES (represented as small circles), and, as in a model incorporating gestures, are grouped
together, under higher nodes. These higher nodes, which are referred to as
class nodes, have essentially the same status as gestures and sub-gestures,
in that they can act as units in phonological rules. In other words, the set
of features grouped under a particular class node can be appealed to in a
phonological rule, just as a set of features forming a gesture or sub-gesture
can be appealed to. Similarly, a segment may lack one or more of the nodes,
and hence all the features dominated by the nodes in question. Compare for
example the representation of English /θ/ in (44a) with that of /h/ in (44b):

(44)   a.

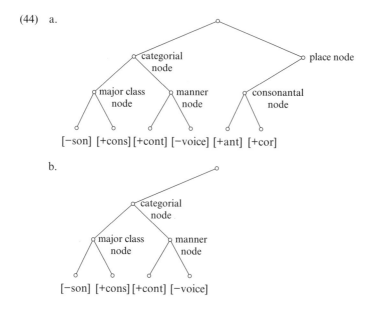

b.

The representation for /h/ lacks a place node, and hence displays none of the
features dominated by that node, while /θ/ and /h/ have identical specifications for those features dominated by the categorial node.[28]

It is clear that structures such as (42) and (43) allow us to make reference
in phonological rules to groups of features. Indeed, if we find rules which
refer to the particular groupings suggested here, we are thereby providing
support for the subdivisions proposed. However, we have not yet addressed
the question of how these structures play a role in the operation of phonological rules, a problem to which we now turn.

---

[28] We are further assuming here that /θ/ and /h/ lack a vowel node. See e.g. Kenstowicz (1994: §9) and
Clements and Hume (1995) for discussion of vowel and consonant place features.

Segments

1.4 Autosegmental phonology

Consider again the formulation of nasal place assimilation in (41). It is clear that this formulation is inadequate in at least three respects. In the first place, it does not show that the two features involved form a group. Secondly, it fails to show that the value for each of the features which is changed by the rule must be the same as the value for the corresponding feature in the segment to which the nasal assimilates. Thirdly, just as in (9) above, there is nothing to prevent us having a rule like (45):

$$(45) \quad [+\text{nas}] \rightarrow \left\{ \begin{array}{l} \begin{bmatrix} +\text{ant} \\ -\text{cor} \end{bmatrix} / \underline{\quad} \begin{bmatrix} +\text{son} \\ -\text{cons} \end{bmatrix} \\[2ex] \begin{bmatrix} +\text{ant} \\ +\text{cor} \end{bmatrix} / \underline{\quad} \begin{bmatrix} +\text{high} \\ +\text{son} \end{bmatrix} \\[2ex] \begin{bmatrix} -\text{ant} \\ -\text{cor} \end{bmatrix} / \underline{\quad} \begin{bmatrix} -\text{round} \\ -\text{voice} \end{bmatrix} \end{array} \right\}$$

(45) is formally just as easy to express as (41).

With respect to the first two objections to (41), the generalisation we are trying to express is that the features of the place gesture must be identical for the two segments. However, the formulation of this generalisation in terms of the kind of notation we have been using up to now is, perhaps not surprisingly, not straightforward: there is no obvious way of expressing the notion of identity, although attempts involving the use of 'Greek letter variables' have been offered, as in (46), where each feature is bound by a variable (see e.g. *SPE*: 352):

$$(46) \quad [\text{nas}] \rightarrow \begin{bmatrix} \alpha\,\text{ant} \\ \beta\,\text{cor} \end{bmatrix} / \underline{\quad} \begin{bmatrix} \alpha\,\text{ant} \\ \beta\,\text{cor} \end{bmatrix}$$

The use of a particular Greek letter variable denotes identity for the feature in question, and the incorporation of this convention takes care of the second objection to (41), by extending the domain of the Greek letter variable convention to all the features dominated by a particular class node, as in (47):

$$(47) \quad [\text{nas}] \rightarrow \alpha[\text{PLACE}] / \underline{\quad} \alpha[\text{PLACE}]$$

However, such linear formulations, even patched up with devices like these, are hardly adequate to characterise assimilation processes, in that they are unable to deal with the third objection raised above. There is again nothing to prevent us replacing the [PLACE] in the environment of (47) by [CATEGORIAL], for example.

30

What we are failing to characterise in (47) is the fact that the nasal preceding a consonant in assimilation cases acquires its specification for place of articulation from the consonant by a process referred to as SPREADING, i.e. it does not have an independent set of features characterising place, but 'shares' its place features with the following consonant. (48) is a formulation of this, using the conventions of non-linear autosegmental phonology (see e.g. Goldsmith 1976, 1990; Clements 1977):

(48)

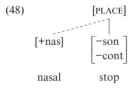

In this formulation, the fact that the two consonants in this environment share a single specification for place of articulation is made explicit. The 'direction' of the assimilation is indicated by the dashed line in (48): the features of the place gesture which are associated with the stop spread from the stop to the nasal.

Cases like these provide the basis for the theory of autosegmental phonology. What we have here is an example of one set of features (the place features) operating *independently* (hence the name of the theory) from the other features. With respect to the place features in (48), there is only one specification – a single **autosegment** – while for all other features there are two specifications, and hence two segments. Among other things, then, autosegmental phonology is concerned with the characterisation of cases where two segments necessarily share the same specification for a feature or group of features.

In this connection, it is perhaps useful to compare words like *camber* and *linger*, which display nasal place assimilation, with English words containing a lateral consonant followed by an obstruent. At first sight, the forms in (49) suggest that such forms do not behave in the same way as the nasals discussed above:

(49) gulp [gʌlp]
      kilt [kɪlt]
      milk [mɪlk]

In all cases in (49) the lateral, which is phonologically alveolar, is phonetically realised as an alveolar, so that English does not seem to have a 'lateral place assimilation' rule of the same type as the nasal place assimilation rule discussed earlier.[29] This raises the question of how the sequence of consonants

---

[29] Notice that the /l/ is velarised in many dialects of English in such contexts; this, however, does not affect the issue at hand.

in *kilt* should be represented. It is of course true that the /l/ and the /t/ have the same place of articulation, and thus the same features in the place gesture, but the /l/ is not alveolar *because* the /t/ is alveolar. Rather, the /l/ is alveolar 'in its own right', as is shown by (49). Thus, in a representation of the same type as (48), it might appear that we should assign a separate (although identical) specification for the place gesture to /l/:

(50)

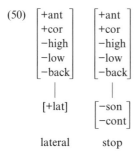

$$\text{(50)}\quad \begin{bmatrix} +\text{ant} \\ +\text{cor} \\ -\text{high} \\ -\text{low} \\ -\text{back} \end{bmatrix} \quad \begin{bmatrix} +\text{ant} \\ +\text{cor} \\ -\text{high} \\ -\text{low} \\ -\text{back} \end{bmatrix}$$

$$\qquad\quad [+\text{lat}] \qquad \begin{bmatrix} -\text{son} \\ -\text{cont} \end{bmatrix}$$

lateral   stop

(Notice that we here introduce a feature [lateral], whose function will be clear.)

However, there are at least three problems associated with a representation such as (50). In the first place, there has been a great deal of discussion as to whether (50) is a well-formed phonological representation, or whether successive identical specifications for particular gestures must eventually be collapsed by what is known as the 'Obligatory Contour Principle', to give a structure more like (48) (see e.g. Odden 1988; Yip 1988). Secondly, the question arises as to whether laterals in English have to be specified underlyingly as having place features at all. English has only one lateral, /l/, and so place of articulation is not distinctive for a segment which is [+lateral] – its place of articulation is always predictable. Thus it may not be appropriate to include a place specification for the lateral in the representation in (50). We return to this aspect when we introduce the notion of underspecification in §2.2.

We devote some space to the third problem at this point. It does not seem to be strictly true that English has no assimilation process affecting laterals. Consider the forms in (51):

(51)　health　[hɛl̪θ]
　　　　kilt　　[kɪlt]
　　　　Welsh　[wɛl̺ʃ]

(We use [l̺] to represent a retracted alveolar lateral.) The forms in (51) appear to be fairly common in English (although notice that many speakers have no central closure at all, especially in the case of a following postalveolar fricative /ʃ/). Thus it appears that there *is* a process of lateral assimilation, which is restricted to cases where the following consonant is a coronal obstruent. This phenomenon lends further support to two aspects which we have been considering. In the first place, we have another case of spreading, and secondly, we have uncovered further evidence for treating [coronal] as one of the major articulation types, as in (35): the features which distinguish the various [+coronal] segments ([anterior], [strident] and [distributed]) form a group, as all and only these features appear to be involved in the spreading process in (51). Thus we can argue that the [coronal] node is what spreads in the English lateral place assimilation process, giving the formulation in (52a), whereas dorsal segments do not spread to laterals, as in (52b):

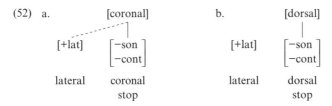

We emphasise at this point that this formulation is a very tentative one, which will be subject to revision in the light of the theoretical developments which we will consider in the remainder of this chapter and in Chapter 2. However, we include it at this point because it throws light on the kinds of considerations that have contributed to these theoretical developments.

We turn now to a more detailed account of autosegmental phonology, starting with a consideration of the ways in which it differs from *SPE*.

In *SPE*, phonological representations are conceived of as unilinear strings of segments, where segments are **unstructured**, **unordered** and **non-overlapping** sets of binary features:

(53) $\begin{bmatrix} +F \\ -G \\ +H \end{bmatrix} \quad \begin{bmatrix} -F \\ -G \\ +H \end{bmatrix} \quad \begin{bmatrix} -F \\ +G \\ +H \end{bmatrix} \quad \begin{bmatrix} +F \\ +G \\ +H \end{bmatrix}$

As we have seen, the introduction of the concept of feature grouping brings some degree of structure to the segment.

The claim that the features in a matrix are sequentially unordered entails that a single segment cannot have two values for a particular feature, as in (54), as this would lead to an anomalous specification:

(54) $\begin{bmatrix} +son \\ +cons \\ +nas \\ -nas \end{bmatrix}$

At first sight, it is not obvious why a feature specification with opposing values for a single feature would be desirable in any case. However, there are a number of phenomena involving **contour segments**, such as prenasalised consonants, affricates (cf. the discussion above) and contour-toned vowels, which appear to point to the desirability of a single segment being able to have two – perhaps sequentially ordered – specifications for a single feature. The term contour segment is generally used to describe two distinct 'events' which appear to function as a single segment in the phonology of a language. Thus, as we have seen, affricates display both a closure phase and a release phase, but behave phonologically as single segments. Similarly, prenasalised consonants involve both a nasal and an oral phase, but, for phonological reasons, are not interpreted as a sequence of two consonants. 'Contour tone' is the term used to describe the interpretation of either a falling or a rising tonal pattern as a sequence of high tone + low tone (H+L) or low tone + high tone (L+H), respectively. As such tonal patterns can be associated with single (short) vowels, we again have two apparently sequentially distinct feature specifications associated with a single segment.

As an example of the relevance of this type of phenomenon for phonology, consider the forms from Apinayé in (55), presented by Anderson (1976):

(55) a. [V b d V]   b. [V b V]
          [Ṽ m d V]   [Ṽ m͡b V]
          [V b n Ṽ]   [V b͡m Ṽ]
          [Ṽ m n Ṽ]   [Ṽ m Ṽ]

These forms illustrate that the nasality of Apinayé consonants depends on the nasality of the contiguous vowel.[30] Those in (55a) show that the first consonant in a sequence of two takes its specification for nasality from a preceding vowel, and the second from a following vowel. In these cases, then, each consonant has simply one specification for nasality. In (55b), however, we see what happens when there is only a *single* intervocalic consonant. If both vowels have the same value for nasality, there is no problem – the consonant has the same value. However, in cases where the vowels have opposite values, it seems that *both* vowels spread their values, to give either a prenasalised or a postnasalised stop. Intuitively, the generalisation here is quite obvious: the first part of the consonant gets its nasality specification from the preceding vowel; the second part from the following vowel. However, such a state of affairs is difficult to express in the formalism of *SPE*,

---

[30] Strictly speaking, the data in (55) only shows that the nasality of the vowels and consonants are not independent, rather than showing the directionality of the relationship. For a discussion of the details of this phenomenon, see Anderson (1976).

which would require the introduction of features such as [prenasalised] and [postnasalised], together with two distinct rules, to express the sequential change within the segment, as in (56) and (57):

(56) a. $\begin{bmatrix} +\text{cons} \\ \vdots \\ +\text{nas} \\ +\text{prenas} \end{bmatrix}$ b. $\begin{bmatrix} +\text{cons} \\ \vdots \\ +\text{nas} \\ +\text{postnas} \end{bmatrix}$

(57) a. $C \rightarrow [+\text{prenas}] / \begin{bmatrix} V \\ +\text{nas} \end{bmatrix} \text{---}$

  b. $C \rightarrow [+\text{postnas}] / \text{---} \begin{bmatrix} V \\ +\text{nas} \end{bmatrix}$

However, (58), in which there are *two* occurrences of [nasal], seems more adequately to express the phonetic state of affairs in Apinayé, which is, quite simply, that at the left prenasalised consonants show the same behaviour as nasals do, whereas at the right they pattern with non-nasals (cf. Anderson 1976):

(58) $\begin{bmatrix} +\text{cons} \\ \vdots \\ +\text{nas}, -\text{nas} \end{bmatrix}$

Such phenomena are often referred to as **edge effects**, and many similar cases can be found. A particularly strong case can be made with reference to contour-toned vowels. Indeed, the analysis of tone systems in languages provided much of the initial impetus for the development of autosegmental phonology (see Goldsmith 1976, for example), and is still commonly used to introduce the theory (e.g. Goldsmith 1990). We look briefly here at the issues involved.

In many languages of the world lexical items are specified as bearing a particular tone. Let us consider a simple system with only two tones, High (H) and Low (L), such as that of Mende, a language spoken in Sierra Leone (cf. Halle and Clements 1983). (59) gives some Mende lexical items, in which the tones are marked on the vowels of each item (we follow the normal convention of marking high tone with an acute accent (´) and low tone with a grave accent (`)):

(59) kɔ́   'war'
    pélé   'house'
    bèlè   'trousers'
    nàvó   'money'

In (59) we see that each vowel has a single tonal specification, so that at first sight we might assume that tone can be dealt with linearly, just like features such as [nasal] in the *SPE* account. Things become more complicated, however, when we consider forms such as those in (60):

(60) mbû   'owl'
      mbǎ   'rice'
      njàhâ 'woman'

These forms display what are referred to as 'contour tones', i.e. falling tones (ˆ) and rising tones (ˇ). Does this mean that we also have to recognise contour tones as basic tonal types in Mende?

This question can be answered by considering what happens to the tonal pattern of the various forms in (59) and (60) when they combine with the suffix -*ma*, meaning 'on':

(61) a. kɔ́-má   b. mbú-mà
          pélé-má   mbà-má
          bèlè-mà   njàhá-mà
          nàvó-má

The forms in (61a) demonstrate that the suffix -*ma* has no independent tonal specification. Rather it acquires its tone by spreading of the tone which is associated with the last vowel of the stem, as in (62):

(62) a. H   b. L L
          ⌐˙˙˙˙˙. | ⌐˙˙˙˙˙.
          kɔ - m a   bɛlɛ - m a

Thus a single tonal specification may be associated with more than one segment. But we can go further than this. Compare (61) with (59) and (60). We see that the tone of the suffix can differ from the final tone of the stem, but only if the final tone of the stem when it occurs without a suffix is a contour tone. Thus, if the final tone of the stem in isolation is a falling tone, the suffix acquires a low tone, while the final tone of the stem changes into a high tone, as is evidenced by [mbû] vs [mbúmà]. If the final tone is a rising tone, exactly the reverse holds ([mbǎ] vs [mbàmá]).

What does this phenomenon tell us about tonal representations? Among other things, it suggests that contour tones are not independent basic entities, but, rather, are realisations of a *sequence* of two tones (H+L or L+H), associated with a single vowel. Thus [mbû] and [mbǎ] might be represented as:

(63) a.   H L   b.   L H

We have now uncovered a case in which a single segment is associated with
two tones, in addition to the cases given in (62), where a single tone is associated to two segments. Thus the tonal specification appears to be independent of the segmental representation, as is further evidenced by the behaviour
of the forms in (61b). These forms not only confirm that contour tones are
sequences of simple tones, but also show that underlyingly the tones are not
associated with individual vowels, but are **floating**: they form part of the
lexical representation of the morpheme in question, but do not link up with
the vowels. Rather, the association of tones to vowels takes place in Mende
only after suffixation.

Before giving an account of how we derive the forms in (61b), let us
consider how the process of association operates. The general principle of
association is clearly that in (64):

(64)   Associate tones to vowels

However, (64) can be seen as the result of a combination of three sub-
principles which ensure that the process of association produces well-formed
surface representations, i.e. representations in which every tone is associated
with at least one vowel, and every vowel with at least one tone. These sub-
principles are given in (65) (cf. van der Hulst 1984):

(65) a. *Mapping*
          Associate each tone with a vowel, working from left to right.
      b. *Spreading*
          If there are fewer tones than vowels, associate the final tone with
          all remaining vowels.
      c. *Dumping*
          If there are fewer vowels than tones, associate all remaining tones
          with the final vowel.

In the light of these principles (which we have formulated here to account
for the Mende data only), we can derive various of the forms given above
as follows. (66a) shows the derivations of stems alone; (66b) of stems when
combined with a suffix. We indicate 'new' associations at each stage with
a dashed line; existing associations at any stage are indicated by a solid
line:

(66) a.   L   H L   L H L

                                  bɛlɛ   m b u   n j a h a

  mapping   L   H L   L H L
  →   bɛlɛ   m b u   n j a h a

  spreading   L
  →   bɛlɛ   —   —

  dumping   H L   L H L
  →   —   m b u   n j a h a

                     [bɛ̀lɛ̀]   [mbû]   [njàhâ]

     b.   L   H L   L H L

                                    bɛlɛma   m b u m a   n j a h a m a

  mapping   L   H L   L H L
  →   bɛlɛma   m b u m a   n j a h a m a

  spreading   L
  →   bɛlɛma   —   —

  dumping
  →   —   —   —

                     [bɛ̀lɛ̀mà]   [mbúmà]   [njàhámà]

What (66) shows us is how Mende responds to a mismatch between the number of tones and the number of vowels, or more correctly the number of **tone-bearing units** (TBUs) in any word. The phonology of the language demands that all tones are realised, and so, where there are more tones than available TBUs, two tones must share a TBU. Equally, though, each TBU must be realised with a tone; spreading ensures that any toneless TBU can share a tone with some other TBU. This means that a stem-final contour tone is split into its two component tones when the toneless suffix *-ma* is attached to the stem.

However, not all tone languages allow contour tones. Goldsmith (1990: 20ff.) considers a dialect of Mixtecan, a tone language of Mexico, which 'has the property of requiring each vowel to have – maximally and minimally – exactly one tone'. What happens in this kind of language when there are more tones than vowels?

Goldsmith illustrates this with the following three words (we use M as a shorthand for Mid tone):

(67)   a. L H   b. MM   c. MMH
          | | | | | |
       s u ʧ i 'child'   k e e 'go away'   k e e 'eat'

This dialect of Mixtecan has High, Mid and Low tones, which are associated on a one-to-one basis with the vowels, as shown in (67a, b). As we would expect, when these two words are combined as in (68), the associations between tones and vowels remains unchanged:

(68)   MM   L H
        | | | |
       k e e s u ʧ i   'the child will go away'

However, certain words, such as *kee* 'eat' in (67c), 'idiosyncratically have a High tone suffixed to them which is not realized when the word is pronounced in isolation, but which is realized when there is a following word for it to associate to'. When this word combines with /suʧi/, there are more tones than vowels, i.e. TBUs:

(69)   MMH   L H
        | | ⸜⸜ |
       k e e   s u ʧ i   'the child will eat'

The final floating H tone of *kee* 'eat' displaces the L tone of /suʧi/, which is then left unassociated. Because, unlike Mende, the language does not permit contour tones, this displaced L tone is simply not realised. Thus different languages may respond to similar situations in rather different ways, depending on the phonological possibilities available to them.

Representations such as the ones we have been developing for tone capture the insight that the phenomena considered are manifestations of a more general property of speech, namely that segmental representations should allow for **overlapping**. In other words, these phenomena suggest that we should abandon what we might refer to as the **strict segment hypothesis**, embodied in representations such as those in (53), and allow single segments to be linked to more than one value of the same feature, and also a single feature to be associated with two segments.

This, then, is the central property of the theory of autosegmental phonology. However, it is of course not the case that feature spreading is an unrestricted process; rather, there are severe restrictions on the way in which features can spread from one segment to another. To illustrate this point in a preliminary way, we turn to the phenomenon of nasal spreading in English. In a word such as *pan*, the vowel is generally phonetically nasalised, to give [pæ̃n], as represented in (70):

(70)

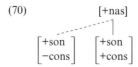

Here a single feature, [nasal], spreads to the preceding vowel. However, spreading is restricted, as is apparent if we consider words such as *kiln*, in which no spreading can take place. A pronunciation such as [kĩln], in which nasality spreads across an intervening liquid, is not possible. If we assume for the moment that the liquid is specified as [−nasal], this possibility is ruled out by a basic principle of autosegmental phonology, which is usually referred to as the **no-crossing condition**, formulated in (71) (see e.g. Goldsmith 1976 and, for discussion, Hammond 1988; Sagey 1988; Coleman 1998):

(71) *The no-crossing condition*
      Association lines may not cross

The condition prevents segments sharing a feature specification if an intervening segment has the opposite value for that feature. Thus in *kiln*, for example, spreading is prevented because the two segments are not **adjacent**, as shown in (72):

(72)   * [−nas]   [−nas][+nas]
         | ------|----⌐
        k   ɪ   l   n

The non-adjacency of the two segments means that the [+nasal] specification for /n/ would have to spread *across* the association line linking the nasality node to the rest of the feature specification for /l/, thus violating (71).[31]

It appears then that the fact that nasality does not spread across the lateral in *kiln* is because spreading must be **local**, i.e. a feature can only spread to an

---

[31] We should note that this treatment of the no-crossing condition is grossly simplified, in that we have not yet introduced the notion of underspecification (see §2.2).

adjacent segment. But it is clearly not the case that spreading processes are necessarily local in this strict sense. For example, in our discussion of Mende tone spreading above, we saw that tones could spread from one vowel to another, ignoring intervening consonants. A very similar situation is found in vowel harmony processes, such as the ATR harmony process of Akan illustrated in (29). Again, consonants are 'invisible' to the spreading harmony feature, so that the appropriate value of the feature [ATR] can spread from one vowel to another. Similar phenomena, involving various features, can readily be found.

Nevertheless, the claim that spreading is local is a sound one. How can we explain such phenomena, without abandoning this hypothesis? Consider a possible representation of the result of the ATR harmony process of Akan:

(73)　　　[+ATR]

　　　／wu b e n u m ? /

We can maintain the hypothesis by assuming that the segments which intervene between the various vowels in (73) have no representation for [ATR]. That is /b/ and /n/ in (73) are 'invisible' to the spreading feature – the vowels, then, are adjacent with respect to [ATR].

We do not at this stage investigate the issue of the circumstances under which segments can lack specifications for particular features. However, notice that this approach suggests that individual features are independent of each other in the sense that the node dominating a feature (or group of features) occupies its own **tier**, and leads to a representation in which adjacency on one tier need not correspond to adjacency on another tier.

On the assumption that each node occupies its own tier, we provide in (74) a representation of the English word *plank*, realised as [pl̥æŋk], and thus displaying spreading processes involving the tiers occupied by the features [voice], [nasal] and [back] (we ignore all other features here, and represent them simply by orthographic symbols):

(74)

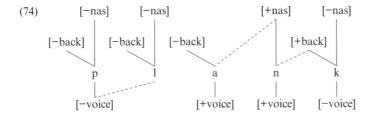

This conception of phonological structure is notoriously difficult to represent on paper, as it is essentially three-dimensional. (75) is an attempt at a more or less complete phonological representation of the English word *cab* /kæb/, in which no feature sharing is involved (as we have not yet developed a theory of the conditions under which segments can lack a specification for particular features, we here provide each segment with a specification for every feature):

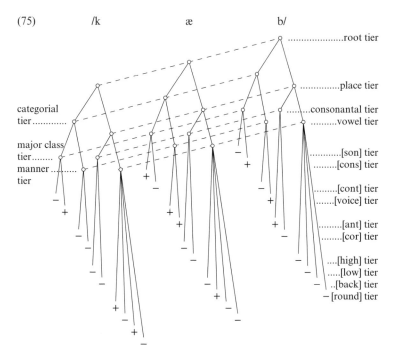

In (75) we see that each tier consists of a set of nodes. Thus, on the major class tier, we find three class nodes, one for each segment, showing that each segment has some specification for the features dominated by the major class node. On the [sonorant] tier, we again find three specifications. These, however, bear a label, i.e. either '+' or '−', given the fact that this is a content tier, rather than a class tier. Thus, for /k/ and /b/ we find the value '−', and for /æ/ the value '+'.

(75), then, shows both the independence of individual features and their grouping. It does not, however, show any examples of the phenomenon we have been discussing, the overlapping of segments. It is, however, clear how this can be achieved, although, again, the representation of what is quite a simple notion is difficult in terms of the kind of formalism proposed in (75).

Let us consider again the phenomenon of assimilation of place of articulation in forms such as *camber*, where the place of articulation of the nasal is determined by that of the stop. As we demonstrated in (48), this state of affairs can be analysed as involving the spreading of the place features of the stop to the nasal, which has no independent place specification.[32] In terms of the formalism in (75), this can be characterised as in (76), which shows the underlying representation for the sequence /Nb/ (i.e. nasal unspecified for place of articulation followed by /b/), and in (77), the surface representation for [mb] after spreading:[33]

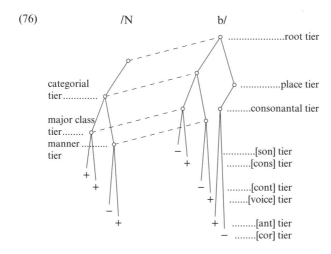

(76)   /N   b/

In (76) we find no place node for the nasal consonant. As a result of spreading, however, we have (77):

---

[32] In terms of a Prague School approach to phonology (see Trubetzkoy 1939), what we have here is a case of neutralisation: an opposition which is found elsewhere in the language (e.g. /ræm/ vs /ræn/ vs /ræŋ/) is not found in a particular environment, as evidenced by (1). In this approach, appeal was also made to a kind of underspecification: the segment occurring in a neutralisation environment was referred to as an 'archiphoneme', i.e. a phonological unit lacking those phonological properties neutralised in the environment in question, in this case the properties characterising place of articulation. Thus the set of words in (1) would be represented in Prague School phonology as /kæNbə/, /kæNtə/ and /kæNkə/, where /N/ is the archiphoneme characterising a nasal consonant, without a specification for place of articulation, which is not distinctive *in this environment*. (For a discussion, see Lass 1984a: ch. 3.) As we shall see in §2.2, the essence of this approach is contained in modern theories of underspecification, although rather different terminology is used; notice that the term 'archisegment' rather than archiphoneme is commonly used.

[33] We assume that non-dorsal consonants such as those in (76) and (77) lack features dominated by the vowel node in (75).

43

(77)   [m   b]

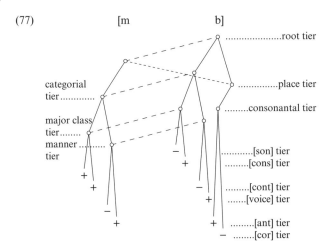

......................root tier

categorial
tier............   ....place tier

major class   ....consonantal tier
tier........
manner......
tier   ....[son] tier
                     ....[cons] tier

                     ....[cont] tier
                     ....[voice] tier

                     ....[ant] tier
                     ....[cor] tier

As in (48), the spreading of the place node of /b/ to the nasal 'segment' is denoted by the dashed line linking the root node of /m/ to the place node of /b/. Notice that, by convention, if a node spreads in this way, all the nodes which it dominates spread as well. In this case all the nodes characterising place of articulation spread as a result of the spreading of the place node, thus assigning labiality to the first of the two segments.

We see in (77) the consequences of abandoning the strict segment hypothesis. Although in the cases of the other tiers in (77) we find two nodes, there is only a single node on the place tier, and on all tiers dominated by it.

It is clear that the formalism used here can be used to account for the various other types of phenomena we have been considering. However, in view of the excessive complexity of diagrams like (75)–(77), we shall henceforth simplify our representations, using instead something rather more like (74) to characterise the notion of segments being made up of independent tiers, with the possibility of 'node sharing'. The reader should be aware, however, that these are merely shorthand representations for the fuller diagrams we have just introduced. Unless the hierarchical structure of the tiers is at issue, then, we will make use of the simpler form of representation.

In this book, we will assume that the kind of feature geometry outlined above is indeed appropriate for the representation of segmental structure, but we will not consider in any detail the question of the exact nature of this structure. In other words, we shall not consider at this point the question of whether the particular structure in (42) or (43), which we have adopted in the immediately preceding discussion, is appropriate, or whether some other organisation of the features into groups is to be preferred. Rather, we now apply the model developed above to two processes which seem particularly susceptible to an autosegmental treatment.

1.4.1   Old English i-*umlaut*

Old English displays a number of morphophonemic alternations, resulting from the operation of a sound-change known as Old English *i*-umlaut (OEIU), which involves various vowel changes triggered by the presence of /i/ or /j/ in a following syllable. These alternations are illustrated in (78), taken from Lass and Anderson (1975: 117):

(78)   *Alternation*

[uː]	[yː]	cūþ	'known'	cȳþan	'make known'
[u]	[y]	burg	'city'	byrig	'city (DAT SG)'
[oː]	[øː] ([eː])	dōm	'judgement'	dēman	'judge'
[o]	[ø] ([e])	ofost	'haste'	efstan	'hasten'
[ɑː]	[æː]	hāl	'whole'	hǣlan	'heal'
[ɑ]	[e]	mann	'man'	menn	'men'
[ɑ]	[æ]	faran	'go'	færst	'go (2SG)'

As will be seen from (78), by the Old English period most of the umlauted forms (those in the second column) had lost the triggering environment /i/ or /j/ (but note *byrig*, which retains /i/). However, whatever the philological details of OEIU, and whether or not it forms part of the *synchronic* phonology of Old English, it is clear that we are dealing here with a (historical) phonological process whereby, among other things, back vowels become front under the influence of a high front vowel or approximant.[34] Thus (79) shows the way in which some of the relevant forms underwent OEIU:[35]

(79)   *cūþ+i+an   > *cȳþ+i+an   > cȳþan
       know-CAUSE-INF
       *hāl+i+an   > *hǣl+i+an   > hǣlan
       whole-CAUSE-INF
       *far+ist   > *fær+ist   > færst
       go-2SG

In terms of an autosegmental approach, it is clear that what we have here is the spreading of an autosegment on the backness tier from the vowel of the suffix. A suitable representation might be that in (80):

---

[34] OEIU also affects low front vowels, as well as various diphthongs, but we ignore this here.

[35] Note the use of * here to denote that we are dealing with a reconstructed, rather than an attested, historical form.

(80)

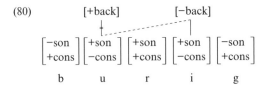

$$\begin{bmatrix} -son \\ +cons \end{bmatrix} \begin{bmatrix} +son \\ -cons \end{bmatrix} \begin{bmatrix} +son \\ +cons \end{bmatrix} \begin{bmatrix} +son \\ -cons \end{bmatrix} \begin{bmatrix} -son \\ +cons \end{bmatrix}$$

b u r i g

There are various aspects of OEIU which differ from certain of the auto-segmental processes which we have previously considered. In the first place, notice that the spreading here is to a segment which apparently already bears a value on the backness tier. The spreading value thus *replaces* the original value, which must then be **delinked** (represented by the double bar through the association line). The process thus appears to be **feature-changing**. No-tice, too, that although the consonants bear no specifications on the backness tier, so that they do not block spreading by violation of the no-crossing condition, it might well be possible to argue that they are also affected by spreading, as in cases where a phoneme may have either a [−back] or a [+back] allophone (e.g. [ç] vs [x] in the case of final *g* in Old English), it is the [−back] allophone which is found in the umlauted cases.

1.4.2 *Vowel harmony in Turkish*
We have just considered a phonological process of English which involves two vowels showing agreement in the values for a particular feature, a situation which is naturally represented within a model incorporating the notion of feature spreading. As we have seen with respect to the feature [ATR] (§1.3.3), however, there are even more spectacular examples of agreement of this sort, in which, within a particular phonological 'domain' in a language − say the word − all the vowels must have the same value for a particular feature (or indeed for a number of features). These vowel harmony phe-nomena have provided a fertile source of exemplification for proponents of autosegmental phonology. For this reason, we consider here in a little detail one of the most familiar processes of vowel harmony, that found in Turkish.

Turkish has a system of eight distinctive vowels, which are classified on phonological grounds into two height classes:[36]

(81)

	[−back]		[+back]	
	[−round]	[+round]	[−round]	[+round]
[+high]	i	y	ɨ	u
[−high]	e	ø	ɑ	o

---

[36] We ignore here the question of the precise phonetic realisation of the non-high series − we make no claim as to the phonetic accuracy of the transcriptions used here.

As shown in (82), all eight vowels can appear in monosyllabic stems, thus implying that the eight-way contrast has phonemic status:

(82) çift [çift] 'couple'
  üç   [yç]   'three'
  ek   [ek]   'affix'
  köy [køj] 'village'
  kız [kɨz] 'girl'
  kurt [kurt] 'worm'
  at   [ɑt]   'horse'
  son [son] 'end'

In polysyllabic words, however, a number of restrictions hold. We give a preliminary formulation of these restrictions as (83):

(83) a. All vowels must have the same value for the feature [back].
      b. A high vowel must have the same value for [round] as the directly preceding vowel (if any).

These requirements hold both in underived stems, i.e. words consisting of single morphemes, and in derived words, i.e. words consisting of a stem and a suffix (although there are many exceptional forms in underived words). The following examples (from van der Hulst and van de Weijer 1991) illustrate some typical derived forms:

(84)	ABS SG	POSS SG		ABS SG	POSS SG	
	son	sonu	'end'	dere	deresi	'river'
	boru	borusu	'pipe'	at	atɨ	'horse'
	køj	køjy	'village'	tat	tadɨ	'taste'
	kurt	kurdu	'worm'	kɨz	kɨzɨ	'girl'
	tilki	tilkisi	'fox'	kap	kabɨ	'container'
	inek	inei	'cow'	yty	ytysy	'iron'

We should notice that Turkish is an agglutinative language, which typically forms words by adding one or more suffixes to the stem. Thus the words in (84) consist of a stem morpheme, which can either occur on its own as the absolute singular form (e.g. *boru*), or be followed by a possessive suffix (which, because of the harmony rules, may have any one of the realisations [i y ɨ u]).[37]

The requirement in (83a) represents the typical situation for vowel harmony: all vowels within some domain (the word, in this case) agree with respect to some feature ([back], in this case). It is clear that this kind of situation can be

---

[37] Notice that other segments in the stem morpheme may be affected by the suffixation process – this need not concern us here.

characterised by the autosegmental mechanism we have been developing, although we should notice that (83a) represents a different state of affairs from OE *i*-umlaut, in that it does not seem to involve spreading from one vowel to another; rather, *all* the vowels within the domain of the harmony process seem to have the same value for the feature in question.

(83b) is a more complicated restriction, which differs from (83a) in two ways. Firstly, the restriction concerns only a subclass of the vowels, the high vowels, and secondly, it has a directional aspect, which is not found in (83a).

The additional set of paradigms in (85) show the effect of (83b): non-high vowels do not display rounding harmony:

(85)	ABS SG	ABL SG	ABS PL	POSS PL	
	son	sondan	sonlar	sonlarɨ	'end'
	boru	borudan	borular	borularɨ	'pipe'
	køj	køjden	køjler	køjleri	'village'
	kurt	kurttan	kurtlar	kurtlarɨ	'worm'
	tilki	tilkiden	tilkiler	tilkileri	'fox'
	inek	inekten	inekler	inekleri	'cow'
	dere	dereden	dereler	dereleri	'river'
	at	attan	atlar	atlarɨ	'horse'
	tat	tattan	tatlar	tatlarɨ	'taste'
	kɨz	kɨzdan	kɨzlar	kɨzlarɨ	'girl'
	kap	kaptan	kaplar	kaplarɨ	'container'
	yty	ytyden	ytyler	ytyleri	'iron'

(where [den, dan] – or [ten, tan] – are the realisations of the ablative morpheme, [ler, lar] those of the plural morpheme, and, as above, [i, ɨ] two of the realisations of the possessive morpheme).

Low vowels, then, need not be in rounding harmony with other vowels, as shown by the ablative singular and absolutive plural forms of *son* [son] 'end', where a back rounded vowel is followed by a low unrounded vowel, and by the same forms for *köy* [køj] 'village', where front vowels are involved.

The restrictions on rounding harmony can be derived from a more general constraint:

(86) The vowels /o/ and /ø/ only occur in initial syllables (i.e. low vowels are never [+round] except in initial syllables).

Let us now turn to the directional aspect of rounding harmony. Consideration of the possessive plural forms in (85) shows that a vowel takes its value for [round] from the immediately preceding vowel, rather than from the first one. Consider *ütüler* [ytyler], the plural form of *ütü* 'iron'. The plural morpheme contains a low vowel, which is therefore unrounded, even though the vowels of *ütü* [yty] are rounded (cf. (86)). The singular possessive form is *ütüsü* [ytysy], with the possessive morpheme being realised as [y] – because it is a high vowel, it undergoes rounding harmony. However, the plural possessive form is *ütüleri* [ytyleri]. Here the possessive morpheme is realised as [i], i.e. the vowel is unrounded. This is clearly because the immediately preceding vowel – the vowel of the plural morpheme – is unrounded, and so the vowel of the possessive morpheme harmonises in the expected way.

Thus the rounding of a high vowel cannot spread across a following low (and therefore unrounded) vowel. As we have already seen, then, harmony statements apply to adjacent vowels. More precisely, in this case rounding harmony only applies to segments which are adjacent *on the roundness tier*.

The harmony processes of Turkish mean that the full set of vowel contrasts need only be specified on initial vowels. In non-initial syllables we only find a contrast between [+high] and [−high], with the values of the features [round] and [back] being determined by spreading from the initial syllable to non-initial syllables.

Many autosegmental treatments of Turkish vowel harmony propose that, lexically, the features [back] and [round] are floating, i.e. they are not lexically associated to a particular vowel. In order to derive the correct surface forms, we need two association rules and one condition, given in (87):

(87)   a.   Associate [back] and [round] to the first vowel (initial association).
       b.   Associate [back] and [round] to the remaining vowels (spreading).
       c.   [+round] may not associate to non-initial non-high vowels
            (condition on target vowel).

Consider now the following derivation of the form *boruları* [borularɨ]:

(88)   [+round]

        b   [−high]   r   [+high]   –   l   [−high]   r   –   [+high]   →

        [+back]

        [+round]

        b   [−high]   r   [+high]   –   l   [−high]   r   –   [+high]   →

        [+back]

        [+round]

        b   [−high]   r   [+high]   –   l   [−high]   r   –   [+high]

        [+back]

Observe that the impossibility of [+round] spreading to the low vowel of the plural suffix also blocks its spreading to the possessive suffix. Furthermore, in order to derive the surface representations, we must assume that all vowels not specified for [round] are automatically assigned the value [−round].

1.5 Summary

This chapter has been concerned with phonological segments, in particular their internal structure. We have shown that segments are not the basic atoms of phonological structure; much of §1.2 dealt with the evidence for postulating units smaller than the segment. These units, commonly referred to as features, are the true atoms of segmental structure, and are primarily motivated by the way in which particular groups of segments recurrently pattern together as natural classes in phonological generalisations (i.e. constraints and processes), generally as a result of some shared phonetic property, which in turn provides the basis for the definition of the relevant feature. For example, the vowels /u o ɔ/ in some language may function as a natural class on the basis of the shared phonetic property of lip-rounding, thus leading us to postulate a feature [round] in our model of representation. The simple enumeration of sets of segments would leave unexplained why these sets of segments form natural classes and why certain changes occur in certain environments.

In §1.3 we discussed a set of features that can be motivated on the basis of various well-known constraints and processes, starting with major class and manner features and then proceeding with vocalic features and consonantal features, respectively. It has not been our intention to suggest that this is the only possible set of features; indeed, we have considered a number of alternatives for features characterising particular phonetic and phonological dimensions. In the domain of vowel features, for example, we proposed that different features may be necessary for several closely related dimensions (height, tongue root position and tenseness). Our discussion of consonantal features included surveys of systems based on place of articulation as well as those based on the active articulator. Nonetheless, the features which we have discussed (or close equivalents) are encountered in most models of segmental representation, and as such provide a general grounding in feature theory. At the end of §1.3, we introduced the idea that the groups that we identified in our survey of features may themselves form part of the segmental structure, which thereby becomes a hierarchical structure, often represented as a tree. This allows rules and constraints to refer not only to the features themselves but also to organisational nodes dominating one or more features.

In §1.4 we showed that in some circumstances an individual feature may simultaneously be assigned to more than one segment. In other words, features are to some extent independent of the notion of segment itself; a single feature may have as its domain a consonant cluster, a syllable or even a complete word. The fact that the consonants in an English nasal + stop cluster such as [mp] or [ŋk] *necessarily* have the same place of articulation, for example, suggests that the two segments involved have only a single feature characterising the place of articulation. We introduced this autosegmental approach to the characterisation of assimilation and harmony processes by looking at tonal phenomena, and illustrated it further with several examples involving umlaut and vowel harmony, in the course of which we also examined some of the principles that govern the association between features and segments. In the following chapter, we will show that our concept of the phonological feature will have to be substantially refined to take account of the full range of phonological processes which we encounter in language; in addition, we will consider the formal nature of features in rather more detail than here.

1.6 Further reading

This chapter has been concerned with the phonological segment and its internal organisation in terms of features. The transcription system of the IPA (see Appendix) reflects a view of phonology in which segment-sized units are the central units in phonological analysis. In this view phonological properties are primarily properties of segments, not of larger units such as syllables.

The view that segments consist of smaller phonological units (§1.2) originates with the work of Trubetzkoy (1939), who proposes to group segments according to the distinctive oppositions in which they participate. Jakobson *et al.* (1951) and Jakobson and Halle (1956) formalise the notion in terms of binary distinctive features (§1.3). See also Ladefoged (1980), Halle (1983). In *SPE* we find a modified system and an emphasis on articulatory definitions. Hyman (1975) and Baltaxe (1978) contain extensive discussion of the binary tradition, and Keating (1988a) provides an overview. See also Jakobson and Waugh (1979) for a study of features in a somewhat wider context. Kaye (1989: ch. 2) discusses the distributional motivation for grouping segments into natural classes. Within the theory of **articulatory phonology**, an approach which we have not considered here, Browman and Goldstein (1986, 1989, 1992) consider the basic units of phonology to be 'articulatory gestures', rather than features. See also Clements (1992).

Major class features (§1.3.1) are discussed in Selkirk (1984b), Anderson and Ewen (1987), McCarthy (1988), Clements (1990), van der Hulst and Ewen

(1991), Kaisse (1992) and Hume and Odden (1995). Manner features include features for voicing (cf. also below) and continuancy (Davis 1989), for the distinctive properties of liquids (Spencer 1985; Lindau 1985; Walsh Dickey 1997) and for nasality (see Anderson 1976 and the papers in Ferguson *et al.* 1975 and Huffman and Krakow 1993). The latter property has received a great deal of attention, particularly in the context of harmony processes; cf. Herbert (1986) and Cohn (1990, 1993), Piggott (1988), Piggott and van der Hulst (1997). Vowel features (§1.3.2) are discussed in Lindau (1978), Wood (1982), Fischer-Jørgensen (1985), van der Hulst (1988), Clements (1989) and Odden (1991). Clements (1991) addresses the issue of vowel height and related dimensions, which he proposes to capture in terms of a single aperture dimension. See also Goad (1993). The discussion on this dimension (and on vowel features in general) often centres around the proper treatment of a large variety of vowel harmony systems; cf. the papers in Vago (1980), as well as van der Hulst (1988) and van der Hulst and van de Weijer (1995). There is extensive literature on ATR harmony systems (§1.3.3); see, e.g., Archangeli and Pulleyblank (1994). The four articulator-based features (§1.3.4) proposed by McCarthy (1988) characterising the major places of articulation ([labial], [coronal], [dorsal], [radical]) have also been adopted in the description of vowels (Sagey 1986; see also Hume 1992, Clements and Hume 1995). The status of coronals has been an issue of some debate; see for example the papers in Paradis and Prunet (1991), as well as Lahiri and Blumstein (1984), McCarthy and Taub (1992) and Hall (1997). For discussion of other consonantal features, see Hayward and Hayward (1989), Ladefoged and Maddieson (1989), Trigo (1991), McCarthy (1994), Ní Chiosáin (1994) and Rice (1995). On proposals for a feature [grave], see Hyman (1973), Vago (1976) and Odden (1978). There is a large amount of literature on the concept of grouping features into some kind of hierarchical structure (§1.3.5). Den Dikken and van der Hulst (1988) and McCarthy (1988) discuss a wide variety of proposals in this area (see also Odden 1991; Halle 1995; Pulleyblank 1995). Developments of the concept of grouping proposed in dependency phonology are discussed in van der Hulst (1995).

All discussion of features depends either on the analysis of phonological processes or on the reliability of information on segment inventories. With respect to the latter, Maddieson (1984) and Ladefoged and Maddieson (1996) are extremely valuable. The former study contains inventories of over 400 languages, and separate chapters dealing with the various classes of segments (e.g. vowels, liquids, etc.). The latter contains a wealth of information on potential contrasting properties of speech sounds. See also Crothers (1978).

In §1.4 we introduced the model of autosegmental phonology. This approach can be traced back to a theory which we have not considered in this chapter, that of the Firthian school of **prosodic analysis** (see e.g. Firth 1948 and the other papers in Palmer 1970; also Langendoen 1968), which is essentially non-segmental in approach. See the series of papers by Goldsmith (1992), Ogden and Local (1994) and Goldsmith (1994) for a discussion of the relationship between autosegmental phonology and prosodic analysis. Firthian phonology has also been combined with work in **declarative phonology** (Ogden 1999; see also Coleman 1998). An alternative model of 'non-segmental' phonology is offered by Griffen (1976). Analyses of the formal properties of autosegmental phonology are offered by Bird (1995; see also Goldsmith 1997), Kornai (1995) and Scobbie (1997).

For work on tone, see the papers in Fromkin (1978), as well as Maddieson (1978). The study of tonal phenomena has been of crucial importance for the development of autosegmental phonology; see the studies in Clements and Goldsmith (1984) and van der Hulst and Snider (1993). Tone features, because of their relationship to laryngeal features, are often discussed together with features for phonation (voicing types), leading to proposals for a unified set of laryngeal features for tonal contrasts and phonation contrasts. See Bao (1990), Duanmu (1990), Odden (1995) and Yip (1995) for further studies on tone.

On airstream mechanisms, see Catford (1977) for a description, and Ladefoged (1971), Lass (1984a), Ladefoged and Traill (1994) on possible feature systems.

Old English *i*-umlaut (§1.4.1) has been the subject of numerous diachronic and synchronic studies; see e.g. Lass and Anderson (1975), Hogg (1992a, b). For Turkish vowel harmony (§1.4.2), see Clements and Sezer (1982) and van der Hulst and van de Weijer (1991).

General overviews of non-linear phonology are given by van der Hulst and Smith (1982a, 1985), Goldsmith (1990) and many of the articles in Goldsmith (1995). A historical overview of some of the developments in non-linear phonology from the mid-eighties up to the mid-nineties can be found in van der Hulst and van de Weijer (1995).

For studies dealing with the structure of the segment in relation to phonological acquisition, see Vihman (1978), Levelt (1994), Stoel-Gammon and Stemberger (1994) and Rice and Avery (1997).

The structure of the segment in the phonology of sign languages is considered by Liddell and Johnson (1989), Sandler (1989), van der Hulst (1993) and Brentari (1999).

2
Features

2.1 The nature of phonological features

In Chapter 1 we established that the atoms of phonological representation must be smaller than the segments expressed in the notational system of, for example, the IPA, and that these atoms are appropriately modelled by units commonly referred to as phonological features. Each phonological feature is defined in terms of some phonetic property, so that any phonological feature system makes a claim as to the phonetic properties which can function in the phonological processes of languages. The value associated with a feature for a particular segment shows that that segment either does or does not bear the phonetic property in question. For example, if we assign a segment the feature-values [+low, −round], we are claiming that it belongs to the **class** of [+low] segments, but not to the class of [+round] segments. Although this may seem trivial, we shall show later in this section that the latter claim is not as straightforward as it may appear. In particular, the corollary of the claim, i.e. that something which does not belong to the class of [+round] segments therefore belongs to the class of [−round] segments, is controversial, and we shall return to this below. However, irrespective of this issue, the tacit assumption we have been making is that there is always a binary choice involved: segments either belong to the set characterised by '+' or the set characterised by '−'. On this assumption, segments never have *more* than two degrees of a particular property, at least from a phonological viewpoint.[1]

This **binarity** claim constitutes an empirical hypothesis, which is not immediately supported by phonetic observations, or indeed by certain phonological analyses. Consider, for example, the phenomenon of nasalisation. It is indisputable that, from a phonetic point of view, we can establish the existence of various degrees of nasalisation, and this might lead us to wonder

---

[1] See, however, our discussion of vowel height in §1.3.3; we return to this below.

whether it is necessary for phonological classification to be strictly binary. Indeed, various phonologists have argued that certain phonological oppositions are clearly **multivalued**, rather than binary, and that this should be reflected by allowing *phonological* features to have more than two values. For example, Ladefoged (1971: 35) suggests that the language Chinantec, spoken in Mexico, may have two contrastive degrees of nasalisation, as in (1) (data from the Palantla dialect of Chinantec; Merrifield 1963):[2]

(1)   a.   *non-nasalised*
           hɑ   'so, such'
           dzɑ e dzɑ si   'he goes to teach reading'
      b.   *lightly nasalised*
           hɑ̃   '(he) spreads open'
           dzɑ ẽ dzɑ hɑ   'he goes to count animals'
      c.   *heavily nasalised*
           hɑ̰̃   'foam, froth'
           dzɑ ḛ̃ dzɑ hɑ   'he goes to chase animals'

It might appear from (1) that a feature with at least three values is required to characterise this state of affairs. That is, we might characterise the nasality by means of a multivalued scalar feature, with the values [0 nasal], [1 nasal] and [2 nasal], in much the same way as suggested for vowel height in (25) of Chapter 1. Nevertheless, many phonologists have adopted the strongest possible version of the binarity hypothesis, i.e. that *all* phonological classification is binary. Proponents of this view, then, analyse apparently multivalued features in terms of two or more binary features. Such a strategy is apparent in the analysis of the vowel-height dimension in (21) in Chapter 1, in which what appeared at first sight to be a single multivalued parameter of vowel height was analysed in terms of the two binary features [high] and [low].

We do not at this point investigate the issue of whether we should allow for multivalued features in phonological descriptions. Rather, we restrict our discussion to the nature and representation of those oppositions which appear to involve no more than two members.

At first sight, the most natural way of representing the binarity hypothesis is to use the binary features which we introduced in Chapter 1, such as [±nasal], [±coronal], etc. In terms of the type of feature geometry which we introduced in §1.3.5, this approach is characterised by (2), which represents the difference between a nasal and a non-nasal sound, say English /m/ and /b/:

---

[2] We ignore tones here.

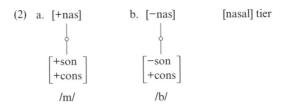

(2)   a. [+nas]   b. [−nas]   [nasal] tier

(Here and in what follows we associate the nasal feature with a node which denotes all other tiers in the segmental representation not relevant for the present discussion, but retain the major class tier.) However, there are other ways in which we might indicate whether a segment either has or does not have a particular property. Alongside specifications consisting of a feature-value and name, such as [+nasal], we might also make use of the contrast in (3):

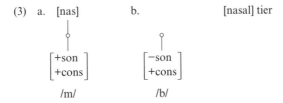

(3)   a. [nas]   b.   [nasal] tier

Here /m/ is characterised by making the feature [nasal] part of its representation, while /b/ has all the properties that /m/ has, except that it *lacks* the feature [nasal], i.e. it is a non-nasal sound. Thus we make no use of the *values* '+' and '−'; rather, /m/ is seen as having a property which /b/ lacks entirely. These two ways of representing a binary opposition may appear to be more or less equivalent. However, they embody two rather different empirical claims, as we will now show.

As we saw in §1.2, sets of segments which recurrently participate in phonological processes are referred to as natural classes. We claimed furthermore that the fact that a particular set of segments forms a natural class is in turn attributable to some shared phonetic property such as nasality, roundness or degree of sonorancy. The shared phonetic property is characterised in our system of phonological representation by a phonological feature, so that in the approach adopted in Chapter 1 all the segments forming a natural class bear the same value for a particular feature. Thus /u o ɔ y w/ in a particular language may take part in a phonological process by virtue of the fact that they form the natural class characterised within the system of phonological representation as [+round], as may /p t k b d g f θ s v ð z/, by virtue of their all being [−sonorant].

On the assumption that any binary feature can have both the values '+' and '−', it appears that the set of segments sharing either value for a particular feature should form a natural class. In other words, it should not matter whether a set of segments is characterised as [+F] or [−F] (where [F] is any feature); in either case, the set can take part in phonological processes. This claim is inherent in (2), the 'traditional' binary approach, which suggests that we can find phonological processes which make reference not only to the set of [+nasal] segments, but also to the set of [−nasal] segments. (3), however, makes a rather different claim, i.e. that only the nasal segments can have this status – there is no means of referring to the set of non-nasal sounds, which have no unique identifying property in (3); rather, the difference between nasal and non-nasal sounds is that the latter simply lack a property which the former possess.

It is clear, then, that the kind of evidence which we must look for in choosing between (2) and (3) consists in showing whether the set of non-nasal segments ever functions as a natural class in languages. If we do not discover such a case, we have, on the assumption that this state of affairs is not accidental but represents a 'real' phonological generalisation, immediately uncovered evidence for rejecting the binarity hypothesis in its traditional form, and, all other things being equal, for introducing segmental representations such as that in (3). The reverse also holds, of course: if the class of non-nasal sounds *does* play a role in the phonology of some language, then representations like those in (2) seem more appropriate.[3]

We have already seen that the set of nasal segments in a language constitutes a natural class. Recall the various examples discussed in §1.2, where all and only the nasal segments agree in place of articulation with a following consonant. Consider too the very common processes whereby nasal consonants spread their nasality to preceding vowels, to give allophonically nasalised vowels, as in English *plank* /plæŋk/ [pl̥æ̃ŋk] (cf. (74) in Chapter 1), or, in some languages, phonemically nasalised vowels, as in French *bon* /bɔ̃/ (with subsequent deletion of the nasal consonant):

(4)

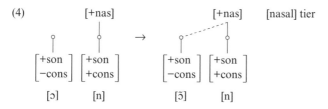

However, examples in which non-nasal sounds function as a natural class are, as far as we know, not attested. We do not find processes affecting, for

---

[3] In fact, evidence allowing us to reject the traditional binarity hypothesis is logically not available – in formal terms, it is a non-falsifiable hypothesis.

example, the class of non-nasal coronals (say /t d s z θ ð l r/) in a language, as opposed to the class of nasal coronals (/n/). For example, rules similar to (4), but with [−nasal] as the spreading node, as in (5), are simply unrecorded:

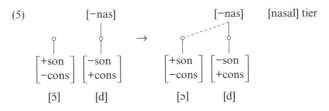

(5), which would change [ɔ̃d] into [ɔd] by spreading of [−nasal], is apparently an impossible rule.[4] This might of course be no more than an accidental gap in our knowledge of phonological processes, but, on the other hand, it might reflect a basic property of the phonological system, i.e. that nasality and the lack of nasality are not equivalent. If this is the case – and there seems little doubt that it is – then a theory of phonological representation which allows us to address either value equally easily seems to be excessively powerful. In general, our aim should be to restrict any part of our phonological theory to describe or generate states of affairs which are actually found in languages, and to prevent it from being able to describe things which are not found. Furthermore, the theory should make it more difficult to describe 'less natural' or 'unnatural' states of affairs. In other words, the generative capacity of our theory should be as limited as possible, always provided that we can adequately describe what *does* take place in the phonologies of the languages of the world.

In this case, then, it looks as if the lack of nasality is not a positive property of a segment, and thus plays no role in the characterisation of sounds, classes and processes. This in turn means that (3) apparently expresses this state of affairs more appropriately than (2), which suggests that [−nasal] is an 'addressable' value, and thus, inappropriately, allows the formulation of rules like (5). A system based on (3), however, does not have anything corresponding to the value [−nasal], and so cannot allow a rule to have the effect of (5); it is therefore to be preferred in this respect. The only way of excluding the possibility of the spreading of the lack of nasality in a system with [+nasal] *and* [−nasal], such as (2), would be to exclude reference to [−nasal] by incorporating some kind of explicit statement to the effect that this value

---

[4] We are not denying here that there are constraints in languages whereby a nasal vowel must be followed by a nasal consonant, while a non-nasal vowel must be followed by a non-nasal consonant. However, these do not result from spreading as such, but rather from general constraints on the well-formedness of particular sequences of vowel + consonant.

cannot function as a natural class – surely an undesirable and arbitrary complication.

However, the apparently asymmetric behaviour of [nasal] does not necessarily have consequences for all other features. Consider [sonorant], for example. We saw in §1.3.1 that there are processes affecting the class of [+sonorant] consonants, but also processes affecting the class of [−sonorant] segments. Thus the natural class of nasals and liquids can be referred to in phonological processes as [+sonorant, +consonantal], and, as we saw in (13) in Chapter 1, [−sonorant] is the feature-value which characterises the class of segments typically involved in final devoicing processes, i.e. stops and fricatives. Clearly, then, the difference between the sets of sonorant and non-sonorant segments is of a different phonological type from that between the sets of nasal and non-nasal segments: *both* [+sonorant] *and* [−sonorant] characterise natural classes.

The notion that features may be of different 'formal types' is obscured in the *SPE* binary approach, and indeed in the Jakobsonian precursor to *SPE*.[5] Nevertheless, it has a long tradition, although the original formulation of this idea was couched in a rather different theoretical framework, which did not incorporate the notion of feature in the form we have been discussing in this book. Trubetzkoy (1939) draws a distinction between two types of binary phonological opposition: **privative** and **equipollent**, in addition to **multivalued** oppositions of the type mentioned in §§1.3.3 and 2.1.[6] In the interpretation we have just given, nasality is an example of a privative opposition, i.e. one involving two classes which are characterised by the presence vs absence of a particular property, or 'mark' (*Merkmal* in Trubetzkoy's terms). As well as nasality, Trubetzkoy characterises contrasts involving rounding and voicing as examples of privative oppositions. In equipollent oppositions, on the other hand, two classes of sounds differ in that *both* classes have some property which the other lacks. The relation between the members of an equipollent opposition is one of 'logical equivalence' (Lass 1984a: 46). In feature theory, this notion has acquired a rather more specific interpretation, as we have seen with reference to the feature [sonorant]. It is used to characterise those binary features of which both values are available in the statement of phonological processes. Thus, for a feature [F], if both [+F] and [−F] form natural classes, the feature [F] is equipollent. In such cases, a representation like (6) (which appears inappropriate for [nasal]; cf. (2)) seems to reflect the equipollent character of the opposition:

---

[5] See Jakobson *et al.* (1951) and Jakobson and Halle (1956).
[6] For a discussion of these and related notions, see Lass (1984a: §3.2).

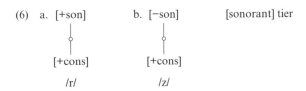

(6) a. [+son]   b. [−son]   [sonorant] tier

    [+cons]   [+cons]

    /r/   /z/

Similarly, if it is the case that vowel frontness and backness, for example, are 'logically equivalent', in that phonological processes can make appeal to either property,[7] the claim would be that there is a single feature, say [±back], which is equipollent: [+back] and [−back] have equivalent phonological status.

In what follows, we will restrict the term **binary** to equipollent features like [sonorant] in (6), with both a '+' and a '−' value, while we will refer to features characterising privative oppositions, as in (3), as **single-valued** features.[8] Single-valued features, then, do not have '+' or '−' values, but are simply present or absent.

2.1.1 *Feature geometry and the nature of features*

In drawing a formal distinction between the different types of features in such a rigorous way, we are going somewhat further than proponents of various of the geometrical models introduced in §1.3.5, where the distinction between the various types of opposition – equipollent, privative and multivalued – is utilised, but often not made formally explicit. Consider again representations like (75) in Chapter 1, a possible feature geometry for English *cab*. We drew a distinction between class nodes, i.e. labels for groups of features, on the one hand, and content nodes, i.e. nodes labelled by individual features such as [back]. We also saw that in a form like *camber*, the nasal had no independent place of articulation; rather, its place of articulation was determined by autosegmental spreading from the following stop. In other words, as we showed in (76) and (77) in Chapter 1, the nasal simply lacked a place node of its own (and hence all the other nodes dominated by it). In terms of the distinction we have just introduced, then, it seems that the place node, like other class nodes, is a single-valued 'feature'.

As we have now seen, some features, and hence content nodes, are also single-valued, in that they express privative oppositions. However, the relations between features are somewhat complex in feature geometry, and we consider here some of the formal aspects of the representation of place of articulation, in terms of the 'articulator theory' introduced in §1.3.4. It will be

---

[7] Such a claim is inherent in *SPE*, which treats neither [+back] nor [−back] as 'marked'; see the discussion of markedness and underspecification in §2.2.

[8] The terms 'unary' and 'monovalent' are also used.

recalled that, following McCarthy (1988), we distinguished a number of major places of articulation, characterised by the features [labial], [coronal], [dorsal] and [radical] (for the sake of the present discussion, we shall ignore radical consonants, i.e. those produced with the root of the tongue as the primary articulator). In feature geometry, each of the nodes characterising these features is dominated by the articulatory, or Place, node, as in (7):

(7)

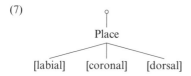

It is clear that a consonant is either [labial], [coronal] or [dorsal]: consonants do not usually have more than one place of articulation.[9] Thus the relationship between the three primary nodes we have introduced in (7) is one of mutual exclusivity. Each of the features is single-valued: it is either present or absent. Equally, though, we can say that the class node Place is multivalued, with three possible values ([labial], [coronal] and [dorsal]). Notice that because the three values are mutually exclusive, they are in a **disjunctive** relationship: only one value of Place can be chosen.

Unlike Place, which is a class node, [labial], [coronal] and [dorsal] are clearly content nodes; to say that something is 'labial' identifies its place of articulation, for example. But these nodes may also dominate other nodes in feature geometry. Recall from §1.3.4 that one of the advantages claimed for a model incorporating [labial], [coronal] and [dorsal] was that a feature such as [anterior], defined as involving a stricture in front of the postalveolar region, could be characterised as being only relevant to segments which are [coronal]. That is, if a consonant is not [coronal], then the question of whether it is [+anterior] or [−anterior] simply does not arise. Similarly, if a consonant is not [dorsal], its values for [high], [low] and [back] (features characterising the position of the body of the tongue) are irrelevant; if the body of the tongue is not involved in the production of a consonant, then its position does not need to be stated. Much the same holds for [strident] and [distributed], restricted to [coronal] consonants, and [round], restricted to labials.

The notion of certain features only being relevant if other features are present is represented in feature geometry as in (8):

---

[9] This is not to say that cases of double articulation (/k͡p, k͡t/) and secondary articulation (/ɫ, pʲ/) do not occur. These are treated in feature geometry by assuming that a single consonant has two distinct place specifications.

(8)

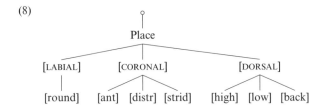

Here [round] is said to be a **dependent** of [LABIAL], while [anterior], [distributed] and [strident] are dependents of [CORONAL], and so on. Thus the occurrence of a specification for [anterior], say, is dependent on the presence of [CORONAL]. Notice that we now represent the features [LABIAL], [CORONAL] and [DORSAL] in a different way from [round], [anterior], etc. This is to show that they are single-valued content nodes which are intermediate between the class node Place and the 'terminal' content nodes, which are binary. The intermediate nodes, being single-valued, may be present or absent. The binary terminal nodes, however, must bear either the value '+' or '−' if they are 'relevant', i.e. if and only if the intermediate feature on which they are dependent is also present.

As Yip (1989: 350) points out, the evidence for the claim that nodes like [LABIAL], [CORONAL] and [DORSAL] appear to be single-valued lies in the natural class behaviour of the various places of articulation: [−coronal] does not occur. In other words, she claims, we do not find phonological processes affecting the set of non-coronals (e.g. /p k q/). If [−coronal], for example, is not a candidate for the definition of a natural class, then we are dealing here with a privative opposition, and thus a single-valued feature. However, the set of labials, velars and uvulars may form a natural class. This, however, is not by virtue of the fact that they do not involve a tongue-blade constriction, but perhaps for acoustic reasons. This leads Avery and Rice (1989: 195) to group [LABIAL] and [DORSAL] together under a Peripheral or Grave node, as in (9):

(9)

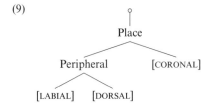

Like the class nodes, then, the intermediate content nodes we have established are single-valued, in the sense that they can be present or absent. However, the relationship between the class node Place and its dependents [LABIAL],

[CORONAL] and [DORSAL] in (8) is different from that between, say, the inter-mediate node [DORSAL] and its dependent terminal features [high], [low] and [back]. We saw that the relationship between the various intermediate features was a disjunctive one: only one feature could be chosen for any one segment. However, the features dominated by [DORSAL] are in a **conjunctive** relationship: dorsal consonants will bear specifications for *each* of the fea-tures [high], [low] and [back]. Thus the representation for English /k/ might be:[10]

(10)

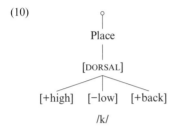

Clearly, then, we have arrived at an analysis in which the [LABIAL], [CORONAL] and [DORSAL] nodes are intermediate, in type as well as position, between 'class nodes' and 'terminal content nodes'. They are single-valued nodes, and may be entirely absent. If they are absent, then any of the content nodes which they dominate will also be absent, in exactly the same way as, if the Place node is absent, none of the nodes [LABIAL], [CORONAL] or [DORSAL] will be present (as in the assimilation examples we have already discussed). How-ever, they have content, unlike class nodes.[11]

2.2 The representation of feature asymmetry

We suggested above that the most appropriate way of handling asymmetry of the type evidenced by privative oppositions involving nasality is to incor-porate single-valued features into our analysis, thus abandoning the strict binarity hypothesis. In the previous subsection we saw that feature geometry, although typically acknowledging that both single-valued and binary nodes are required, fails to make a clear formal distinction between the various types of phonological oppositions we have encountered. Later in this chap-ter, we shall examine a system which makes use of single-valued features, but,

[10] Notice that (9) is a feature geometry representing a number of 'choices'; it is not the representation of an individual segment. (10), however, is the representation of a particular segment (English /k/), in which these choices have been made. Thus [DORSAL] has been chosen from the set of nodes dominated by the Place node, while each of the binary nodes under [DORSAL] has been assigned a value.

[11] For a discussion of the various types of dependency relationships in feature geometry, see Ewen (1995: §3).

before introducing this system, we must first consider the fact that there have been influential attempts to represent the kind of asymmetry involved in privative oppositions without giving up the strict binarity hypothesis.

The kind of approach which maintains strict binarity in the face of asymmetry might be desirable on one of two grounds. On the one hand, it restricts the number of feature types, and hence is to be preferred over a theory with a proliferation of feature types, all other things being equal. On the other, it has been claimed that, even though many features are 'basically' privative, in the manner discussed above for [nasal], there are nevertheless circumstances, however rare, in which reference to the opposite pole is required. In other words, even though '+' is the pole of [nasal] to which phonological rules and processes normally refer, they may sometimes also refer to [−nasal]. A harmony process in which spreading was blocked by any segment with the value [−nasal] would also provide evidence that, contrary to what we have claimed, [−nasal] can be an active value in the phonology of a language. If this state of affairs is indeed found in languages, i.e. that reference to the 'opposite pole' is required, then it can be claimed that all features are binary.

We consider now how the notion of asymmetry between feature-values can be accounted for within a theory which maintains the binarity hypothesis. Notice first that the asymmetry between the values of at least some of the binary features which we have been discussing has always been recognised as something which needs to be accounted for, even in strictly binary theories. In *SPE*, for example, a complex set of **marking conventions** was established. On the basis of the kinds of considerations introduced above, and some to which we will return in the course of this section, one of the two values of certain binary features was characterised as *m* (marked), and the other as *u* (unmarked), instead of the normal '+' and '−' values. In cases where it was claimed that there was no reason to assume asymmetry, such as [back], the latter values were retained. Associated with this was an 'evaluation metric', whereby features having the value *u* for a particular segment were 'cost-free', and those with the value *m* contributed to the 'cost' (i.e. phonological complexity) of the segment in question. In (11) we give the matrices for the vowel features for a system containing the vowels /i e ɑ o u y/, in terms of this approach:

	/i/	/e/	/ɑ/	/o/	/u/	/y/
(11)						
[high]	u	m	u	m	u	u
[low]	u	u	u	u	u	u
[back]	−	−	u	+	+	−
[round]	u	u	u	u	u	m
complexity	1	2	0	2	1	2

The 'cost' of a segment is established simply by adding the number of marked specifications to the number of '+'s and '–'s. As noted above, such representations were associated with a set of marking conventions, which spelled out the value of *u* and *m* for particular features. (12) (from *SPE*: 405) is an example of such a convention:

(12)

$$[u\ \text{low}] \rightarrow \left\{ \begin{array}{l} [+\text{low}] \,/\, \left[\begin{array}{l} \overline{} \\ u\ \text{back} \\ u\ \text{round} \end{array}\right] \\[1.5em] [-\text{low}] \end{array} \right\}$$

Thus the unmarked value for [low] is '+' for a vowel which is unmarked for backness and roundness, and '–' otherwise (i.e. /ɑ/ ([+low]) is unmarked, but for all other vowels [–low] is unmarked).

We leave it to the reader to examine the kinds of claim that are being made with respect to relative complexity in (11), i.e. claims of the following sort: for front vowels it is unmarked to be unrounded, and for non-low vowels it is unmarked to be high. Indeed, we shall devote no further space to markedness theory in this form, as it has largely been replaced by an alternative approach within Binary Feature Theory, to which we now turn.[12]

2.2.1   *Underspecification*

Recent approaches within the binary model to the asymmetry problem have utilised the notion of **underspecification**. In this conception of segmental structure, the marked value for a feature is underlyingly specified, while the unmarked value is absent in phonological representations, and is filled in by rule in the course of the derivation of the surface phonetic representations. We can represent this position formally as in (13), where we return to the kinds of representations introduced at the beginning of this chapter:

(13)   a.   [+nas]   b.   [nasal] tier

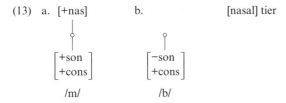

Thus the nasal consonant is underlyingly specified for nasality, but the oral consonant is **unspecified** for this feature, so that the segment as a whole is

---

[12] For a demonstration of the inadequacy of markedness theory as formulated in *SPE*, see e.g. Lass and Anderson (1975: App. IV), Kean (1980).

'underspecified', i.e. it does not bear a specification for every feature. It will be clear that this position comes very close in spirit to that in (3). Both approaches express the fact that non-nasality is not a positive property, but the claim in (13) is that this is no more than the 'normal' case; it is still formally possible to characterise cases where non-nasality apparently functions in the characterisation of phonological processes, by appealing to the value [–nasal], which can be introduced by a rule. A 'strict privativist', however, clearly has to show that analyses making use of [–nasal] are flawed. Equally, though, it is incumbent on a 'binarist' employing underspecification to show that such analyses are in fact required in the phonology of some language.

In underspecification theory, then, only the marked value of a feature is underlyingly specified; the unmarked (or **default**) value is added in the course of the derivation, so that the *surface* representation of (13) will be identical to (2).

2.2.2 *Redundancy*

We should notice at this point that the mechanism of underspecification can also be used to express something other than relative markedness. English, for example, is a language in which all non-low back vowels are rounded, as there are no vowels such as */ɯ ɤ/. In other words, if a vowel has the features [–low, +back], then we know it must be [+round]. Halle (1959) pointed out that it is thus not necessary to specify non-low back vowels as [+round] phonologically: as the feature [round] is not distinctive (or contrastive) for non-low back vowels, it can be left underlyingly unspecified. The value [+round] is thus **redundant**, i.e. predictable on the basis of other feature specifications. Notice that this is a different type of claim from those we have been considering with respect to markedness and asymmetry, in that we are not making any general claims about whether it is more natural for non-low back vowels to be rounded or unrounded. Rather, it is an automatic consequence of the structure of the vowel system of English that the value of this particular feature should be non-contrastive, and thus predictable and phonologically redundant.

Such a state of affairs can be represented by a **redundancy constraint** such as that in (14):

(14)   if [–low, +back] then [+round]

However, although the two reasons for not specifying a particular value for a binary feature in phonological representations – lack of markedness and redundancy – are logically independent, they are not unrelated. Consider the two potential redundancy constraints in (15), for example:

(15) a. if [+low] then [+round]
      b. if [+low] then [–round]

While (15b) characterises a state of affairs frequently encountered in languages of the world, (15a) would be unexpected: there are virtually no languages without an /a/ or an /ɑ/-type vowel. In other words, on the basis of (15b), which expresses a redundancy (non-contrastiveness) in many languages, [–round] can be left unspecified for low vowels. On grounds of markedness, we would reach exactly the same conclusion: [–round] is in general the unmarked value for low vowels, and could therefore be left unspecified.

However, unmarked values are not *necessarily* non-contrastive in a particular system. Consider the feature [nasal], for which, as we have seen, [–nasal] is the unmarked value. In English, however, [–nasal] is a contrastive value: the only difference between English /m/ and /b/, let us assume, is that /m/ is nasal, while /b/ is not. In an approach to binary features which does not incorporate considerations of markedness, both values will be lexically specified, as in (2).

In the following two sections we consider underspecification approaches in more detail. Let us first, however, consider a slightly different way in which phonological representations can be simplified. It will be quite obvious that no single language makes use of the whole set of features (whatever its content) to classify the inventory of contrastive segments (i.e. phonemes). Languages like English or Dutch, for example, do not make use of lexical contrasts which require the use of laryngeal features characterising *degree* of glottal opening, which does not play a contrastive role in these languages. There is no opposition between breathy and creaky voiced segments, or between aspirated and unaspirated stops, for example. This means that the features involved, whatever their precise character, are redundant 'as a whole', and do not require to be specified lexically. Notice that this situation is different from those which we have just been discussing, where one of the *values* of a feature may be redundant in some context. Features which are redundant at the phonological level, however, may be used phonetically, for example to express allophonic variation. In most dialects of English, initial voiceless stops become aspirated before stressed vowels. This implies that voiceless stops in this context are assigned a value for whatever feature characterises aspiration (see §2.7 for discussion of the features characterising these laryngeal phenomena, though in a different framework). The same process does not take place in Dutch, for example.

However, in the remainder of this chapter we consider the underspecification of values, rather than features which may be absent from the lexical specification. In the next two sections we discuss two approaches to the notion of underspecification introduced above. In §2.2.3 we discuss underspecification on the basis of redundancy (**contrastive specification**) and in §2.2.4 underspecification on the basis of markedness (**radical underspecification**).

2.2.3   Contrastive specification

Consider a language which has a system of five contrastive vowels, as in (16):

(16)

	/i/	/u/	/e/	/o/	/a/
[high]	+	+	–	–	–
[low]	–	–	–	–	+
[back]	–	+	–	+	+
[round]	–	+	–	+	–

This feature matrix contains redundant information. The feature [round] can be omitted entirely from the lexical specification, since no pair of vowels is distinguished by this feature; cf. the discussion in the previous section.[13]

To distinguish the vowel /a/ from all the other vowels in (16) it is sufficient to specify it as [+low], since there are no other vowels which are [+low]. We can leave out the other specifications for this vowel, and fill in these values using the redundancy statements or constraints in (17):

(17)   a.   if [+low] then [–high]
         b.   if [+low] then [+back]

Notice that redundancy constraints do not express phonological *processes* as such. Rather, they constitute statements about a particular inventory of segments. Because of this, the existence of a redundancy constraint in a particular language allows us to derive from it another redundancy constraint by the following principle, familiar from formal logic:

(18) $(A \rightarrow B) \rightarrow (\sim B \rightarrow \sim A)$

(i.e. if $A \rightarrow B$ is true then $\sim B \rightarrow \sim A$ is also true). This entails that if the redundancy constraints in (17) are true for a particular system, then those in (19) must also be true:

(19)   a.   if [+high] then [–low]
         b.   if [–back] then [–low]

---

[13] We might have chosen to omit [back], rather than [round]. On grounds of contrastiveness, there is no reason to choose one rather than the other as the feature to be omitted from (16): in either case, we end up with an underspecified display like (20) below. See Schane (1973) for discussion of the relationship between the two features.

These statements allow us to simplify the matrix in (16) as in (20), in which all non-contrastive values and features are omitted:

(20)		/i/	/u/	/e/	/o/	/a/
[high]	+	+	–	–	
[low]				–	+
[back]	–	+	–	+	

We should note that the status of the (a) and (b) sets of constraints in (17) and (19) is different. The constraints in (a) must be true in every language, given the definitions of the features [high] and [low]. Hence these redundancy constraints express 'universal' properties of the system.[14] Those in (b), on the other hand, are only true if the language in question lacks a contrast between low front and low back vowels. Thus if a language has both /a/ [+low, −back] and /ɑ/ [+low, +back], then the (b) constraints do not hold. Hence these constraints are part of language-specific grammars. Languages with the same number of vowels tend to have very similar systems, resulting from the fact that certain feature specifications are preferred over others.

In the approach to underspecification known as **Contrastive Specification Theory** (cf. Steriade 1987; Clements 1988; Archangeli 1988a; Mester and Itô 1989), only redundant values can be left unspecified, and the possibility of underspecification on grounds of markedness is not utilised.

Contrastive Specification Theory differs in one crucial way from early models of generative phonology. In these earlier models, phonological rules could make reference only to 'fully specified matrices', i.e. those in which all feature-values were specified.[15] Contrastive Specification Theory, on the other hand, allows rules to operate on segments for which redundant values have not yet been specified by the application of redundancy constraints. This position allows us to provide a more satisfactory characterisation of various types of phonological phenomena, in particular those involving assimilation processes. Recall from §1.4 that assimilation is characteristically viewed in non-linear phonology as the spreading of a feature to another segment, in the manner represented in (21):

(21)

---

[14] We might argue that the need to state universal redundancies of this sort is a reflection of the inadequacy of the feature system in question. It seems more desirable to have a model of segmental structure in which universally impossible states of affairs cannot be described, rather than one in which we require extra mechanisms of this sort.

[15] See for discussion Stanley (1967), Ringen (1975), Kiparsky (1982).

However, assimilation of this sort need not involve *strictly* adjacent segments, in spite of examples such as (72) in Chapter 1, which, we argued, showed that nasality could not spread from a consonant to a vowel across an intervening lateral, for example. Indeed, in our discussion of the vowel harmony phenomena of Turkish in §1.4.2, we tacitly assumed that segments could be skipped, as is shown by an examination of (88) in Chapter 1. There we see that the spreading feature ignores all intervening consonants.

The same kind of trans-segmental transparency holds for umlaut processes such as the Old English case discussed in §1.4.1. Again, consonants intervening between the vowels involved in this kind of spreading process typically seem to take no part in the process. That is, they are not in themselves affected by the spreading – they remain unchanged – nor do they prevent the spreading feature from reaching the 'target' vowel. In a feature system like that discussed in §1.3.2, vowel features such as [high], [low] and [back] are, within Contrastive Specification Theory, not required for the lexical specification of consonants (except in languages which display contrasts between tongue-body (i.e. dorsal) consonants, e.g. between palatals and velars, or which have contrasts involving secondary articulations such as velarisation or palatalisation, which might involve a contrast between [+back] and [−back]). In Hungarian, for example, the feature [back] is lexically contrastive for vowels, but its specification is redundant for consonants: there are no contrasts between consonants involving just the feature [back]. Like Turkish, Hungarian is a vowel harmony language. The feature involved in Hungarian harmony, [back], spreads from vowel to vowel, but leaves intervening consonants unaffected:

(22)	NOM SG	DAT SG		
	ház	háznak	[hɑːznɔk]	'house'
	öröm	örömnek	[œrœmnɛk]	'joy'

Contrastive Specification Theory allows us to say that the consonants in the dative forms in (22) are unspecified for the feature involved in the spreading process. Thus the absence of any specification for [back] straightforwardly accounts for the fact that the backness property of a stem vowel can spread to the vowel of an affix, even though this involves spreading across another segment:[16]

---

[16] An issue which arises here is the motivation for treating the specification of 'vowel' features on consonants as redundant, and hence added in the course of the derivation by redundancy rule, rather than as being omitted entirely from consonantal specifications, even at the surface level.

(23)

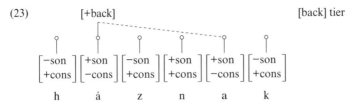

Further evidence for skipped segments being unspecified for features involved in spreading can be found from processes involving voicing assimilation among consonants. In Dutch, for example, syllable-final voiceless obstruents become voiced if a following syllable-initial obstruent is also voiced, as illustrated in (24):

(24) zakdoek 'handkerchief' /zɑkduk/ → [zɑgduk]
      kasboek 'cashbook'   /kɑsbuk/ → [kɑzbuk]

The details of how this process operates, and the restrictions on it, need not concern us here, but it clearly involves the leftward spreading of [+voice], a process which, at first sight, we might formalise as in (25):

(25)

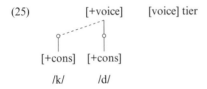

However, voiceless obstruents followed by a *sonorant* consonant do not become [+voice], as shown in (26):

(26) kruidnagel 'clove'   /krøydnaːɣəl/ → [krøytnaːɣəl][17]
      Parklaan   (street name)   /pɑrklaːn/   → [pɑrklaːn]

At first sight this seems unexpected, since sonorants (like voiced obstruents) are phonetically [+voice]. The most straightforward way of characterising the process would seem to be to say that the process simply requires the trigger to be [–sonorant], as in (27):

(27)

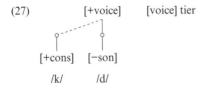

---

[17] Notice that the final consonant of *kruid*, which is underlyingly voiced, undergoes Final Devoicing (cf. (12a) in Chapter 1).

This certainly accounts for the facts, and as such is adequate, but it is also very unrevealing. In particular, it fails to show *why* the spreading process should be restricted to obstruents, and what it is about sonorant consonants which prevents them from spreading voice into a preceding obstruent.

In an approach which allows underspecification, such as Contrastive Specification Theory, there is a straightforward way of representing the phenomenon. In Dutch there is no contrast between voiced and voiceless sonorants: Dutch does not have segments such as */l̥/ or */m̥/. Thus [+voice] is phonologically redundant for sonorant consonants, and need not be specified. Because sonorant consonants lack the [+voice] specification, then, they do not trigger voicing assimilation. Thus our original formulation in (25) is adequate: any consonant which is marked as [+voice], i.e. any voiced obstruent, spreads [+voice] to a preceding consonant, while any consonant which is *not* [+voice], i.e. either a voiceless obstruent, which is of course [−voice], or a sonorant consonant, which is simply unspecified for the feature, does not participate in the assimilation process.

It is interesting to notice the behaviour of sonorant consonants with respect to voicing assimilation in Russian (see Hayes 1984b; Kiparsky 1985). In Russian, the value for the feature [voice] of all members of an obstruent cluster is determined by the final member of the cluster, as shown by the forms in (28) (from Hayes 1984b: 318; Kiparsky 1985: 103; notice that (28) shows that the assimilation process takes place both word-internally and across various types of morphological boundaries):

(28) a. zub-ki   'little teeth'   /zubki/   → [zupki]
     b. Mcensk#by   'if Mcensk'   /mtsɛnskbɨ/ → [mtsɛnzgbɨ]
     c. Mcensk##byl   'it was Mcensk'   /mtsɛnskbɨl/ → [mtsɛnzgbɨl]
     d. mozg   'brain'   /mɔzg/   → [mɔsk]

In *zubki* in (28a), the voiced labial stop is devoiced under the influence of the following voiceless /k/. That this is not a question of final devoicing, which is found in other contexts in Russian, is demonstrated by (28b, c), where the morpheme-final voiceless obstruent cluster is voiced by spreading from the /b/. Indeed, final devoicing may feed the assimilation process; in (28d) /g/ is devoiced in final position, and then triggers voicing assimilation of the preceding fricative.

Consider now the forms in (29):

(29) a. iz Mcenska 'from Mcensk'   /iz mtsɛnska/ → [is mtsɛnska]
     b. ot mzdy   'from the bribe'   /at mzdɨ/   → [ad mzdɨ]

Here we see that the voicing specification of an obstruent spreads across an intervening sonorant, which we must therefore assume is unspecified for [voice].

That is, in *iz Mcenska* in (29a), the voiced alveolar fricative is devoiced under the influence of the following voiceless /ts/, even though a sonorant consonant intervenes. In *ot mzdy* in (29b), the morpheme-final voiceless alveolar stop is voiced by spreading from the /z/. On the analysis given here, such a case is similar to the harmony and umlaut cases considered above.

Another case of this type is discussed by Yip (1988: §5.4). In Cantonese Chinese there are various constraints on the co-occurrence of labial consonants and rounded vowels in the same syllable. One such constraint states that a syllable-final labial consonant cannot be preceded by a rounded vowel, so that sequences such as */tup, køm/ are impossible, whereas forms like /tip/ are permitted. This is an example of a dissimilation constraint, which states that two segments cannot be associated to the same value for a particular feature.[18]

A second constraint involves syllable-initial labial consonants, which can be followed by /u/ or /o/, but not by /y/ or /ø/ (/puk, mou/ vs */pyk, møy/). This constraint is thus weaker than the previous one, in that back rounded vowels may combine with labial consonants, but not front rounded ones. Why should this be?

As we have seen, labial consonants are dominated by the [LABIAL] node (cf. (8) above). Phonetically, of course, all the vowels /u o y ø/ are [+round], and thus also dominated by the [LABIAL] node. However, for the (non-low) back vowels, this is a redundant feature, because there are no back unrounded vowels corresponding to rounded /u o/ in Cantonese. Underlyingly, then, /u o/ are unspecified for [LABIAL], and thus a sequence of a labial consonant and /u/ or /o/ does not violate the dissimilation constraint in question, as shown in (30a). However, the same does not hold for the front rounded vowels, which are in opposition with /i e/, and for which [LABIAL] is lexically contrastive (30b):

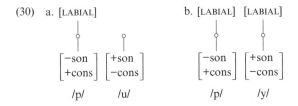

(30)   a. [LABIAL]   b. [LABIAL]   [LABIAL]

$$\begin{bmatrix} -son \\ +cons \end{bmatrix} \quad \begin{bmatrix} +son \\ -cons \end{bmatrix} \qquad \begin{bmatrix} -son \\ +cons \end{bmatrix} \quad \begin{bmatrix} +son \\ -cons \end{bmatrix}$$

      /p/   /u/   /p/   /y/

Because both labial consonants and front rounded vowels are lexically specified as [LABIAL] in Cantonese, a sequence of the two violates the dissimilation constraint.

---

[18] Yip ascribes this to the operation of the Obligatory Contour Principle (cf. §1.4), which prohibits 'adjacent identical elements'.

Examples like these suggest that allowing rules to make reference to representations in which redundant feature-values are omitted is more than a mere notational economy. It straightforwardly expresses the observed fact that redundant information *behaves differently* from non-redundant information, i.e. it is simply ignored by spreading processes and constraints.[19]

Notice that the redundancies we have been considering up to now are **intrasegmental**, i.e. certain feature-values of a segment are predictable, regardless of the environment in which this segment occurs, purely on the basis of other specifications of the same segment. Such constraints are also referred to as **segment structure constraints**. Certain specifications may also, however, be predictable on the basis of the context in which a particular segment occurs, either with respect to the value(s) of particular features in neighbouring segments, or because of its position in, say, the syllable. Thus, given a syllable-initial sequence of three consonants in English, we know that the first one can only be /s/, and so all feature-specifications except [+consonantal] are redundant. This kind of situation is characterised by **phonotactic constraints**.[20]

In this section we have shown that Contrastive Specification Theory restricts the non-specification of feature-values to situations in which that value is not contrastive in the language in question. We turn now to a theory of underspecification which, in addition, extends the non-specification mechanism to cases of relative markedness.

2.2.4   *Radical underspecification*

In our discussion in §2.1 we introduced the notion of asymmetry. We saw that the two values of a binary feature often behave differently, in that only one of the two typically occurs in the characterisation of phonological constraints and processes, the other doing so less typically or not at all. In other words, only one of the values may define a natural class, as we illustrated with respect to the feature [nasal]: the set of [+nasal] sounds forms a class which can be appealed to in phonological processes, while the set of [−nasal] sounds is apparently not available. In §2.2 we gave a brief sketch of how relative markedness of this kind was dealt with in *SPE*.

In recent approaches to asymmetry, underspecification has been employed instead of the marking conventions of markedness theory. This theory is

---

[19] Clearly, we also need to establish whether there are phonological processes which do make reference to redundant information. It has been argued that such cases do in fact exist, which would imply that at some stage in the derivation redundancy rules apply, which then feed a second class of phonological rules.

[20] In *SPE* phonotactic constraints were referred to as morpheme structure constraints; later treatments (e.g. Vennemann 1972) characterise them as syllable structure constraints. The term 'phonotactic constraints' is more general than either.

commonly referred to as **Radical Underspecification Theory** (see e.g. Archangeli 1988a; Archangeli and Pulleyblank 1994). Radical Underspecification Theory goes a step further than Contrastive Specification Theory, which eliminates only those feature-values which are redundant. For any 'asymmetric' feature, such as [nasal], Radical Underspecification Theory specifies only one value of a feature in underlying representations, leaving the other value to be added by rule in the course of the derivation. The value which is found underlyingly is the one which typically defines a natural class in that language. For the feature [nasal], then, the underlying value would normally be [+nasal]. Thus, as we noted in §2.2.1, in underspecification theory, it is the marked value of a feature which is underlyingly specified; the default value is added by rule. Within Radical Underspecification Theory, in the vast majority of cases, *no* feature has both values underlyingly specified in a particular language; effectively, then, Radical Underspecification Theory claims that in general all features are asymmetric: no feature is underlyingly equipollent.

This latter claim means that we will have to decide for each feature which value can be left underlyingly unspecified, i.e. which of the two values is the 'expected' one. This is not straightforward, especially as the theory allows different solutions for different languages, as we shall see. However, let us first explore the mechanism employed within Radical Underspecification Theory for relating underlying representations to surface representations. Feature asymmetry is expressed by a set of **default rules**. The set in (31) would generate the **fully specified** matrix in (16) for a language with the vowel system /i u e o ɑ/:

(31)   a.   [   ] → [–high]
       b.   [   ] → [–low]
       c.   [   ] → [–back]

The value of a feature which is added by a default rule is the one that is not referred to by the phonological rules of the language in question, while the opposite value of that feature is the one that is present in the underlying lexical representation of a segment. Thus the claim made in (31c), for example, is that it is [+back], rather than [–back], which is involved in processes such as spreading. Assuming the set of default rules in (31), (32) gives the underlying representations of the vowels in (16):

(32)

	/i/	/u/	/e/	/o/	/ɑ/
[high]	+	+			
[low]					+
[back]		+		+	+

Crucially, only one of the values for each feature in (32) is found; none of the features is underlyingly specified for both values.

If we compare (32) with (20), in which only the non-contrastive (i.e. redundant) feature-values were omitted, we see that the default rules render many of the redundancy constraints superfluous. Every redundancy constraint which fills in a value identical to that filled in by default, such as (17a) and (19), will apply vacuously. This filling in of the default value is the typical pattern, so that in Radical Underspecification Theory, only one redundancy constraint is still required for the system in (16), that in (33):

(33)   if [+low] then [+back]

This means that (34), rather than (32), is the 'radically underspecified' underlying representation of the vowel system in (16):

(34)

	/i/	/u/	/e/	/o/	/a/
[high]	+	+			
[low]					+
[back]		+		+	

The properties of a radically underspecified underlying system are formally rather different from the corresponding system in Contrastive Specification Theory, where only the redundant specifications have been removed. The underlying representations are no longer formally contrastive, in the sense of Contrastive Specification Theory, in that the representation of a particular segment may in (34) formally 'include' the representation of some other segment. Thus, although the phonological representation of /i/ contains only the specification [+high], it is not the only [+high] vowel in the system. Similarly, the vowel /e/ is entirely unspecified, and therefore its representation is not formally contrastive. Such a state of affairs would be impossible in Contrastive Specification Theory, as in (20), where no representation can be formally 'ambiguous'. Notice, though, that in Radical Underspecification Theory, the underlying representation of each vowel in a system is still unique: there are no pairs of segments with identical feature specifications, and therefore the representation of any segment is different from all others.

It is clear that the choice of which value is present in underlying representations determines both the lexical representation of a segment and the set of default rules in a language. If we were to assume different default rules for the example which we have been considering, say by taking [−high] as underlyingly specified, we would have the set of default rules and redundancy constraints in (35):

(35)   a.   *Default rules*   b.   *Redundancy constraints*
              [   ] → [+high]   if [+low] then [−high]
              [   ] → [−low]   if [+low] then [+back]
              [   ] → [−back]

These would yield the lexical representations in (36):

(36)   /i/   /u/   /e/   /o/   /ɑ/
       [high]   −   −
       [low]   +
       [back]   +   +

Archangeli (1988a) argues that both options (and indeed others) are available, although only one of them will be 'expected'. Thus it is assumed that [+high] *generally* represents the default rather than [−high]. On grounds of complexity we might prefer (35), which yields a set of underlying representations in which the relatively simple high vowel /u/, for example, has a less complex representation than its mid counterpart, /o/.

Proponents of Radical Underspecification Theory claim that in any system there is typically one segment which is underlyingly *completely* unspecified. In other words, phonological systems tend to have one 'special vowel', i.e. one that fails to take part as expected in various phonological processes, in particular behaving as if it were absent, or invisible to phonological processes such as vowel harmony, or one that typically occurs as the default **epenthetic** vowel, i.e. the vowel that is inserted in contexts in which for some reason a vowel is required, but where its particular specifications for the vowel features are unimportant. Thus Khalkha, a Mongolian language, displays a vowel harmony process by which low vowels agree in roundness with the first vowel of the word, as in [dɔlɔːn-ɔːs] 'seven (ABL)' and [gərəːsn-əːs] 'antelope (ABL)'.[21] However, a non-initial /i/ behaves as if it is invisible to rounding harmony: if the initial vowel is round, an /i/ in the second syllable neither undergoes harmony (i.e. it surfaces as [i]) nor prevents roundness from spreading to following syllables, as is evidenced by the form [ətʃigdər] 'yesterday'. The status of this vowel can be reflected in the underlying representations of Khalkha Mongolian by leaving it completely unspecified, i.e. 'empty'. In turn, the identity of the empty vowel in any system will determine the choice of which value of a particular feature should be underlyingly present and which should be added by default rule. Thus in (34) it is /e/ which is unspecified for all features, and therefore predicted to behave as the empty vowel; in (36) it is /i/.

Let us now look at a slightly more complicated example, the vowel system in (37), which represents one stage of Old English (see Hogg 1992a):

---

[21] See Svantesson (1985) for a discussion of vowel harmony in Khalkha.

(37)

	/i/	/y/	/u/	/e/	/ø/	/o/	/æ/	/a/
[high]	+	+	+	−	−	−	−	−
[low]	−	−	−	−	−	−	+	+
[back]	−	−	+	−	−	+	−	+
[round]	−	+	+	−	+	+	−	−

We use the same set of default rules as in (31) and furthermore assume that '−' is the unmarked value for [round]. This gives the set of default rules and redundancy constraints in (38):

(38) a. *Default rules*
    [ ] → [−high]
    [ ] → [−low]
    [ ] → [−back]
    [ ] → [−round]

    b. *Redundancy constraint*
    if [+back, −low] then [+round]

This allows the Old English system to be represented as in (39):

(39)

	/i/	/y/	/u/	/e/	/ø/	/o/	/æ/	/a/
[high]	+	+	+					
[low]							+	+
[back]			+			+		+
[round]		+			+			

Finally, consider a vowel system like that of Turkish, with both back rounded and back unrounded vowels:

(40) *Default rules*
    [ ] → [−high]
    [ ] → [−back]

Notice that (40) does not contain a default rule for [round], so that we have (41) for the Turkish vowel system:

(41)

	/i/	/y/	/ɨ/	/u/	/e/	/ø/	/a/	/o/
[high]	+	+	+	+				
[back]			+	+			+	+
[round]		+	−			+	−	

(41) differs from the other radically underspecified underlying systems which we have considered, in that we find both [+round] and [−round], i.e. *both* values of a single feature. However, although it may appear that we are thereby abandoning the radical underspecification claim, i.e. that each feature has only one value present in underlying representations, this is in fact not quite the case. Rather, the suggestion here is that whether or not a particular value is marked is partially a function of the other features involved

in the representation of a segment. As far as roundness is concerned, it is unmarked for non-low back vowels to be [+round], whereas for front vowels [–round] is the unmarked value. English is not atypical in this respect, in having no front rounded vowels such as /y ø/, and no non-low back unrounded vowels such as /ɯ ɤ/. This means that we can add the default rules in (42) to the set in (40):

(42) *Default rules*

$$[\ ] \rightarrow [+\text{round}] \ / \left[\begin{array}{c} \overline{} \\ +\text{back} \end{array} \right]$$

$$[\ ] \rightarrow [-\text{round}] \ / \left[\begin{array}{c} \overline{} \\ -\text{back} \end{array} \right]$$

Notice that the rules which we have added to (42) are indeed default rules: they only apply to a segment which does not bear a value for [round] underlyingly. Thus, /y/ in (41), which already bears the marked value [+round], will not be subject to the default rule affecting [–back] vowels.

We have seen that Radical Underspecification Theory goes further than Contrastive Specification Theory, in allowing underspecification on the basis both of redundancy (i.e. non-contrastiveness) and of relative markedness. It is clear that this approach leads to a situation in which, typically, only one value for a particular feature is required underlyingly (in spite of cases such as that just mentioned, where binarity seems to play a crucial role), and it might be asked whether this approach is not largely the same as one in which the notion of binarity is abandoned, and replaced by a system incorporating features which can only have one value *anywhere* in the phonology. We now turn our attention to this matter.

2.3 Single-valued features

As we have seen, proponents of Radical Underspecification Theory claim that there are various grounds for claiming that features must have two values, even though only one value per feature is required underlyingly. This means that we require various formal mechanisms such as default rules for linking underlying representations involving underspecification to fully specified surface representations.

The reasons for retaining the binarity assumption in Radical Underspecification Theory are of various types, as we have observed. Firstly, some languages appear to take the normally unmarked value of a feature as the one that is lexically specified, i.e. as the one which is marked. This seems to be the case in the harmony system of Yoruba, which we discuss in some detail in §2.4.3. Secondly, there seem to be processes in languages which show

79

evidence that we have to refer to *both* values of some feature, either under-lyingly or at some point in the course of the derivation. Our analysis of the feature [round] in Turkish in (41) provides an example of this. Thirdly, as observed by Chomsky and Halle (1968), markedness can be context-dependent. So one value may be marked in context A, while the other is marked in context B. Thus it is unmarked for obstruents to be voiceless in syllable-final position, but voicelessness is marked in intervocalic position, at least following a stressed syllable. Fourthly, a spreading process may be blocked by the presence of a segment bearing the 'opposite value' of the feature involved in the spreading.

As we have already observed, an alternative to an approach incorporating the radical underspecification of binary features would be one based on the notion of single-valued features. A system based on binary features, such as Radical Underspecification Theory, is, all other things being equal, a more complex theory of representation than one in which every feature is single-valued, i.e. has only one value at *all* levels of the derivation. In a single-valued approach, the vowel /y/ in a language might differ from /i/ in having a specification [round], which /i/ would lack altogether, both at the phono-logical and at the phonetic level. Thus the fact that it is marked for front vowels to be round (see the discussion in the previous section) would be reflected by the fact that, throughout the phonology, /y/ would have an extra property, roundness, as compared with /i/. This approach to vowel features is the same as that implied by (3), in which we characterised the distinction between nasal and non-nasal sounds as involving the presence vs the absence of a single-valued feature [nasal].

Notice that adopting single-valued features would mean that the set of default rules would become superfluous, and that the interpretation of the 'non-specification' of a feature would not be a phonological issue, but would be a matter entirely for the phonetic component.[22] This would clearly consti-tute a formal simplification, if the arguments which suggest that binary features are required can be successfully refuted.

A single-valued feature approach can be seen as an extreme form of Rad-ical Underspecification Theory, in which the idea that one of the values of a feature is typically the default value is carried to its logical conclusion. The claim of **Single-valued Feature Theory** is simply that default values play no role in the phonology whatsoever, and so features do not have such default values: each feature is single-valued. Thus a single-valued system reflects the

---

[22] We assume here that the output of the phonological component – let us call it the 'surface phono-logical representation' – forms the input to a 'phonetic component', whose function is to provide a detailed set of phonetic instructions for the realisation of the string being generated.

spirit of underspecification in expressing markedness considerations directly, but it does so in a more rigorous way.

Single-valued features have been introduced in various ways into phonological analyses. Some approaches, such as the model of feature geometry considered in §2.1.1, allow certain features to be single-valued, while others are binary. Another approach is that of Goldsmith (1985), who proposes a model in which a particular feature may be single-valued in one language, but binary in another, according to the behaviour of the feature in phonological processes in the languages in question. Still other phonologists claim that *all* features are single-valued.[23]

As we have seen, the use of single-valued features seems to lead to a reduction of the complexity of the phonological machinery. Consider the various mechanisms which we associated with the underspecification theories discussed above. We distinguished 'redundancy constraints', associated with Contrastive Specification Theory, and 'default rules', associated with Radical Underspecification Theory. As we have already noted, if we introduce consistently single-valued features, the category of default rules is no longer required. Clearly, as the function of default rules is to 'fill in' the value of the feature which is not specified in lexical representations, they have no role in a single-valued approach, where each feature only has one value. Let us illustrate this by considering the vowel system in (43), for which we give first a radically underspecified representation in which the redundancy constraints have not applied:

(43)		/i/	/e/	/a/	/o/	/u/	/y/	/ø/
	[high]	+				+	+	
	[low]			+				
	[back]			+	+	+		
	[round]				+	+	+	+

In anticipation of our arguments for a particular set of single-valued features for characterising the vowel space, let us construct a single-valued equivalent of (43), using three features. These are [front], [low] and [round] (where we assign [low] a rather wider interpretation than in a binary approach; we will say that any vowel which is not [+high] in binary terms is [low] in single-valued terms).[24] This gives us the system in (44), where we represent [front] as

---

[23] This position has been defended most extensively by proponents of dependency phonology (e.g. Anderson and Jones 1974, 1977; Anderson and Ewen 1987) and government phonology (e.g. Kaye *et al.* 1990; Harris 1994), but has been increasingly adopted in various forms in recent years. See also the approach within the model of particle phonology of Schane (1984), and the work of Rennison (e.g. 1986).

[24] A more appropriate definition might be in terms of acoustic properties, specifically relative sonority, whereby low vowels are, all other things being equal, more sonorous than high vowels. For ease of exposition, however, we will continue to use the articulatory label.

i, [low] as **a** and [round] as **u** (from now on, we indicate single-valued features by the use of boldface):

(44) /i/ /e/ /a/ /o/ /u/ /y/ /ø/

i	i				i	i	i tier
	a	**a**	**a**			**a**	**a** tier
			u	**u**	**u**	**u**	**u** tier

The representations in (44) are underlying, but are nevertheless 'fully specified', in the sense that there is nothing that can be added. 'Default rules' are simply not formally relevant in a single-valued approach. On the other hand, redundancy constraints may still be required in systems, although on a much more restricted scale than in underspecification theories: (44), for example, displays no such redundancies, whereas (43) contains redundancies which can be filtered out by virtue of the constraints in (45):

(45) *Redundancy constraints*
    a. if [+low] then [+back]
    b. if [+back, −low] then [+round]

We consider the matter of redundancies in relation to a single-valued system in §2.4.3; however, we notice at this point that if we were to find a three-vowel system containing the vowels /i u æ/, the representation of /æ/ would contain a redundancy even in a single-valued system: its surface representation would contain both **i** and **a**, while **i** would be omitted from its underlying representation, in that its occurrence would be predictable, and therefore redundant.

Single-valued Feature Theory essentially makes the claim that the difference between the underlying lexical phonological representation and the surface phonological representation is minimal – in the case under discussion here, they are identical. It is in this sense that the phonological 'machinery' is simplified by the adoption of a single-valued model.

As we have already anticipated, single-valued feature systems generally differ from the *SPE* system not only in feature type, but also in the choice of different parameters for characterising the vowel space. As we showed in (21) of Chapter 1, the *SPE* system is essentially rectangular, in that the features divide up the vowel space into points on the high–low and the front–back dimensions, with lip-rounding being superimposed on these two dimensions. The feature systems associated with Single-valued Feature Theory, however, are generally **tridirectional**, in accordance with the traditional view of the vowel space as triangular, as in (46):

(46)   high   high
       front   round

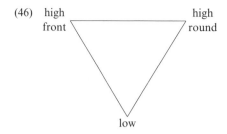

                    low

As is illustrated by (46), the three basic primes which tridirectional feature systems characteristically employ in their feature set correspond to the three extremes of the vowel triangle. As suggested above, the articulatory realisations of these three primes are typically high front, high round and low, as shown in (47):[25]

(47)   *Single-valued vowel features*
       i   'high frontness'
       u   'high roundness'
       a   'lowness'

From a phonetic point of view, these features, which on their own would represent the vowels /i/, /u/ and /ɑ/ (as in (44)), are clearly basic. They correspond to the **quantal** vowels (Stevens 1972, 1989), i.e. those vowels which are acoustically particularly 'stable' in that their acoustic effect can be achieved with a fairly wide range of articulatory configurations. In addition, these three vowels are maximally distinct, both from an acoustic and an articulatory point of view. Moreover, /i/, /u/ and /ɑ/ are also basic as far as phonology is concerned. Systems containing just three vowels typically have vowels in the /i/, /u/ and /ɑ/ regions, and these are also the first vowels that children acquire. Hence the choice of **i**, **u** and **a** as basic vocalic features is well motivated, both phonetically and phonologically.

The fact that a single-valued feature in isolation characterises a complete segment has often been claimed to be a major advantage of the system. That is, each feature is in itself a phonetically interpretable 'element'.[26] In binary models, however, feature-values do not have this property; the fact that a segment has the value [−back] says nothing about the values for any other

---

[25] Other features beside these three have been proposed (see §§2.4.3 and 2.5 below). However, for the present, we restrict the discussion to the characterisation of the vowel set described in binary terms by the features [high], [low], [back] and [round].

[26] Single-valued features are generally referred to as elements within government phonology (see §3.8). For discussion of the desirability of the notion that elements should be phonetically interpretable, see e.g. Harris (1994: §3.2.3).

features. Contrast this with the single-valued model, where **i** on its own is the representation for the vowel /i/. Inherent in this approach is the claim that vowels which are not represented by a single feature are 'mixtures' of the basic vowels /i/, /u/ and /a/. Thus Harris (1994: 97) refers to /i u a/ as 'simplex' and /e o y/ as 'compound', while Donegan (1973), although working with binary features, refers to 'pure' and 'mixed' vowels. A mixed vowel such as /e/, then, contains the element which in isolation characterises /i/ as well as the element which in isolation characterises /a/, but each element is less 'strong' than it would be when it occurs alone in the representation of a vowel. In simple articulatory terms, /e/ is front, but less front than /i/, and low, but less low than /a/.[27]

Processes involving diphthongisation or monophthongisation have often been cited in support of these claims. In a binary approach, a diphthongisation process involves the addition of a new feature-matrix, whereas in a single-valued model it is claimed that the only change involves the rearrangement of features which are already present. For example, the change from Middle English /klɑu/ to Modern English /klɔː/ 'claw' can be represented as in (48):

(48)

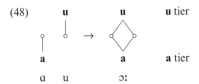

The association of the features to the root nodes is the only change that takes place. A similar process is cited by Jones (1989: §2.4.4) and by Hogg (1992b: 215), who note that the Old English diphthong /eo/ in e.g. *eorþe* 'earth' monophthongised to a front rounded vowel /ø/ in certain dialects of Middle English, as represented in (49):

(49)

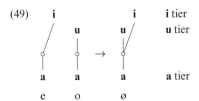

Here, as before, the two segments have undergone **fusion**, so that the various features are now associated with a single segmental node.

---

[27] As we saw in note 24, an articulatory definition of **a** is less revealing than one based on acoustic properties; indeed, it is probably the case that this also holds for **i** and **u**.

Unlike the vowel system in (44), many systems do not have front rounded vowels. The incorporation of single-valued features in a feature geometry approach to the representation of segments allows us to characterise this in terms of **tier conflation** (see e.g. Kaye *et al.* 1985; Harris 1994: 102). In a system without front rounded vowels the **i** and **u** features share a single tier, and so can never combine, as in the system in (50):

(50) /i/ /e/ /a/ /o/ /u/
     i   **i**   **u**   **u**   **i/u** tier
          a   **a**   **a**   **a** tier

Similarly, in a vowel system with only the three 'basic' vowels, such as that of Alaskan Eskimo (see e.g. Lass 1984b: 85), the three vowel feature tiers are conflated into one:

(51) /i/ /a/ /u/
     i   **a**   **u**   **i/u/a** tier

We have seen that the three single-valued features introduced here allow us to characterise the seven vowels in (44). However, at first sight this seems to be the maximum, given that the features simply co-occur in the representation of a vowel; there are apparently no other combinations of the three features available. It will be obvious that these seven representations do not exhaust the maximum number of different vowels found in the language systems of the world. The existence of systems containing more than seven vowels means that there must be some way in which the total number of vowels describable in terms of (combinations of) the three basic vocalic components can be increased. We return to this issue in §2.5.

2.4   Umlaut and harmony processes

In this section we consider a number of cases involving umlaut and harmony which will illustrate the workings of Underspecification Theory and Single-valued Feature Theory, and will address some of the issues raised in previous sections.

2.4.1   Umlaut

In §1.4.1 we saw that Old English *i*-umlaut (OEIU) involved the autosegmental spreading of [−back], in binary terms, from a suffix to a stem. We formulated the spreading in the word *byrig*, the dative singular form of *burg* 'city', as (80) in Chapter 1, repeated here in slightly adapted form as (52):

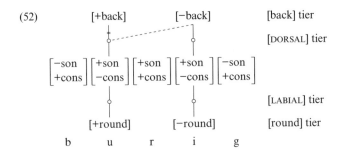

(52)

(For reasons which will become clear, we have included the feature [round] in (52).) Spreading of [−back] necessarily involved a second process, the delinking of the lexically associated [+back] value on the first vowel. In a radically underspecified approach, this latter stage is no longer required. On the assumption that [−back] is the value which is active in the phonology of Old English, as is evidenced by the fact that it spreads, it is the marked value, and therefore lexically present. [+back] is the default value, and therefore not present when the umlaut process applies, so that the formulation in (53) is sufficient in Radical Underspecification Theory:

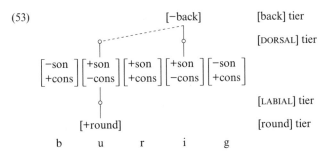

(53)

(We further assume that [+round] is the marked form, and so omit [−round].) As the first vowel is now associated with a specification on the [back] tier, the default rule will not apply to it.

Consider now a single-valued formulation of the same process, which at first sight looks more or less identical:

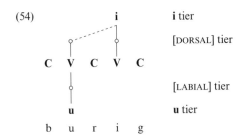

(54)

(For illustration, we replace the binary feature [consonantal] with the single-valued features **C** and **V**; this does not affect our argument here, but see §2.6 for discussion.)

Just as in Radical Underspecification Theory, the process involves the spreading of a feature from the suffix vowel to the stem vowel. The feature involved is the frontness feature; underlyingly, the lexically back vowel is not associated with a feature on this tier (hence its renaming as the **i** tier).

In what sense do (53) and (54) differ, then, other than in the 'name' of the feature involved? In both cases, 'frontness' is characterised as the spreading property involved, either as [−back] or as **i**. The Radical Underspecification approach means that [−back] is the underlyingly present value for Old English. However, the possibility that another language might exist with a process which is identical, except that [+back] is the spreading value, and therefore the underlyingly present value in that language, is not excluded. The single-valued approach, on the other hand, makes the prediction that 'backness' can never spread, as it is not an addressable feature in the system.

Before we consider whether this prediction is correct, we examine another umlaut process, Old Norse *u*-umlaut (ONUU), which involves front vowels becoming rounded under the influence of a following /u/ or /w/. Some examples are given in (55):

(55) i > y   /systur/   'sister'   (< *swistur)
      e > ø   /tøgr/   'ten'   (< *tegur)
      ɑ > ɔ   /lɔndum/   'land (DAT PL)'   (< *lɑndum)

The philological details of ONUU are highly complex (cf. Gordon 1957: 273; Benediktsson 1963), and, as in the case of OEIU, the triggering environment (/u/ or /w/) is often lost, and is therefore not to be found in the orthography. A possible representation of the umlaut of *systur* in terms of Radical Under-specification Theory is given in (56):

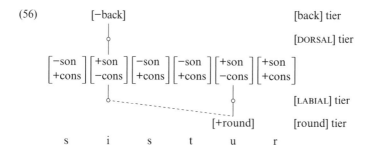

while a single-valued equivalent is given in (57):

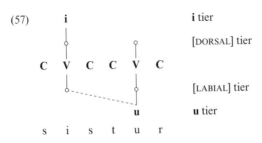

(57)

Just as in the case of OEIU, the choice of [+round] as the underlyingly present value in (56) suggests that in a Radical Underspecification approach to this phenomenon [+round] is the underlying value in Old Norse, but, equally, that it would be possible to find a language in which the spreading value was [−round]. The single-valued approach, on the other hand, predicts that we will not find such a language: 'unroundedness' is not a property in the system.

In this respect the single-valued approach seems to make the correct prediction. While the umlaut processes in (58a) are indeed recorded, as we have seen, those in (58b), as far as we know, are simply not attested:

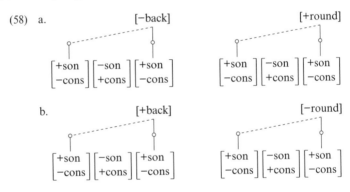

(58)

While it is possible to formulate the rules in (58b) for the two putative but unattested types of umlaut, which must therefore be excluded in Radical Underspecification Theory by explicit statement, in Single-valued Feature Theory it is simply impossible to formulate rules which would represent these processes, as there is nothing corresponding to the spreading values [+back] and [−round]. All other things being equal, then, the latter theory seems to give a more adequate account of umlaut processes.

2.4.2 *Vowel harmony in Yawelmani*

We turn now to a case which has been influential in the development of Radical Underspecification Theory (see Archangeli 1984), but which also provides interesting support for a single-valued approach (Ewen and van der Hulst 1985). This concerns the analysis of vowel harmony in Yawelmani, a dialect of Yokuts, a language spoken in California. As this language has a small vowel system (having only /i/, /u/, /a/ and /o/), and a relatively straight-forward harmony rule, we will consider the analysis of this phenomenon in terms of each of the three approaches we have introduced in this chapter, viz. Contrastive Specification Theory, Radical Underspecification Theory and Single-valued Feature Theory.

The Yawelmani vowel system can be given the fully specified feature representation in (59):

(59)	/i/	/u/	/a/	/o/
[high]	+	+	−	−
[round]	−	+	−	+
[low]	−	−	+	−
[back]	−	+	+	+

The vowel harmony process involves the rounding of an unrounded vowel in a suffix after a rounded vowel in the stem with the same value for the feature [high], as illustrated in (60), from Kenstowicz and Kisseberth (1979: 78ff.):

(60)	a.	xat-nit	'will be eaten'
		bok'-nit	'will be found'
		xil-nit	'will be tangled'
		dub-nut	'will be led by the hand'
	b.	xat-xa	'let us eat'
		bok'-xo	'let us find'
		giy'-xa	'let us touch'
		dub-xa	'let us lead by the hand'

(60a) shows that /i/ in a suffix is realised as [u] if the stem contains /u/; (60b) shows /a/ in a suffix being realised as [o] if the stem contains /o/. This state of affairs can be characterised in a linear formulation as in (61):

(61)   a.   /i/ → [u] / /u/ C __
       b.   /a/ → [o] / /o/ C __

Archangeli (1984) gives the non-linear formulation of the rule as (62):

(62)   [+round]

       [α high]   [α high]

(where the use of 'α' indicates that the two vowels must have the same value for the feature [high]).

Consider now the analysis of this system within Contrastive Specification Theory. Recall that only feature-values which are redundant, in the sense that they are non-contrastive, can be omitted from the phonological representation. Given the vowel system in (59), it is clear that we can omit all the values for the features [low] and [back], according to the following set of redundancy constraints:[28]

(63) a. if [+high] then [−low]
     b. if [+round] then [+back]
     c. if [+round] then [−low]
     d. if [−high, −round] then [+back, +low]
     e. if [+high, −round] then [−back]

This leaves us with the non-redundant specifications in (64):

(64)	/i/	/u/	/ɑ/	/o/
[high]	+	+	−	−
[round]	−	+	−	+

None of the remaining feature-values can be omitted within a Contrastive Specification approach, as each is required to distinguish one segment from at least one other.

As the harmony rule in (62) is formulated in terms of the spreading of [+round], and all vowels are specified for the feature [round] in a Contrastive Specification approach, then it is clear that the application of the rule will involve feature *change*, as shown in (65):

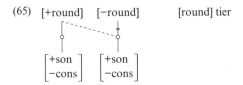

(For convenience we ignore the fact that the two vowels must have identical height specifications.) The [+round] specification spreads from the first vowel to the second, with subsequent delinking of the second vowel from its original [−round] specification.

(66) shows the derivation of the various vowels from their underlying representations within a Contrastive Specification approach. (66a) show the derivation of vowels when not affected by harmony; (66b) the derivation of /i ɑ/ when they are affected by rounding harmony:

---

[28] A different set of redundancy rules might be chosen, e.g. if [+low] then [−high, −round, +back]. This would, of course, yield a different set of phonological representations.

(66)

	a. *no harmony*				b. *harmony*		
	/i/	/u/	/a/	/o/	/i/	/a/	
[high]	+	+	−	−	+	−	underlying
[round]	−	+	−	+	−	−	representation →
[high]	+	+	−	−	+	−	harmony (65) →
[round]	−	+	−	+	+	+	
[high]	+	+	−	−	+	−	redundancy (63)
[round]	−	+	−	+	+	+	
[low]	−	−	+	−	−	−	
[back]	−	+	+	+	+	+	
	[i]	[u]	[a]	[o]	[u]	[o]	

Let us now consider the same problem, analysed within a Radical Underspecification approach, which dispenses with the need to change features. In accordance with the claim that no feature has both values specified underlyingly, Archangeli (1984) proposes the following two default rules for Yawelmani, in addition to the redundancy rules in (63):

(67)   a.   [ ] → [+high]   b.   [ ] → [−round]

Thus the underlying representations are:

(68)

	/i/	/u/	/a/	/o/
[high]			−	−
[round]		+		+

Notice that /i/ is now underlyingly unspecified for all features.

As (68) is radically underspecified, we can revert to the original formulation of the harmony rule in (62), where delinking plays no role. The derivation of the harmonising vowels in Yawelmani then involves the stages shown in (69):

(69)

	a. *no harmony*				b. *harmony*		
	/i/	/u/	/a/	/o/	/i/	/a/	
[high]			−	−	−		underlying
[round]		+		+			representation →
[high]	+	+	−	−	+	−	default (67a) →
[round]		+		+			
[high]	+	+	−	−	+	−	harmony (62) →
[round]		+		+	+	+	
[high]	+	+	−	−	+	−	default (67b) →
[round]	−	+	−	+	+	+	
[high]	+	+	−	−	+	−	redundancy (63)
[round]	−	+	−	+	+	+	→
[low]	−	−	+	−	−	−	
[back]	−	+	+	+	+	+	
	[i]	[u]	[a]	[o]	[u]	[o]	

Notice that we first apply the default rule for [high], as the harmony rule in (62) makes reference to this feature. Within the Radical Underspecification approach, this ordering is regulated by a convention referred to as the **Redundancy Rule Ordering Constraint**, formulated in (70):

> (70) *Redundancy Rule Ordering Constraint* (RROC)
> Any [redundancy or default] rule assigning [αF], where 'α' is '+' or '−', applies before the first rule in which reference is made to [αF].

According to the RROC, the Yawelmani harmony rule, which makes reference to the feature [high], triggers the previous application of the default rule assigning [+high].

After application of (62), the default rule for [round] applies, assigning [−round] to any segment not specified as [+round] (either underlyingly or as a result of harmony), and finally, as in Contrastive Specification theory, the redundancy rules operate.

Finally, we consider how we can deal with Yawelmani vowel harmony in terms of a single-valued feature system. We assume the three single-valued features introduced above, viz. **i** (frontness), **u** (roundness) and **a** (lowness). On this assumption, the *surface* representation of the Yawelmani vowel system will be as in (71):

> (71) [i]   [u]   [ɑ]   [o]
>   **i**   **u**   **a**   **u,a**

(Here and elsewhere we adopt the convention that two single-valued features appearing in the representation of a segment are linked by a comma, so that **u,a** is a vowel containing both the features **u** and **a**.)

Up to now we have been assuming that Contrastive Specification Theory, Radical Underspecification Theory and Single-valued Feature Theory are distinct, although related, theories of phonological representation. However, it is clear that within Single-valued Feature Theory we can envisage two approaches. In the approach which we have been adopting in the discussion above, the representations in (71) would also be the underlying representations, since no redundancies are involved. As we have argued, in this form of single-valued theory, no 'redundancy rules' corresponding to (63) are required: underlying representations already meet the criterion of 'contrastive specification'.

We have also argued that the default rules of Radical Underspecification Theory are not required in a single-valued approach. This is certainly true if default rules are merely required to 'fill in' the value of a feature which is not lexically specified. These rules are sometimes referred to within Radical

Underspecification Theory as **complement rules**, because the value which is filled in is the complement of the value which is lexically specified. However, as we have seen, Archangeli's 'radical' analysis of Yawelmani in (68) involves the claim that /i/ is the 'unspecified' vowel and thus has no underlying specification. It is possible to adopt this aspect of Radical Underspecification Theory in a single-valued approach, by omitting the frontness component from underlying representations, to give (72):

(72) [i] [u] [ɑ] [o]
         u   a   u,a

where only /i/ differs from its corresponding surface representation. We can then formulate the default rule to assign the frontness component as (73):

(73) V
      |
         → **i**

i.e. a vowel which remains empty is assigned the frontness component, and surfaces as [i]. Notice that this is not a 'complement rule', but a rule which makes a specific claim about the nature of the 'unmarked' feature in Yawelmani.

The Yawelmani harmony rule simply involves spreading of **u**, as in (74):

(74) **u**   **u** tier

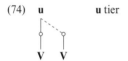

The derivation of the various surface vowels in a single-valued framework involves the application of the two rules in (73) and (74), as shown in (75):

(75) a. *no harmony*   b. *harmony*

	/i/	/u/	/ɑ/	/o/		/i/	/ɑ/	
		u	a	u,a			a	underlying representation
		u	a	u,a		u	u,a	harmony (74)
	i	u	a	u,a		u	u,a	default (73)
	[i]	[u]	[ɑ]	[o]		[u]	[o]	

2.4.3 *Vowel harmony in Yoruba*

We turn now to a rather more complex case of harmony. This involves Yoruba, a Niger-Congo language spoken in Nigeria, the analysis of whose harmony system has played an important role in establishing and motivating Radical Underspecification theory (e.g. Pulleyblank 1988a; Archangeli and Pulleyblank 1989).

Standard Yoruba has a seven-vowel system, in which the mid vowels are generally analysed as differing from each other in their value for the feature [Advanced Tongue Root] ([ATR]; see §1.3.3):

(76)	/i/	/e/	/ɛ/	/a/	/ɔ/	/o/	/u/
[high]	+	–	–	–	–	–	+
[low]	–	–	–	+	–	–	–
[back]	–	–	–	+	+	+	+
[ATR]	+	+	–	–	–	+	+

Yoruba has a vowel harmony system involving the feature [ATR]. Mid vowels (/e ɛ o ɔ/) must agree in their value for [ATR], as shown by (77); the forms in (77a) show the combinations of mid vowels which are permitted by the harmony constraints, while the corresponding forms in (77b), containing two mid vowels with *different* values for [ATR], are prohibited (data from Archangeli and Pulleyblank 1989: 177; ′ = high tone, ` = low tone, mid tone is not marked and /p/ is realised as [k͡p]):

(77)	a.	ebè	'heap for yams'	ɛsɛ̀	'foot'
		epo	'oil'	ɛ̀kɔ	'pap'
		olè	'thief'	ɔbɛ̀	'soup'
		owó	'money'	ɔkɔ́	'vehicle'
	b.	*ɛbè		*esɛ̀	
		*ɛpo		*ɛ̀ko	
		*ɔlè		*obɛ̀	
		*ɔwó		*okɔ́	
	c.	*eba		*osa	

In addition, the sequence in (77c), i.e. a [+ATR] mid vowel followed by [–ATR] /a/, is prohibited.

We might expect from this data that any pair of vowels in a Yoruba disyllabic word would have to have the same value for this feature. But this is not so, as we summarise in (78):

(78)　a.　/i/ and /u/ ([+ATR]) can combine with any preceding or following vowel.

　　　b.　/a/ ([–ATR]) can be followed by /e/ or /o/ ([+ATR]).

We give some representative forms in (79):

(79)	a.	ilè	'land'	ɛ̀bi	'guilt'
		itɔ́	'saliva'	ɔkín	'egret'
		ilá	'okra'	àdí	'palm nut oil'
	b.	ate	'hat'	àwo	'plate'

We will now, following Archangeli and Pulleyblank, examine the assumptions we need to make regarding formal representations in order to deal with the facts within a Radical Underspecification approach. We can propose the default rules and redundancy constraints in (80):

(80) a. *Default rules*   b. *Redundancy constraints*
     [ ] → [+high]   if [+low] then [–high]
     [ ] → [–low]   if [+low] then [+back]
     [ ] → [–back]   if [+low] then [–ATR]
     [ ] → [+ATR]   if [+high] then [+ATR]

This gives the radically underspecified representations in (81):

(81)   /i/ /e/ /ɛ/ /a/ /ɔ/ /o/ /u/

	/i/	/e/	/ɛ/	/a/	/ɔ/	/o/	/u/
[high]	–	–			–		–
[low]				+			
[back]					+	+	+
[ATR]	–			–			

As can be seen in (81), Archangeli and Pulleyblank take [–ATR] to be the underlying value. Consider first words containing the low vowel /a/. We have seen that /a/ can be followed by any mid vowel, whether [+ATR] or [–ATR], but cannot be *preceded* by a [+ATR] mid vowel (/e/ or /o/). (82) gives the derivation of two words containing /a/, [àwo] 'plate' and [ɔjà] 'market' (we use capital letters to indicate lexical representations in which the feature [ATR] is unspecified):

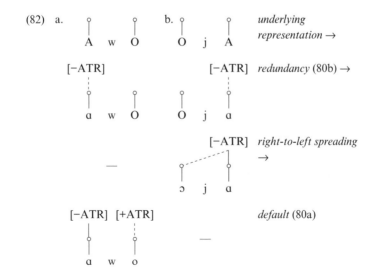

95

If Yoruba had left-to-right [–ATR] spreading, (82a) would incorrectly be realised as *[awɔ]. Notice that the redundant [–ATR] specification for low vowels is assigned before the harmony rule spreading [–ATR] applies, by virtue of the Redundancy Rule Ordering Constraint (70). If this were not the case, then spreading would be unable to operate.

However, a word such as [awɔ] would also be well formed in Yoruba, as we would expect, given that both the vowels here are [–ATR], so that there is no question of a harmony violation. Thus we find forms such as [aʃɔ] 'cloth' and [ajɛ] 'paddle'. Archangeli and Pulleyblank suggest that forms such as these can be generated by allowing a morpheme in Yoruba to have a floating feature on the [ATR] tier in the underlying representation. In other words, just as in our discussion of Turkish vowel harmony in §1.4.2, a morpheme may contain a [–ATR] feature which is initially not associated with a vowel. Furthermore, mapping (cf. our discussion of tone in §1.4) must target the final vowel of the morpheme. On this assumption, the derivation of [aʃɔ] proceeds as in (83):

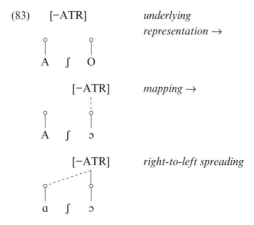

A similar account is available for words in which high vowels co-occur with [–ATR] vowels, as in (79a) above. These words, too, will have a floating [–ATR] autosegment. However, [–ATR] will not be able to associate to a high vowel, because of the redundancy constraint in (80b) which rules out high [–ATR] vowels. If the high vowel is final, as in [ɛ̀bi] 'guilt', floating [–ATR] associates with the first available vowel, i.e. the preceding non-high one. By default (80a), the final vowel becomes [+ATR], as in (84a). If, however, the high vowel is in the first syllable, as in [ilɛ̀] 'land' in (84b), [–ATR] is mapped onto the final vowel as normal, but fails to associate with the first vowel, which is high.

(84)   a.   [−ATR]   b.   [−ATR]   *underlying*
                                         representation →

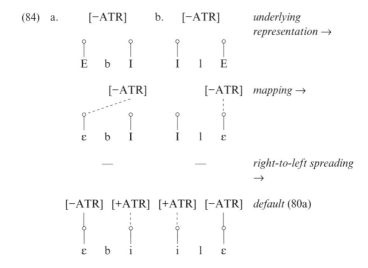

However, although (84a) shows that floating [−ATR] can skip a final high vowel, and be mapped onto a preceding non-high vowel, it apparently cannot spread *across* a high vowel. Evidence for this comes from trisyllabic words such as those in (85):

(85)   a.   èlùbɔ́   'yam flour'   b.   *ɛlubɔ
            odíde   'grey parrot'   *ɔdidɛ

On the assumption that these words again have a floating [−ATR], the first step in the derivation of [èlùbɔ́] involves mapping [−ATR] onto the final vowel:

(86)   [−ATR]   *mapping*

As before, [−ATR] cannot spread to the high vowel in the second syllable, However, it also does not spread to the vowel in the first syllable, as we see from the unacceptability of (85b). This possibility is excluded by the assumption that a spreading rule cannot simply skip a segment to which it cannot associate, as this would involve **discontinuous feature sharing**, as in (87):

(87)   *   [−ATR]   *right-to-left spreading*

Facts like these provide further evidence for an important property of phonological representations, viz. that feature sharing must involve adjacent class nodes (cf. the discussion in §1.4 with respect to line crossing).[29] At first sight, though, the form in (88) appears to violate this constraint, in that here the first and third vowels are [–ATR], while the second is [+ATR]:

(88) àkùrɔ̀ 'a type of farmland'

However, no violation is in fact involved. As in [èlùbɔ́], [–ATR] cannot spread to the vowel in the second syllable because it is [+high], and cannot cross this vowel to spread to the vowel in the first syllable. Thus at this point the two derivations are essentially identical:

(89)   [–ATR]   *mapping*

In (86) the [ATR] values for the vowels in the first two syllables is determined by default (80a): they are both [+ATR]. This also holds for the second vowel in (89). However, (89) is subject to the redundancy constraint in (80b), which determines that [+low] vowels are [–ATR]. This redundancy constraint applies before the default specification is determined, so that the derivations continue as follows:

(90) a.   b. [–ATR]   [–ATR] *redundancy*
                                                           (80b) →
      —

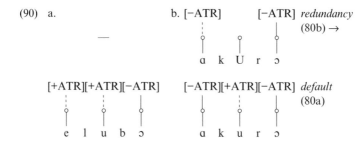

These forms do not involve spreading, then, but are rather the result of the interaction of the default rules and redundancy constraints of Yoruba given in (80).

The analysis we have just given is one in which [–ATR] is the lexically specified feature-value, and [+ATR] the default value. This is cross-linguistically an atypical situation; most languages in which [ATR] plays a role in the

---

[29] Notice that, here as elsewhere, we assume that consonants, which do not participate in vowel harmony processes, simply lack the class node with which [ATR] associates. The fact that they are ignored by vowel harmony processes is not a violation of this constraint, then.

phonology would select [+ATR] as the underlying value. If the analysis given is the appropriate one, as Archangeli and Pulleyblank argue, then we have clear evidence in favour of the view that this is a binary feature, with both values being available in phonological processes. This analysis of Yoruba thus presents an interesting challenge to the claim that all features are single-valued.

Alternative analyses are possible, however. Indeed, an analysis of Yoruba vowel harmony in which no reference is made to [−ATR] is available in a system making use of the single-valued features **i**, **u**, **a** and ATR. This analysis depends on treating the vowels /e/ and /o/ not as the [+ATR] counterparts of /ɛ/ and /ɔ/, as in Archangeli and Pulleyblank's account, but as the [−ATR] counterparts of the high vowels /i/ and /u/. There are good phonetic grounds for this claim: high [−ATR] vowels and mid [+ATR] vowels are acoustically very similar, and are notoriously hard to distinguish.

Assuming a single-valued system with a feature ATR, this would yield the following representation of the Yoruba vowel system:

(91) /i/ /e/ /ɛ/ /a/ /ɔ/ /o/ /u/

i	**i**	**i**					**i** tier
		a	**a**	**a**			**a** tier
				u	**u**	**u**	**u** tier
ATR					ATR		ATR tier

Thus the only ATR vowels are /i/ and /u/. Abandoning [−ATR], of course, means that the harmony process of Yoruba must be reanalysed as involving the spreading of some other feature. We suggest that this feature is **a**.

Let us consider how such an analysis might work. In Archangeli and Pulleyblank's analysis, as we have already seen, [−ATR] was not allowed to associate with a high vowel. Something similar is required here; we have to prevent **a** from spreading to /i/ and /u/. This can be achieved by the mechanism of tier conflation introduced in §2.3:

(92) /i/ /e/ /ɛ/ /a/ /ɔ/ /o/ /u/

i	**i**	**i**					**i** tier
ATR		**a**	**a**	**a**		ATR	**a**/ATR tier
			u	**u**	**u**		**u** tier

That is, the features **a** and ATR, which share a tier, cannot combine in the representation of a segment, so that spreading of **a** to a high vowel is formally impossible. In addition, we assume that the Redundancy Rule Ordering Constraint of Binary Feature Theory (70) operates in the single-valued model to assign a default feature to a vowel which is completely empty, prior to the first application of any rule which mentions the feature. For Yoruba, the default rule is that in (93) (cf. the default rule for Yawelmani in (73)):

(93)   V
       |
       |
         → **a**

This allows the following derivations of the Yoruba bisyllabic words in (82) and (83) above, where we retain Archangeli and Pulleyblank's analysis in terms of a floating feature, in this case **a**:

(94)   a.   b.   c.   **a**   **a**/ATR tier

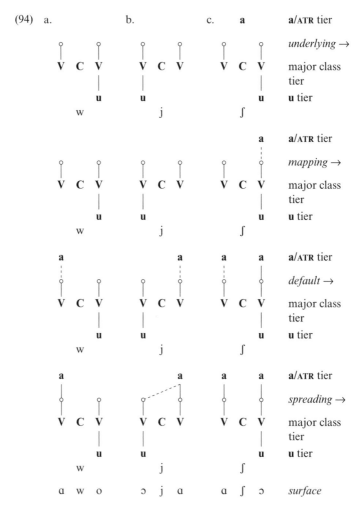

Mapping takes place in (94c), as before. Before spreading takes place, empty vowels are assigned the default feature **a**. This renders spreading in (94c) vacuous.

Consider now the forms containing high vowels in (84). In the single-valued analysis their derivations proceed as in (95):

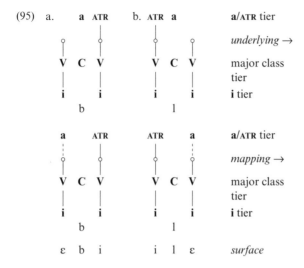

a cannot be mapped on to the high vowel /i/ in (95a), which already has a specification (ATR) on the relevant tier, nor can it spread to the first vowel in (95b), for the same reason. The trisyllabic forms [èlùbɔ́] and [àkùrɔ̀] are dealt with as might be expected:

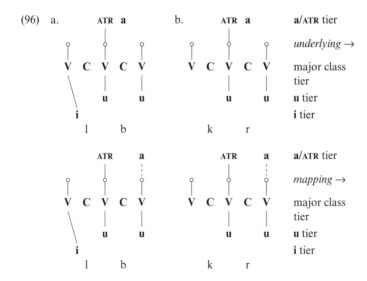

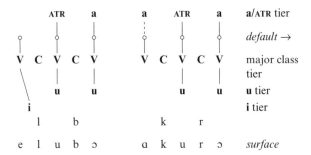

As in (94), there is no spreading.

Although it is not our concern here to argue the relative merits of the binary and single-valued models in any detail, we have shown here that what appears at first sight to be a clear case of the spreading of an 'unexpected' binary feature value ([–ATR]) can be given an interpretation within single-valued theory by attributing the spreading to a different feature, which already forms part of the feature inventory for the language in question.

2.5 Dependency within the segment

We noted in §2.3 that the combinations of the three single-valued features **i**, **u** and **a** apparently allow a maximum of seven distinct representations, those given in (44). However, especially in view of our discussion in §1.3.3, it is clear that we must consider how we should view vowel systems with a more extensive array of vowels. Recall that in §1.3.3 we suggested that vowel systems can be organised in different ways. In one kind of system, that in (28) in Chapter 1, the vowels divided into two sets, a [+ATR] set and a [–ATR] set. Alternatively, the two sets can involve an opposition between peripherality and centrality, which we characterised in terms of a tense vs lax opposition, as in (26) in Chapter 1. Lastly, we observed that there is evidence that we can identify a multivalued scalar vowel-height opposition in certain systems, involving four distinctive vowel heights.

Let us first consider systems organised in terms of ATR oppositions. In our discussion of Yoruba in §2.4.3 we introduced a single-valued feature ATR, and it will be clear that it is the presence of this feature which distinguishes the members of the two sets of this kind of system, as shown in (97):

(97)

	/i/	/e/	/ə/	/o/	/u/	/ɪ/	/ɛ/	/a/	/ɔ/	/ʊ/	
	i	i				i	i				i tier
		a	a	a			a	a	a		a tier
				u	u				u	u	u tier
	ATR	ATR	ATR	ATR	ATR						ATR tier

We are assuming here a system in which ATR is a 'positive' property, rather than one like Yoruba, which is atypical in this respect. A system such as (97) allows a straightforward interpretation of harmony in terms of the spreading of the ATR feature.

As yet, however, we do not seem to be able to account within single-valued theory for the second type of system, that involving a distinction between peripheral and central vowels. Most proponents of Single-valued Feature Theory have suggested that a further feature is necessary to deal with these systems, a feature which on its own is interpretable as a schwa-like vowel. This feature is referred to variously as **neutral** (Harris 1994: §3.3.5), **centrality** (Anderson and Ewen 1987: §6.2) and **cold** (Kaye *et al.* 1985: §1.2), because of the fact that central vowels have less well-defined acoustic properties than peripheral vowels. Following Harris (1994), we represent the neutral feature here as @. A system organised in terms of a tense vs lax opposition, such as (26) in Chapter 1, can now be characterised as in (98):

(98) /i/ /e/ /a/ /o/ /u/   /ɪ/ /ɛ/ /ə/ /ɔ/ /ʊ/
    i **i**   **i** **i**   *i* tier
        a **a** **a**   **a** **a** **a** *a* tier
             u **u**   **u** **u** *u* tier
                     @ @ @ @ @ *@* tier

The lax vowels differ from the tense vowels in the presence of @.

Accounting for a system in which we have a scalar opposition of vowel height is less straightforward, however. It does not seem appropriate simply to add a new feature (or to utilise either ATR or @), as we have argued that a *single* phonetic parameter is involved here. Rather, it seems that we have to increase the combinatorial potential of the three features **i, u** and **a**.

There are in principle two ways in which this can be achieved. Either we can assume that features can occur more than once in a particular representation, or we can take the view that one of the features in a feature combination can be in some sense more prominent than the other feature(s). The first of these two positions is defended by Schane (1984), while the concept of **dependency** is used to create a larger number of possible representations in various approaches.

For Schane, who refers to his single-valued features as **particles**, each step down the vowel-height scale involves the addition of **a**, so that a low vowel contains more than one occurrence:

(99) /i/ /e/ /ɛ/ /a/
    i **ia** **iaa** **iaaa**

Dependency-based theories adopt a different approach. In these theories, the difference between pairs of mid vowels in a scalar system is achieved by allowing one of the features to contribute more to the segment than the other. The features which are required in the representations of /o/ and /ɔ/, say, are identical (**u** and **a**), but **u** is more 'important' in the representation of /o/ than **a**, while for /ɔ/ the roles are reversed. In other words, one feature is the **head** and the other the **dependent**. We give the representations for a typical seven-vowel system lacking front rounded vowels in (100), where we indicate the head in any representation by underlining.[30]

(100) /i/ /e/ /ɛ/ /a/ /ɔ/ /o/ /u/

i	i̲	i		u	u̲	u	i/u tier
	a	a̲	a	a̲	a		a tier

Within this approach, scalar processes such as lowering and raising can be characterised as changes in the relationships between the features on the two tiers, such that, as we move along a scale, one feature becomes more 'important' in the representation of the segment than another. Thus, the scale from /a/ to /u/ is characterised as an interaction between the two features **a** and **u**, whereby **a** is initially maximally prominent in the representation (it is the only feature for /a/) and ultimately minimally prominent (it is absent for /u/).

The introduction of dependency allows us to refine our analysis of the monophthongisation process in (48). There we saw that the monophthongisation of /au/ to /ɔː/ involved simply the rearrangement of features. Now, anticipating our discussion of suprasegmental structure in Chapter 3, we can show why the expected outcome of the monophthongisation is indeed /ɔː/, rather than /oː/, which also contains the features **u** and **a**. For /ɔː/, the head is **a**, while for /oː/ it is **u**. The output /ɔː/ is therefore expected, as /au/ is a 'falling' diphthong, in which the first element is more prominent than the second, and therefore can be interpreted as the head, as in (101):

(101)

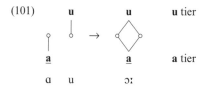

---

[30] Headship is denoted in various ways in the literature on dependency relations in phonology. In the approach known as **dependency phonology** (Anderson and Jones 1974, 1977; Ewen 1980a; Anderson and Ewen 1987), heads are placed higher in the segmental representation than their dependents. This formalisation is difficult to combine with autosegmental representations incorporating tiers, so we adopt here the underlining convention of, e.g., Harris (1994: §3.3.3).

The dependency relation can also be invoked to provide a more satisfactory relationship between the representations of the tense (peripheral) and lax (central) vowels in (98), where the lax vowels were characterised as containing an extra feature @ in comparison with their tense counterparts. Thus a change from /i/ to /ɪ/, say, could involve the addition of a feature. It is not immediately obvious that it is appropriate to treat central vowels as containing more features than peripheral ones, and this leads Harris (1994) to suggest that all vowels, both 'tense' and 'lax', contain @, with @ being the head in the representation of a lax vowel, and a dependent otherwise, as in (102):[31]

(102) /i/ /e/ /ɑ/ /o/ /u/   /ɪ/ /ɛ/ /ə/ /ɔ/ /ʊ/

i̲	i̲				i	i				i tier
	a̲	a				a	a	a		a tier
			u̲	u̲				u	u	u tier
@	@	@	@	@	@	@	@	@	@	@ tier

Furthermore, Harris claims that @ only contributes to the interpretation of a segment if it is a head; in dependent position it has no interpretation.

2.6   Consonants and single-valued features

A claim that has often been made in support of Single-valued Feature Theory is that it provides a simple metric for measuring the inherent complexity of a segment: the more features a segment requires in its specification, the more complex it is. Thus the 'pure' vowels /i u ɑ/, each characterised by a single feature, are less complex than 'mixed' vowels such as /e o y ø/, which require two or three features. We do not pursue this here with respect to vowel features, but we will examine briefly how the notion has been utilised in accounting for lenition processes such as those considered in §1.3.1. We saw there that intervocalic lenition involves movement along what seemed to be a sonority-based hierarchy, such that a voiceless stop might first pass through a voiced stop or voiceless fricative stage, then a voiced fricative stage, on its way to a sonorant consonant. Each stage has been typically viewed as assimilation in some property to the surrounding vowels; indeed, the sonorant consonant often vocalises in this context. At first sight, then, we might expect lenition to be characterised in terms of spreading from the surrounding vowels. However, it has often been observed that lenition ultimately leads to deletion; indeed, an often quoted definition is that of Hyman (1975: 165):

(103)   A segment X is said to be weaker than a segment Y if Y goes through an X stage on its way to zero.

[31] For the sake of exposition, we treat **i** and **u** as the head of /e/ and /o/, respectively. A full account would have to consider the relationship between these features and **a**, however.

This fact has been utilised in treatments of lenition as involving reduction in complexity of a segment, such as that of Harris (1990, 1994). Harris notes that lenition as defined in (103) is not restricted to intervocalic position, but is also found in initial and final position. In initial position we find developments such as that in (104a), and in final position (104b), as well as the intervocalic 'trajectories' in (104c, d):

(104) a. (voiceless) fricative > [h] > Ø
       b. (voiceless) plosive > [ʔ] > Ø
       c. voiceless plosive > voiceless fricative > voiced fricative > liquid > Ø
       d. voiceless plosive > voiced plosive > voiced fricative > liquid > Ø

In Harris's terms, each of these changes must involve the removal of a feature from the representation. This in turn means that segments at the consonantal end of the sonority hierarchy have maximally complex feature representations; those at the vocalic end have minimally complex representations. It would take us too far here to examine the full set of features which Harris proposes; we restrict our account to showing in (105) some examples of lenition in the model which he proposes:

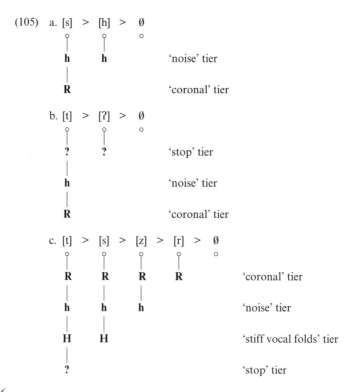

The set of features which Harris employs certainly allows a uniform treatment of the various processes in (104) as involving reduction in the number of features. However, the resulting representations of consonants seem to be at odds with a single-valued feature system which characterises the vowel space in terms of the three features **i**, **u** and **a**. These features were claimed to be appropriate because they correspond in isolation to the most basic vowels, those at the 'corners' of the vowel triangle. With respect to the sonority hierarchy, it would seem that the two extremes of the hierarchy, voiceless stops and vowels, should have the same status as these basic vowels. However, it follows from Harris's model that voiceless stops must have the most complex representation, which is in conflict with this claim.[32]

The claim that voiceless stops and vowels are the maximally simple categories obviously means that intermediate categories are more complex, in the same way that mid back vowels are more complex than /u/ or /ɑ/. On this assumption, lenition cannot be interpreted as involving an across-the-board decrease in complexity (or, indeed, an increase in complexity). Indeed, we believe that it is mistaken to equate lenition and complexity, either inversely or directly, and that this results from the assumption that all the lenition processes in (104) have the same cause. Those in (104a) and (b) are indeed cases of reduction of complexity, as we suggested in our characterisation of [h] in §1.3.5 as a 'defective' segment, lacking a place specification of its own. The same account would be appropriate for [ʔ]. However, as we have noted, intervocalic changes seem to be triggered by assimilation to some property of the surrounding vowels; there seems to be no *a priori* reason to expect that spreading should lead to reduction in complexity. Indeed, in a single-valued approach, we would expect the reverse, if anything.

How, then, might we represent the assimilation involved in intervocalic lenition within a single-valued model? Notice that lenition in these terms does not involve place of articulation, and so we assume that features such as Harris's **R** (coronality) play no role. Rather, the features involved are those corresponding to the binary features dominated by the **categorial** class node in (43) in Chapter 1, i.e. [sonorant], [consonantal], [continuant] and [voice] (cf. our discussion in §1.3.5).

Earlier in this chapter we introduced, but did not discuss, the single-valued features **C** and **V**, which may be taken as corresponding to [+consonantal] and [+sonorant], respectively. By analogy with the interpretation of single-valued vowel features when they occur alone, these two features in isolation

---

[32] It is interesting to notice that other models (e.g. that of K. D. Rice 1992) incorporate a system of representation in which complexity *increases* as a segment becomes more sonorous.

are interpretable as the extremes of the 'categorial space', i.e. as stops and vowels, respectively. Other categories of segments, e.g. fricatives and sonorant consonants, can be represented as various combinations of the two features, as in (106), where we take the coronal series as examples:

(106) /t d/ /s z/ /l r n/ /i/
     C   <u>C</u>   C   C tier
     V   <u>V</u>   V   V tier

As before, we introduce the dependency relation into the representations; as we would expect, in the representation for sonorant consonants **V** is more prominent than for fricatives. As in the case of vowels, as we move from one end of the hierarchy to the other, one feature becomes more 'important', at the expense of the other. In a model like this, we can characterise weakening as an increase in the prominence of **V**, i.e. as an assimilation to the **V** feature of the surrounding vowels.

Clearly, as we have presented it, the model only defines a few of the categories on the sonority scale. As in our presentation of Harris's model of consonantal features, we will not consider the way in which this model deals with the full range of possibilities, especially as there is an extensive literature within dependency phonology which deals with this issue (although this generally adopts a rather different notation).[33]

2.7 Laryngeal features

Up to this point we have been assuming that the feature [voice] is adequate for the characterisation of what are often referred to as laryngeal oppositions. In a binary approach, segments have been considered to be either [+voice] or [−voice]. In a model incorporating underspecification, a segment may bear no value for [voice], as in our account in §2.2.3 of voicing assimilation in Russian. If this feature is appropriate, it is obviously relevant for single-valued theory to establish which value is 'active' in languages; i.e. whether it is [+voice] or [−voice] which is typically involved in spreading, for example. However, even within binary theory, it has long been recognised that a simple binary feature is inadequate to express the full range of laryngeal oppositions which are found in languages. Indeed, Halle and Stevens (1971) propose replacing [voice] by no fewer than four binary features, [spread glottis], [constricted glottis], [slack vocal folds] and [stiff vocal folds]. However, as Ladefoged (1973) points out, these four features in fact characterise

---

[33] See for example Anderson and Ewen (1987: §4.4), Ewen (1995: §2.2), van der Hulst (1995).

two ternary parameters, in the same way as the binary features [high] and [low] are the expression of the single parameter of vowel height.

Consider first the parameter spread/constricted glottis. This parameter characterises the degree of glottal opening, independent of whether the vocal folds are in vibration. A feature is required for this parameter to represent the opposition which some languages display between different types of voiced or voiceless segments, as in (107) (data from Ladefoged 1973: 80):

(107)		$\begin{bmatrix} -\text{spread} \\ +\text{constr} \end{bmatrix}$	$\begin{bmatrix} -\text{spread} \\ -\text{constr} \end{bmatrix}$	$\begin{bmatrix} +\text{spread} \\ -\text{constr} \end{bmatrix}$
a.	*Hausa*	ḅ	b	
b.	*Uduk*		p	pʰ
c.	*Beja*	ḍ	d	ḍ
d.	*Sindhi*		b	ḅ

The various types of contrasts in (107) are appropriately characterised in terms of glottal opening, i.e. between laryngealised (creaky voiced) and 'normal' voiced plosives in Hausa (107a), between 'normal' voiced and breathy voiced plosives in Sindhi (d) and between voiceless unaspirated and voiceless aspirated plosives in Uduk (b). The contrast in Beja in (107c) involves a three-way opposition between different types of voiced plosives, viz. creaky voiced, 'normally' voiced and breathy voiced.

In terms of laryngeal oppositions, the second parameter, stiff/slack vocal folds, is responsible for the difference between the presence and absence of vocal fold vibration: voiced sounds are [+slack vocal folds], voiceless sounds [+stiff vocal folds]. Lenis sounds, however, are neither slack nor stiff, so that Korean has the opposition in (108d):

(108)		$\begin{bmatrix} -\text{stiff} \\ +\text{slack} \end{bmatrix}$	$\begin{bmatrix} -\text{stiff} \\ -\text{slack} \end{bmatrix}$	$\begin{bmatrix} +\text{stiff} \\ -\text{slack} \end{bmatrix}$
a.	*Hausa*	ḅ/b		p
b.	*Uduk*	b		p/pʰ
c.	*Beja*	ḍ/d/ḍ		t
d.	*Korean*		ḍ̥	t/tʰ

One of the reasons for claiming that three oppositions are required here is that there appears to be a close relationship between vocal fold vibration and tone. It is claimed that [+slack] corresponds to low tone, and [+stiff] to high tone, while a mid tone corresponds to a lenis unvoiced consonant. This is not an issue which we will pursue here, except to note that, although the evidence for having distinct features for glottal opening and vocal fold vibration is convincing, it is not entirely clear that we require a three-way opposition for the vocal fold vibration parameter; as Ladefoged (1973: 82) points out, we have no simple way of specifying the difference between voiced and voiceless sounds.[34] Moreover, it appears that the feature combinations in (107) and (108) can describe a much larger set of laryngeal oppositions than is ever found in languages.

2.7.1 Single-valued laryngeal features

Within single-valued theory, it has been generally assumed that a feature corresponding to [voice] is not in itself sufficient for the characterisation of laryngeal contrasts. Nevertheless, something corresponding to [voice] is usually incorporated, so that we now need to address the question raised in the previous section: is [+voice] or [–voice] the active value?

Harris (1994: §3.6) cites evidence which appears to show that languages differ in this respect, even though, unlike the languages in (107) and (108), they only have a two-way laryngeal opposition. In English, he observes, the 'voiced stop' series /b d g/ is in fact very rarely voiced, but is often phonetically voiceless and lenis. The /p t k/ series, on the other hand, is always voiceless, and in initial position is aspirated. Furthermore, some property of the voiceless series seems to be 'active' in English, as evidenced by the devoicing of a following liquid:

(109) /krɪb/   [kɹ̥ɪ̬b̬]   crib
       /pliːz/   [pl̥iːz̬]   please

(we also indicate the devoiced nature of the final 'voiced' obstruents).

In French, however, Harris observes that the series /b d g/ is always fully voiced, and the /p t k/ series unaspirated, and suggests that this means that in French /p t k/ is the 'neutral' series, while in English it is /b d g/ – the two series are, he observes, 'to all intents and purposes [phonetically] identical'. In this connection, it is instructive to consider again the Dutch data in (24), where we analysed the realisation of *zakdoek* /zɑkduk/ 'handkerchief' as [zɑgduk] as involving spreading of [+voice]. Notice that Dutch, like French, does not aspirate the voiceless series.

These facts lead Harris to propose two single-valued features, one corresponding to [+slack vocal folds], **L**, and one to [+stiff vocal folds], **H** (the choice of symbols reflects the relationship with tones discussed above). There is no feature corresponding to the parameter of glottal opening, but Harris observes of **H** that 'aspiration is the particular interpretation this [feature] receives when it is present in an expression defining a fortis plosive'. (Aspiration

---

[34] Indeed, Ladefoged casts doubt on a number of the phonetic claims supporting the [stiff vocal folds] feature.

is associated with a fully open glottis.) Most languages will only require one of these features, the choice between which will depend on which is active in the phonology of the language in question. In English, **H** is active, so that the voiceless series contains an extra feature in comparison with the 'neutral' lenis series, while in French and Dutch **L** is active, and the voiceless series is 'neutral':

(110) a. *English*   b. *French*   c. *Dutch*
         /p t k/ /b d g/   /p t k/   /b d g/   /p t k/   /b d/
         H   **H** tier
                              L   **L**   **L** tier
         cool   ghoul   peau   beau   tuin   duin
                         'skin' 'beautiful'   'garden' 'dune'

Languages with more than a simple two-way opposition utilise both features, and indeed both may appear in the representation of a single segment (data from Harris 1994: 135):

(111) a. *Thai*
         /pʰ/   /p/   /b/
         H   **H** tier
                   L   **L** tier
         /pʰàa/ /pàa/   /bàa/
         'split' 'forest' 'shoulder'
     b. *Gujarati*
         /pʰ/   /p/   /b/   /b̤/
         H   **H**   **H** tier
                   L   **L**   **L** tier
         /pʰɔdz/ /pɔɾ/   /baɾ/   /b̤aɾ/
         'army' 'last year' 'twelve' 'burden'

Although this approach gives a perspicuous account of the way in which different languages deal with laryngeal contrasts, the actual choice of features raises some questions. It is difficult to see that **L** and **H** represent *distinct* phonetic parameters; both their articulatory definition (slack vs stiff vocal folds) and what Harris calls their 'signal mapping' (low vs high fundamental frequency) appear to suggest that a single parameter is involved. This in turn would imply that the opposition is an equipollent one, contrary to the fundamental claim of Single-valued Feature Theory.

We think that this problem can be avoided by abandoning **H**, and replacing it by a feature of glottal opening, which we label **O**.[35] Notice that this allows us to characterise laryngeal contrasts in terms of two distinct parameters, and

---

[35] For earlier proposals along these lines, see Ewen (1980b); Anderson and Ewen (1987: §5.1).

also to give up [stiff vocal folds] as an active value, which seems desirable on phonetic grounds (cf. again Ladefoged 1973). However, the representations in (110) and (111) need not change, except for the substitution of **H** by **O**.

Consider now the analysis of the English 'devoicing' processes in (109). English, as we have seen, has **O** as an active feature. The fortis stop series contains **O**, which will be realised as aspiration in syllable-initial prevocalic position. However, when a fortis stop is followed by a liquid, spreading of **O** takes place, as in (112):

(112)

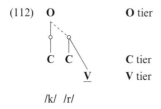

The representation of the sonorant which results from the spreading of **O** is such that the specification for glottal opening overrides the inherent voicing of the sonorant; spread glottis in English is incompatible with vocal fold vibration. It is interesting to notice that voiceless sonorants tend to occur only in those languages in which **O** is the active feature; Dutch, for example, in which the voiceless stop series is 'neutral', does not display devoicing of this sort.

2.8 Summary

Chapter 1 was concerned with the way in which features characterise segments. In this chapter we have been focusing on the nature of the features themselves, in particular on the question of how many of the phonetic properties of segments should be encoded in phonological structure. In §2.1 we examined the claim that features should characterise binary oppositions rather than gradual oppositions, and that the most natural way of representing such opposition is in terms of binary features. We considered evidence which appeared to challenge the idea that both the presence and the absence of a phonetic property is *necessarily* encoded in terms of the two opposing values of a binary feature. One such piece of evidence involved the properties of nasality and orality. We argued that the property of orality does not have to be encoded in any other way than in terms of the absence of nasality. In other words, orality is not a 'positive' property, and we therefore require no explicit means of characterising it, e.g. as the absence of nasality. We suggested that the feature characterising the oral–nasal dimension can therefore be considered to be single-valued.

The asymmetry between the two poles of phonetic dimensions has received different formal treatments in the phonological literature, some of which maintain the hypothesis that all phonological features are binary. These we considered in §2.2, in particular with reference to approaches incorporating the concepts of redundancy and underspecification. In §2.3 we considered feature asymmetry in terms of single-valued feature theories, our focus being on the characterisation of vowel structure, and in §2.4 we demonstrated how the various theories considered in §§2.2 and 2.3 dealt with the analysis of a number of umlaut and harmony processes.

§2.5 saw the introduction of a further concept in the representation of the segment: dependency. Dependency is a relation holding between features in a segmental representation, such that a feature may occupy a head position or a dependent position. We demonstrated how this concept can be used in the representations of vowels, while §2.6 was concerned with how single-valued features and, to a lesser extent, dependency can be used in the characterisation of consonantal structure, in particular with respect to their major class and manner properties. Finally, in §2.7 we applied the same notions to the representation of laryngeal properties.

2.9   Further reading

Much of the further reading mentioned in §1.6 is also relevant to this chapter.

On the nature of phonological features (§2.1), see Trubetzkoy (1939: ch. 3) for the fundamental notions of the 'logical classification of distinctive oppositions'. See Anderson (1985: ch. 4) for discussion. On multivalued features, see Ladefoged (1971), Vennemann and Ladefoged (1973) and Williamson (1977). Clements (1985) and McCarthy (1988) are basic references for feature geometry. See also Padgett (1995), and, on the different types of features and tiers in feature geometry, Avery and Rice (1989).

There is a substantial body of literature on the various theories dealt with under the heading 'feature asymmetry' (§2.2). Chomsky and Halle (1968: ch. 9) lay out their theory of the 'intrinsic content of features'. Cairns and Feinstein (1982) and Cairns (1988) propose refinements on the markedness theory of *SPE*. For critical accounts of markedness theory, see Lass (1975), Lass and Anderson (1975: App. IV) and Kean (1980).

Steriade (1995) provides an overview of the issues involved in markedness and underspecification (§2.2.1). For early arguments against allowing binary features to be unspecified (§2.2.2), see Stanley (1967). For work on contrastive specification (§2.2.3) and radical underspecification (§2.2.4), see Kiparsky (1982), Archangeli (1984, 1988a), Pulleyblank (1988a, b), Ringen (1988), Abaglo and Archangeli (1989), Mester and Itô (1989), Mohanan (1991),

Archangeli and Pulleyblank (1994), Pulleyblank (1995). Itô *et al.* (1995) consider the role of underspecification in Optimality Theory. Keating (1988b) shows the relevance of underspecification in phonetic representation. See also Stevens *et al.* (1986), Stevens and Keyser (1989).

Much has been written on single-valued vowel features, and on the notion that the vowel space is triangular (§2.3). See for example Sanders (1972), Anderson and Jones (1974), Schane (1984), Goldsmith (1985), Rennison (1986, 1990), Anderson and Ewen (1987), Kaye *et al.* (1990), Harris (1994), Harris and Lindsey (1995), Lombardi (1996) and Cyran (1997).

For reading on umlaut and harmony processes (§§2.4, 2.4.1), see the papers in Vago (1980) and van der Hulst and Smith (1988a), as well as Aoki (1968), Anderson (1973), Ultan (1973), Vago (1973), Ringen (1975), Halle and Vergnaud (1981), Hume (1990), van der Hulst and van de Weijer (1995) and Polgárdi (1998).

For accounts of Yawelmani harmony (§2.4.2), see Kuroda (1967). Archangeli (1984), Pulleyblank (1988a) and Archangeli and Pulleyblank (1989, 1994) give accounts of harmony in Yoruba (§2.4.3). For a discussion of harmony in Nez Perce, in particular whether it involves spreading of ATR or of **a**, see Anderson and Durand (1988).

The notion of segment-internal headedness (§2.5) originates in the model of dependency phonology (Anderson and Jones 1974; Ewen 1980a; Anderson and Ewen 1987; van der Hulst 1989). See Lass (1984a: ch. 11) for an overview. Essentially the same concept is employed in government phonology (Kaye *et al.* 1985, 1990; Harris 1994). The term 'dependency' is used in different senses elsewhere, particularly in feature geometry; see e.g. McCarthy (1988), Mester (1988) and Piggott (1992). For an overview of dependency in phonology, see Ewen (1995).

For proposals on the representation of consonants in single-valued feature theory (§2.6), see, besides the dependency and government references given above, Smith (1988), Harris (1990, 1997) and Harris and Kaye (1990). Ladefoged (1975: ch. 12) offers an account in terms of a multivalued feature [place], whose values correspond to the traditional articulatory labels for place of articulation.

For binary treatments of the representation of laryngeal features (§2.7), see Halle and Stevens (1971), Ladefoged (1973), Iverson (1983), Lombardi (1991) and Steriade (1996). For analyses in terms of single-valued features, see Ewen (1980b), Davenport and Staun (1986) and Harris (1994).

3
Syllables

3.1 Introduction

In the first two chapters of this book we considered the internal structure of
the segment in some detail. In the course of our discussion, we saw that
certain features may be relevant to stretches of speech larger than just a
single segment. This generally involved cases where two adjacent segments
agreed in their specifications for place or voicing, for example. In other cases,
such as vowel harmony, the two segments involved appeared not to be immediately adjacent, in that consonants could intervene which did not appear to
be affected by the harmony process in question. However, we argued that the
adjacency condition was in fact met, provided that we interpreted adjacency
to refer to successive elements on some tier.

There are still other types of cases in which stretches of adjacent segments
appear to agree with respect to a certain property. For example, in the South
American Indian language Terena (or Tereno), spoken in Brazil (cf. Bendor-
Samuel 1960), the 1st person singular morpheme is realised by spreading
nasality from left to right throughout the word. Thus the form for 'his brother'
is [ajo], while the form for 'my brother' differs only in the fact that all the
segments are nasalised, giving [ãj̃õ]. In the kind of notation we have been
developing (ignoring considerations of underspecification, etc.), we can show
that sequences of segments can share a single nasal feature or autosegment as
shown in (1) (we are assuming that nasality is expressed by a single-valued
feature **N** (cf. §2.3); we also use the single-valued features **V** and **C**):

(1) **N**   **N** tier

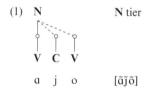

      V **C** **V**

      ɑ   j   o   [ãj̃õ]

In cases like this, a single feature appears to be the property of a sequence
of segments, rather than of an individual segment. This raises the question

of whether there are particular strings of segments which are involved in processes like this more regularly than others, perhaps strings which form independently motivated constituents of some kind. In other words, do certain strings regularly form **domains** for the application of such processes, or is it the case that *any* string of segments is a candidate for feature sharing of the type illustrated in (1)?

It certainly seems to be the case that the 'word' is a constituent which acts as a domain of this sort. Word-bound nasal agreement processes like those in (1) are not uncommon, although they may be more complex than is the case in (1). In Terena, for example, the situation is not as straightforward as we have suggested. Rather, nasality spreads from the beginning of the noun only as far as the first obstruent (which is realised as a prenasalised stop or fricative), as shown in (2) (examples from Bendor-Samuel 1960: 350):

(2) a. owoku   'his house'   õw̃õŋgu   'my house'
    b. piho   'he went'   mbiho   'I went'
    c. emoʔu   'his word'   ẽmõʔũ   'my word'

In (2a), nasality spreads as far as the velar stop, where it is blocked from spreading any further, while in (b) it cannot spread beyond the first segment, a bilabial stop. In these cases the stop is realised as prenasalised, i.e. as a complex segment (cf. §3.6 below). Notice that the glottal stop in (c) does not block the spreading, even though it is not itself affected.[1] (3) gives the representation after spreading for the form 'my house':

(3) N   N tier

      V   C   V   C   V

      o   w   o   k   u   [õw̃õŋgu]

We ignore here the question of the details of how the **N** autosegment is associated with the voiceless stop to give a prenasalised stop. What appears to be involved here is similar to the effects discussed for Apinayé in §1.4; in Terena the stop 'accepts' the spreading feature, but blocks its further spreading, yielding a segment whose left edge is nasal, but whose right edge is oral. What (3) demonstrates is that the *domain* of nasal spreading is the whole word, even though there is an extra restriction – the presence of a stop – which can block the spreading from reaching to the end of the domain in question.

---

[1] The transparency of glottal stops to the spreading of nasality in Terena is perhaps due to the fact that such segments lack a place node in their feature representation (cf. the discussion of /h/ in §1.3.5).

We can find many other processes of feature agreement whose application
is determined by whether or not the string of segments involved is within a
particular domain. Thus, in English, obstruents in a cluster must agree in
voicing, but only if they occur within a simple word (i.e. one containing only
a single morpheme; (4a)) or in words containing a stem and certain types of
affix (e.g. the plural suffix; (4b), where we represent the boundary in question
by +). Agreement is not found in compound words, as is shown by the forms
in (4c), where the boundary is represented by #:[2]

(4)   a.   Brigden   [brɪgdən]
           tactile   [tæktaɪl]
      b.   dogs   DOG+PL   [dɒgz]
           cats   CAT+PL   [kæts]
      c.   matchbox MATCH#BOX [mæʧbɒks]
           textbook TEXT#BOOK [tɛkstbʊk]
           pigsty   PIG#STY   [pɪgstaɪ]

In terms of the autosegmental representations developed in Chapter 1, then,
(5a) and (b) are the only possibilities; (5c) and (d) do not occur within the
simple English word; rather, they are only found when # intervenes:

(5)   a.   b.   L

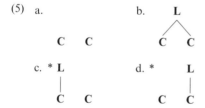

(We use here the single-valued feature **L** to represent voicing (cf. §2.7); voicelessness is therefore unmarked, so that (5c) represents a sequence of a voiced
and a voiceless obstruent.)

The phenomenon of nasal place assimilation in English discussed in §1.2
provides another example of the applicability of a process being dependent
on a domain. The constraint that a nasal is obligatorily homorganic with a
following stop at the end of a word holds only within the monomorphemic
word, as in (6a): it does not hold if the final stop is a realisation of a past
tense suffix, say, as in (6b), nor in compound words, as in (6c), and is thus, in
the analysis of Borowsky (1993), a word-level rule:

[2] For discussion of the relationship between the morphology and phonology of suffixation and compounding, in particular within Lexical Phonology, see e.g. Kaisse and Shaw (1985). For a different
kind of approach, see Harris (1994: ch. 1).

(6)	a.	kind		[kaɪnd]
		lamp		[læmp]
	b.	climbed	CLIMB+PAST	[klaɪmd]
		banged	BANG+PAST	[bæŋd]
	c.	gumdrop	GUM#DROP	[gʌmdrɒp]
		moonbeam	MOON#BEAM	[muːnbiːm]
		gangbang	GANG#BANG	[gæŋbæŋ]
		Sten gun³	STEN#GUN	[stɛngʌn]

We are, of course, not denying that optional assimilation may occur in forms like those in (6c), giving for example [muːmbiːm] for *moonbeam* and [stɛŋgʌn] for *Sten gun*; however, such assimilation is largely restricted to coronal nasals, with labials and velars being much less likely to undergo assimilation, so that *[gæmbæŋ] for *gangbang* and *[gʌndrɒp] for *gumdrop* are improbable realisations. Thus, these examples differ from those in (6a), where homorganicity is obligatory, and in (6b), where it is impossible.

Processes like these appear to show that morphological and syntactic structure may be relevant to phonological processes. In the examples which we have been considering, the domains within which feature agreement holds appear to be morpho-syntactic in nature. However, many phonologists would argue that the role of such morpho-syntactic units is indirect, and that the relevant domains are phonological units, usually referred to as **prosodic** or **phonological words** or **phrases**.

One well-known process of this kind is that of *Raddoppiamento Sintattico* (RS) in Italian (see Nespor and Vogel 1986). This is a process which lengthens a word-initial consonant when it follows a word-final stressed vowel.⁴ Nespor and Vogel (1986: 38) give the following examples:

(7)	a.	La scimmia aveva appena mangiato metá [b:]anana.
		'The monkey had just eaten half a banana.'
	b.	Il gorilla aveva appena mangiato quáttro [b]anane.
		'The gorilla had just eaten four bananas.'

RS applies in (7a), as the final vowel of *meta* is stressed, but not in (7b), because *quattro* has penultimate stress. However, RS fails in many contexts in which the segmental conditions appear to be met:

(8)	a.	La volpe ne aveva mangiato metá [p]rima di addormentarsi.
		'The fox had eaten half of it before falling asleep.'

---

³ Note that although the spelling of *Sten gun* would suggest that it consists of two separate words, its stress pattern (/sténgʌn/) shows that it behaves as a compound word in English.

⁴ Writers on RS observe that there is a great deal of regional variation in the way in which the process operates. We are not concerned here with these variations.

b. Ho visto tré [k:]olibrí [k]osí [b:]rutti.
   'I saw three such ugly humming birds.'

As part of an argument for positing prosodic (phonological) constituents
which are distinct from syntactic constituents, Nespor and Vogel argue that
RS only takes place if the two words are part of the same **phonological
phrase**, a unit which, as noted, does not necessarily correspond to any syntactic constituent. Thus RS again provides an illustration of a process whose
application depends on whether or not the elements affected are within the
same suprasegmental domain.

This is a very simplified statement of RS, but it serves as an illustration of
the importance of non-syntactic suprasegmental domains to certain phonological processes. In the remainder of this chapter, we will discuss in some
detail what is probably the most familiar of these phonological domains, or
phonological constituents, the **syllable**. In Chapter 4, we consider a larger constituent, the **foot**, and its interaction with the placement of stress and accent
in languages. In this book, we will not consider constituents such as the
phonological phrase, but will limit our attention to the **phonological word**.
Underlying our discussion is the assumption that suprasegmental constituent
structure has the general form in (9), where φ is the phonological phrase, ω
the phonological word, F the foot and σ the syllable:

(9)

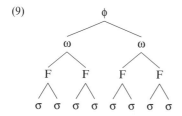

The **prosodic hierarchy**[5] in (9) shows a consistent structure, in that, at any
level, a constituent splits into two identical constituents at the immediately
lower level. This is a reflection of the principle formulated by Nespor and
Vogel (1986: 7) as follows: 'A given nonterminal unit of the prosodic hierarchy,
X^p, is composed of one or more units of the immediately lower category,
X^{p-1}.' Thus the phonological phrase consists of two phonological words, the
phonological word consists of two feet, and the foot of two syllables.

The syllable, then, is the smallest element in this hierarchy. It is clear that
speakers in some sense know about the syllabic structure of the words in
their language, i.e. they can decide both how many syllables there are in a

---

[5] Hence also the terms **prosodic word**, **prosodic foot**, etc.

word and and, very often, where one syllable ends and the next begins. Most speakers of English, for example, will syllabify the words in (10) as shown:

(10) albatross [æl]$_\sigma$[bə]$_\sigma$[trɒs]$_\sigma$
      America   [ə]$_\sigma$[mɛ]$_\sigma$[rɪ]$_\sigma$[kə]$_\sigma$
      slender   [slɛn]$_\sigma$[də]$_\sigma$

The existence of the syllable might seem a straightforward matter, given the discussion above. Nevertheless, things are not quite as simple as we have suggested. It is certainly not the case that native speakers agree on the exact location of syllable boundaries in all the words of a language, as is evidenced by the various syllabifications in (11):

(11) master   [mɑː]$_\sigma$[stə]$_\sigma$ *or* [mɑːs]$_\sigma$[tə]$_\sigma$
      revels   [rɛ]$_\sigma$[vəlz]$_\sigma$ *or* [rɛv]$_\sigma$[əlz]$_\sigma$
      pastry   [peɪ]$_\sigma$[strɪ]$_\sigma$ *or* [peɪs]$_\sigma$[trɪ]$_\sigma$ *or* [peɪst]$_\sigma$[rɪ]$_\sigma$

Furthermore, it is not immediately apparent what it is that native speakers are counting when they say that, for example, *eccentricity* has five syllables and *remarkable* four – although there will seldom be disagreement between speakers on this point. From a phonetic point of view, it is often claimed that what is involved here is **relative sonority**, in particular the notion of **sonority peak**: each syllable has one sonority peak, i.e. a segment which is more sonorous than any of the others. Sonority is thus a relative, rather than an absolute, property. In auditory terms, the sonority peak is more prominent than the surrounding segments, and forms the **syllabic** element.[6] As we anticipated in §1.3.1, vowels are inherently more sonorous than consonants, and so the vowel, if there is one, in a syllable will be the **syllabic peak**. However, in syllables which do not contain a vowel the most sonorous consonant will be the syllabic peak. For example, in the pronunciation of English *bottles* as [bɒɬz], the [ɬ] will be syllabic in the second syllable, giving [bɒɬz]. Notice that a sonorant consonant will only form the peak if there is no segment immediately preceding or following it with greater sonority. In the word *confusion*, pronounced [kənfjuːʒn̩], there are three sonorant consonants ([n], [j] and [n]). Only the final [n] is a syllabic peak, however, as shown in (12), in which we distinguish three degrees of sonority (vowels, sonorant consonants and obstruents); the peaks are indicated by an open circle, non-peaks by a closed circle:

(12) k   ə   n   f   j   uː   ʒ   n

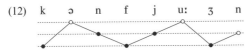

---

[6] As we have seen, the phonetic interpretation of sonority is not as uncontroversial as we are suggesting here. For discussions, see Malsch and Fulcher (1989), Nathan (1989).

The final [n] is the only sonorant consonant which is neither preceded nor followed by a more sonorous segment (the previous consonant is less sonorous, and there is no following segment), and so forms a syllabic peak, as do the vowels, which are more sonorous than their neighbours. In English, syllabic consonants are restricted to unstressed syllables, by virtue of the fact that stressed syllables tend to contain full vowels, while in unstressed syllables we typically find vowel reduction, with further optional deletion of the reduced vowel when it is followed by a sonorant consonant. Thus, as well as [kənfjuːʒn̩], we also find the pronunciation [kənfjuːʒən].

Even obstruents can be syllabic in English, but typically only in fast speech. Thus, pronunciations such as [sp̩ɪʃ̩s] for *suspicious* can be heard. In addition, English has items such as *psst!* [ps̩t] and *ssh!* [ʃ̩]. In other languages, though, syllabic obstruents (and indeed sonorants) are more widespread, in the sense that they may occur regularly in stressed as well as unstressed syllables (see e.g. Hoard 1978 on Northwest Indian languages, and Dell and Elmedlaoui 1985 on Berber).

On the one hand, the syllable divisions in (10) clearly demonstrate that syllabification is independent of the *number* of segments in a word: there are no languages, for example, which organise every sequence of, say, three segments into a syllable to give syllable divisions like *[ælb]$_\sigma$[ətr]$_\sigma$[ɒs]$_\sigma$. On the other hand, organisation into syllables equally clearly cannot be derived from any independently given morphemic structure, since the words in (10) are all simple, i.e. they contain only a single morpheme. Indeed, syllabic structure can even be in conflict with morphological structure:

(13) lending   LEND+ING   [lɛn]$_\sigma$[dɪŋ]$_\sigma$
      writer   WRITE+ER   [raɪ]$_\sigma$[tə]$_\sigma$

The morpheme boundary falls after the stop in (13); the syllable boundary falls before it.

In some cases, morpho-syntactic boundaries may prevent the application of the 'normal' phonological syllabification rules of a language. In an intervocalic biconsonantal cluster in English, we expect the syllable boundary to fall before the first consonant (cf. *albatross* in (10)) or between the consonants (*slender*). We find exactly the same pattern in Dutch, as shown in (14):

(14) sterker   STERK+ER   'stronger'   [stɛr]$_\sigma$[kər]$_\sigma$
      avontuur   AVONTUUR   'adventure'   [a]$_\sigma$[vɔn]$_\sigma$[tyːr]$_\sigma$

However, if the morphological boundary is strong enough, syllabification does not operate in the expected way, as shown in (15):

(15) avonduur   AVOND#UUR   'evening (hour)'   [a]$_\sigma$[vɔnt]$_\sigma$[yːr]$_\sigma$

Dutch *avonduur* is a compound word, in which the last consonant of the first element is underlyingly voiced, as is evidenced from the fact that the plural form of the first element is *avonden* [avɔndən] (cf. singular *avond* [avɔnt], with syllable-final devoicing; (12) in Chapter 1). The fact that the final stop of *avond* is also voiceless in *avonduur* shows that here too it is syllable-final. Both intervocalic consonants must then precede the syllable boundary. Thus the only segmental distinction between *avontuur* and *avonduur* is the placement of the syllable boundary; they are otherwise homophonous.[7] If syllable division is in itself bound to the prosodic word domain, then we must assume that each member of a compound word constitutes a phonological word.

We will now try to establish whether the native speaker's ability to parse a string into 'syllables' has any relevance to phonological theory. Can we, by invoking the notion of the syllable, explain phonological facts which we could not otherwise explain? In other words, are there properties of the phonological organisation of segments which lead us to formalise the syllable as a unit within our theory of phonology? If the answer to this question is negative, we do not require a unit of this kind in our theory of phonological representation, even though it seems to reflect a particular kind of organisation which speakers of a language attribute to strings of segments. In §3.2 we consider arguments which appear to support the need for the syllable as a unit in our *phonological* representations. We then discuss the question of how syllable structure is most adequately represented (§§3.3–3.7), and in so doing will address a variety of issues concerning the relation between syllable structure and segmental structure, and will provide further motivation for the syllable by showing that it may form the domain for the application of certain phonological rules. In §3.8, however, we consider one school of phonological thought which holds that some of the arguments in support of the syllable as a unit are spurious, while accepting that there is evidence for prosodic units smaller than the syllable.

3.2 Why syllables?

Although it is clear that there is a unit which native speakers recognise as a syllable, we still have to demonstrate that it is required in phonological analysis. One kind of evidence involves the native speaker's ability to judge whether or not an arbitrary string of segments is a possible word in the language. As we will show, this ability hinges crucially on the fact that the native speaker can only assign a well-formed syllabic organisation to a string of segments if the string in question is a possible word of the language.

---

[7] Suprasegmentally, however, there is a difference between the stress patterns of the words: *avon'tuur* vs *'avonduur*.

What would happen if our native speaker had no access to syllable structure, and could do no more than identify sequences of segments as being well formed or ill formed in his or her language? The native speaker of English, for example, would identify the string */lmɒk/ as ill formed because the consonant cluster /lm/ cannot occur at the beginning of any English word. In other words, the initial sequence */lm/ violates the **phonotactic constraints** of English. Similarly, */lɒpk/ is ill formed because the consonant cluster /pk/ cannot occur at the *end* of any English word, and */lɒpkmɜ:/ is unacceptable because /pkm/ is not a well-formed English medial cluster, i.e. a sequence occurring between two sonority peaks. Thus it might appear that part of the phonological knowledge of a native speaker involves the specification of which consonant clusters are ill formed in the language, as in (16):

(16) *initial*   *medial*   *final*
     *lm-   *-pkm-   *-pk
     *mr-   *-kmr-   *-km
     *nw-   *-tnw-   *-tn
     ...   .

However, the list in (16), even if it were complete, displays a fairly obvious redundancy. The constraints on medial clusters in a language are not *independent* of those on initial and final clusters. Rather, if we split any of the medial clusters in (16) into two parts (wherever the split is made), the first part is an illicit final cluster and/or the second part is an illicit initial cluster:

(17) *-pkm-   *pk+m *or* p+*km
     *-rtdl-   *rtd+l *or* rt+*dl *or* r+*tdl

Medial clusters, then, are not independent units, but consist of two parts, a 'final cluster' followed by an 'initial cluster'. However, because these clusters are word-medial, 'initial' and 'final' here cannot refer to word-initial and word-final, or even morpheme-initial and morpheme-final. Rather, we must regard the ill-formed cluster as consisting of the initial and final parts of some unit distinct from the word or morpheme. This unit is the syllable, whose well-formedness depends purely on phonological factors.[8]

A second type of argument for the existence of the phonological syllable involves the fact that phonological processes can be shown to be conditioned by the syllabic organisation of the string of segments, and also the fact that

---

[8] We are ignoring here the fact that word-initial syllables can have initial clusters which can appear *only* at the beginning of words (e.g. /kn/ in Dutch *knuffel* 'cuddle'). Thus **alkne* would be ill formed in Dutch. Furthermore, certain word-final clusters cannot appear as the final cluster of a non-final syllable. For example, although an English word may end in the sequence /rst/ in a rhotic dialect (as in *burst*), there are no monomorphemic words in which a non-final syllable ends in this cluster.

there are many processes which affect segments at the 'edges' or 'margins' of syllables. A case in point would be final devoicing in Dutch, which we considered in §1.3.1. Given the organisation of segments into syllables, the generalisation is quite simply that a syllable-final obstruent (or obstruent cluster) is never voiced. If we do not have the syllable as a phonological unit, we are still able to describe the process, but we are forced to state a disjunction in the rule: devoicing takes place in *two* environments, as demonstrated in (18). On the one hand, obstruents are voiceless in word-final position (18a), and on the other, there are no voiced obstruents in the environment in (18b):

(18) a. /bɑd/   [bɑt]   'bath'
          /lœyd/   [lœyt]   'loud'
          /lœyt/   [lœyt]   'lute'
      b. /atlɑs/   [atlɑs]   'atlas'
          /ɔrtnər/   [ɔrtnər]   'folder'
          /prɪsmaː/ [prɪsmaː]   'prism'

In an *SPE*-type formalism, in which the syllable was given no formal recognition, such apparent disjunctions were represented as in (19):

$$
(19) \quad / - \begin{Bmatrix} \# \\ C \end{Bmatrix}
$$

i.e. the environment of the process is defined as preceding *either* a word-boundary *or* a consonant. A formulation such as (19), however, like any other involving a disjunction in the environment, betrays the fact that we have failed to find what it is that is shared in that environment.

Notice that the question of the *underlying* value for voicing is not at issue: in (18a), as we have seen, the obstruent may be underlyingly voiced (e.g. /lœyd/) or voiceless (e.g. /lœyt/), depending on its behaviour in other contexts ([lœydə] *luide* 'loud (INFLECTED)' vs [lœytən] *luiten* 'lutes'), while in (18b) there is no evidence available to decide whether the obstruent is underlyingly voiced or voiceless, given the fact that there are no alternations to be found.

In a non-syllabic formulation, it is, in spite of (19), very difficult to identify the environment in (18b) in which 'final' obstruents must be voiceless. The environment is not in fact 'immediately preceding a consonant', as (19) suggests, because of the existence of the forms in (20a), which do not display devoicing of the medial obstruent. Indeed, a voiceless obstruent can also occur in what appears to be the same environment, i.e. preceding /l/ or /r/ (20b):[9]

---

[9] Here and elsewhere, we indicate stress by placing ' before the stressed syllable; see Chapter 4 for discussion of stress and accent.

(20)   a.   /'koːbraː/   cobra   'cobra'
             /sjaː'bloːn/ sjabloon   'template'
       b.   /'meːtroː/   metro   'metro'
             /paː'troːn/   patroon   'pattern'

Rather, the generalisation is that an obstruent in a medial cluster does not undergo devoicing if the cluster is a well-formed syllable-initial. If this is not the case, as in *atlas* (there are no syllable-initial */tl-/ clusters in Dutch), the first syllable ends before the /l/, and so the obstruent is syllable-final. The difference in syllabification is shown in (21), in which the (a) forms show the obstruent in syllable-final position, where it must be voiceless, while the (b) forms show that the second syllable begins *before* the obstruent, so that the obstruent is syllable-initial, and hence does not devoice if it is underlyingly voiced:

(21)   a. $[\text{ɑt}]_\sigma[\text{lɑs}]_\sigma$ b. $[\text{koː}]_\sigma[\text{braː}]_\sigma$
             $[\text{ɔrt}]_\sigma[\text{nər}]_\sigma$ $[\text{paː}]_\sigma[\text{troːn}]_\sigma$

Thus devoicing in Dutch takes place in the single environment in (22), i.e. in syllable-final position, rather than in the two apparently unrelated environments in (19):

(22)   __ $]_\sigma$

The aspiration of voiceless stops in English provides another example of a syllable-edge process.[10] Aspiration takes place when the stop is followed by a primary or secondary stressed vowel, but only if the stop is the first element in the syllable. Thus no aspiration takes place if the stop is preceded by /s/ (the only consonant which can precede the stop to yield a well-formed syllable-initial cluster), irrespective of whether the consonants involved are in word-initial position (23a) or word-medial position (23b). However, a word-medial stop preceding an unstressed syllable is unaspirated, whether or not it is preceded by /s/ (23c):

(23)   a.   tile $[\text{t}^\text{h}\text{aɪl}]_\sigma$
             stile $[\text{staɪl}]_\sigma$
       b.   retire $[\text{rɪ}]_\sigma[\text{'t}^\text{h}\text{aɪə}]_\sigma$
             distend $[\text{dɪ}]_\sigma[\text{'stɛnd}]_\sigma$
       c.   mutter $[\text{'mʌ}]_\sigma[\text{tə}]_\sigma$
             muster $[\text{'mʌ}]_\sigma[\text{stə}]_\sigma$

[10] For a fuller account of aspiration in English as a syllable-based process, see Spencer (1996: §6.2.1).

Thus the environment in which aspiration is found is $_\sigma[$ __, i.e. at the beginning of a stressed syllable.[11]

Another source of evidence for the status of the syllable as a phonological unit can be found in the behaviour of Dutch vowels which are often referred to as 'lax' or 'checked' (cf. the discussion of lax vowels in §1.3.3). This is the set of vowels which cannot occur in syllable-final position in Dutch, i.e. in **open** syllables. Thus (24) would be ill formed in Dutch, because the vowel in the final syllable is lax:

(24) *[maː]$_\sigma$[krɔ]$_\sigma$

Lax vowels are not found in word-final position, then. But they are also not found preceding a cluster which is a well-formed syllable-initial, as in (25a), although they *can* precede a cluster which is not a well-formed initial cluster, such as /rk/ in (25b):

(25) a. *[mɑ]$_\sigma$[kroː]$_\sigma$
      b. [mɑr]$_\sigma$[koː]$_\sigma$ Marco (name)

Furthermore, if the following syllable starts with a vowel, the preceding vowel cannot be lax, as in (26a):

(26) a. *[hɪ]$_\sigma$[aːt]$_\sigma$
      b. [maː]$_\sigma$[kroː]$_\sigma$ macro 'macro'
          [hiː]$_\sigma$[aːt]$_\sigma$ hiaat 'hiatus'

Tense vowels are required in all these contexts, then, giving for example the forms in (26b).[12]

We should notice that the existence of constraints of this kind removes an ambiguity with respect to syllabification. The fact that *macro* cannot be realised with a lax vowel in the first syllable indicates that the syllabification which we have been assuming is indeed correct; i.e. both the /k/ and the /r/ are assigned to the second syllable, rather than the first, even though syllables ending with /k/ are well formed in Dutch, as are syllables beginning with /r/.

The fact that the /k/ in, for example, *macro* is assigned to the second syllable is due to a principle which appears to hold true of languages in general: given an intervocalic consonant or consonant cluster, assign it to the

---

[11] In a later section, we will show that the structure of syllables with an initial /s/ + obstruent cluster is more complex than that of 'normal' syllables. This in turn will lead us to adopt a slightly different view of the environment in which aspiration in English is found.

[12] In Dutch, /ə/ is anomalous with respect to the tense/lax distinction. Although it is phonetically short, like the lax vowels, it can occur in the same environments as the set of tense vowels, e.g. word-finally ([kaː]$_\sigma$[də]$_\sigma$ *kade* 'quay') and in hiatus, albeit only in morphologically complex environments ([bə]$_\sigma$[aː]$_\sigma$[mən]$_\sigma$ *be+amen* 'to confirm'). For discussions of the status of /ə/ in the phonology of Dutch, see e.g. Trommelen (1983), van der Hulst (1984) and van Oostendorp (1995).

beginning of the second syllable, unless an ill-formed syllable-initial cluster is thereby formed.[13] Anything preceding a well-formed initial cluster is then assigned to the end of the previous syllable. This is usually referred to as the **maximal onset principle**.[14]

In English, the assignment of stress provides further evidence for the existence of the syllable. Syllables which are closed or contain a long vowel attract stress, whereas syllables ending in a short vowel do not. This restriction is illustrated by the examples in (27), taken from Chomsky and Halle (1968: 71):

(27) arena $[ə]_σ[\text{'riː}]_σ[nə]_σ$
      agenda $[ə]_σ[\text{'ʤɛn}]_σ[də]_σ$
      America $[ə]_σ[\text{'mɛ}]_σ[rɪ]_σ[kə]_σ$

The rules of stress assignment in English are highly complex, and we will not go into details of their operation here (but see, e.g., §4.3). However, we can observe that different classes of words have different syllables as their 'targets' for stress. The target in the class of nouns illustrated in (27) is the penultimate syllable, as illustrated by *arena*, whose penultimate syllable contains a long vowel, and *agenda*, with a penultimate syllable closed by a consonant. However, the penultimate syllable of *America* contains a short vowel and is not closed by a consonant, and so it rejects stress, which is then shifted to the antepenultimate syllable. Notice that the distinction we have just drawn can be characterised in a unitary fashion if phonological sequences are indeed divided into syllables. In other words, the application of the stress rules of English depends on whether a consonant following a short vowel belongs to the same syllable as the vowel (as in *agenda*, for example) or to the following syllable (as in *America*). This is not just a matter of the *number* of consonants following a short vowel, as might at first be thought, but, just like the Dutch examples in (20), involves placement of the syllable boundary, as is shown in (28) for the English word *algebra*:

(28) algebra $[\text{'æl}]_σ[ʤə]_σ[brə]_σ$

---

[13] A language which does not allow consonant clusters at the beginning of a syllable will have to assign the first element of a consonant cluster to the previous syllable, however.

[14] Dutch does allow lax vowels immediately preceding a CV sequence. One common source of this is the inflection of nouns and verbs: compare /pɑd/ [pɑt] *pad* 'toad' with /pɑd+ən/ [pɑdə] 'toads' and /lɛk/ [lɛk] *(ik) lek* '(I) leak' with /lɛk+ən/ [lɛkən] *(wij) lekken* '(we) leak'. (This is a lexical matter: compare /pɑd/ [pɑt] *pad* 'path' with /paːd+ən/ [paːdə] 'paths'.) Standard analyses of Dutch assume either that the intervocalic consonant syllabifies to the left, i.e. it forms part of the first syllable, giving e.g. $[pɑd]_σ[ən]_σ$, or that it is ambisyllabic, e.g. $[pɑ[d]_σən]_σ$. The first consonant of a well-formed initial cluster cannot be considered ambisyllabic in such analyses, as this would yield $*[kɔ[b]_σraː]_σ$, rather than the well-formed $[koː]_σ[braː]_σ$ *cobra* 'cobra'. The second consonant of a well-formed final cluster, however, is ambisyllabic, e.g. $[mɑr[m]_σər]_σ$ *marmer* 'marble'. By analogy with forms with final clusters, it is also possible to analyse *padden* and *lekken* as containing a double (i.e. geminate) consonant, giving $[pɑd[d]_σən]_σ$ and $[lɛk[k]_σən]_σ$. For discussion, see van der Hulst (1984, 1985).

Here the vowel of the penultimate syllable occurs in an open syllable, even though it is followed by two consonants, and so the syllable rejects stress, which shifts to the antepenultimate.

The example of stress assignment in English has been extensively used to show the superiority of an approach to stress which incorporates the syllable over the treatment given by Chomsky and Halle (1968). In *SPE*, as noted above, there is no phonological unit corresponding to the notion of syllable, so that any cluster which is a well-formed syllable-initial, and therefore cannot be preceded by a stressed short vowel, must be specified individually in the stress rules. This is tantamount to incorporating the syllabification rules of a language in every rule which makes reference to syllable boundaries in one way or another, and clearly misses the generalisation illustrated by the forms in (27).

3.3 The representation of syllable structure

We have seen that the syllable is a unit which is required in phonological theory, and that segments can be seen as the constituents of which syllables are constructed. Using a common formalism, we can represent this in terms of the tree structures in (29a), a possible representation of the syllables making up English *albatross*:

(29) a. σ   σ   σ   b. [æl]$_\sigma$[bə]$_\sigma$[trɒs]$_\sigma$

æ l b ə t r ɒ s

Thus /æ/ and /l/ are constituents of a unit labelled **syllable** (σ), and similarly for the other segments. The tree structure in (a) and the labelled bracketing in (b) are equivalent. Notice, crucially, but perhaps confusingly, that the constituent trees in (a) have a quite different interpretation from representations such as (1), although they are apparently formally identical. Here the lines linking the levels denote **constituency**, whereas those in (1) and similar diagrams denote **association**. In other words, /æ/ and /l/ in (29a) are part of a larger unit σ, while no such claim is made in (1), which merely shows that the feature **N** is a property of each of the segments with which it is associated. This notational ambiguity, although unfortunate, is now so widespread that it seems pointless to try to avoid it here.[15]

We have already seen that there is evidence to suggest that syllables themselves may be grouped into constituents larger than the syllable, but smaller than the word. We consider this question in Chapter 4, where we discuss the

---

[15] We should notice, though, that Kahn (1976) considers the syllable node to be 'associated' to segments.

foot. Here, however, we consider first the nature of the *internal* structure of the syllable.

In the representations in (29) it is assumed that the syllable is a **flat** constituent, without any internal structure. This is evident from the structure given in (29a) for the syllable /trɒs/, in which each of the segments is an *immediate* constituent of the syllable node, with no intervening nodes. This is by no means uncontroversial, however, and various proposals regarding the internal structure of the syllable have been put forward.

We will distinguish three proposals in this area. The differences between the proposals is illustrated in (30), three representations of the internal structure of the English monosyllabic morpheme /træmp/ *tramp*. For the present, we use the symbol 'X' to label nodes which are intermediate between the syllable and the segment:

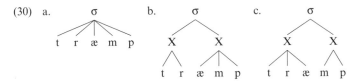

(30a) is a flat structure, like (29a), and as such is the minimal constituent structure which we might assign to the syllable. However, (30b) and (c) show two different ways of assigning further constituent structure within the syllable. (30b), in which we see a major split before the vowel of the syllable, illustrates the **onset–rhyme theory** of syllable structure, while (30c), where the split comes after the vowel, is one interpretation of an approach referred to as **mora theory**. We now consider these two approaches in some detail.

3.4   Onset–rhyme theory

As the name suggests, in onset–rhyme theory the syllable is analysed as consisting of two immediate constituents: the **onset**, containing any consonants preceding the vowel, and the **rhyme**, containing the vowel and whatever follows it:

(31)

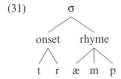

Various arguments have been put forward for the division of the syllable into two constituents of this sort. Notice first, however, that although the name of the phonological constituent 'rhyme' is derived from the term traditionally used in verse, we cannot equate the two concepts: the elements which rhyme in the traditional sense are not necessarily just parts of the syllable, as might be suggested by a pair such as *bill–mill*, but may also involve something larger, as is evidenced by rhyming pairs such as *older–colder* and *higgledy–piggledy*. In the latter cases, the rhyming element is not just the rhyme of the syllable; apparently we are dealing with identity between the rhyme of the stressed syllable and any following unstressed syllables. (We will see in the following chapter that this state of affairs provides evidence for constituent structure *above* the syllable.) However, although the two notions of rhyme are different, the rhyming tradition does indicate the relevance of the onset–rhyme division as far as the *stressed* syllable is concerned.

Further evidence for the validity of the onset–rhyme division has been found in the apparent independence of the two constituents. That is, on the assumption that a syllable can be seen as a sequence of onset and rhyme, it has been claimed that the constraints on the co-occurrence of segments holding *between* onset and rhyme are much less severe than those holding *within* each of the two constituents. That is, given a list of well-formed onsets and well-formed rhymes, these can combine quite freely to form well-formed syllables.[16] Thus onsets and rhymes are seen as autonomous units, each with their own constraints on their internal structure.

The combination of onsets and rhymes is not in fact entirely free, as is evidenced by a number of restrictions on the well-formedness of English syllables, of the type given in (32), from Clements and Keyser (1983: 20–1):

(32) a. Stop + /w/ clusters are excluded before /uː ʊ ʌ aw/: */kwuːt/, etc.
       b. English has virtually no words consisting of the form $sC_a\breve{V}C_a$, that is, *s*, a consonant, a short vowel, and the consonant again.

The second of these two constraints means that words such as **spop*, **skick* and **stit* are apparently ruled out, even though the same sequences without the initial *s* are well formed in English.

Nevertheless, although the existence of restrictions such as (32) leads Clements and Keyser to reject the onset–rhyme approach to syllable structure in favour of a flat syllable structure, it is clear that the relationship between the vowel and the following consonants, if any, in a syllable is closer than that between the vowel and the preceding consonants. Restrictions of the type in (32) are much more common *within* the onset or the rhyme than between the two constituents. English, for example, does not allow onsets consisting of a stop followed by a nasal (33a), rhymes consisting of a tense vowel followed

---

[16] In fact, we should restrict this to 'non-peripheral' syllables, because word-initial and word-final syllables typically display extra material before the onset and after the rhyme, respectively. We return to this in §3.4.4.

by /ŋ/ (33b) or, as we have seen, final consonant clusters in which a nasal is not homorganic with a following stop, at least within a single morpheme (33c):

(33) a. */kn-/, */pn-/, */gm-/
      b. */-iːŋ/, */-ɑʊŋ/
      c. */-mg/, */-ŋb/

Another argument in favour of identifying the rhyme as a constituent involves stress assignment. In English and Dutch, as in many other languages, the location of stress depends on the structure of the syllable; certain syllables may reject stress in contexts where we would otherwise expect it. In determining whether a syllable is stress-attracting or not, it appears that the number and type of consonants in the onset are entirely irrelevant, as is shown by an examination of the forms in (34), which belong to the same class as those in (27), i.e. the target syllable for stress is the penultimate:

(34) a. arena $[ə]_\sigma['riː]_\sigma[nə]_\sigma$
          verbena $[vər]_\sigma['biː]_\sigma[nə]_\sigma$
          angina $[æn]_\sigma['ʤaɪ]_\sigma[nə]_\sigma$
      b. America $[ə]_\sigma['mɛ]_\sigma[rɪ]_\sigma[kə]_\sigma$
          orchestra $['ɔː]_\sigma[kə]_\sigma[strə]_\sigma$
          cholesterol $[kə]_\sigma['lɛ]_\sigma[stə]_\sigma[rɒl]_\sigma$
      c. agenda $[ə]_\sigma['ʤɛn]_\sigma[də]_\sigma$
          appendix $[ə]_\sigma['pɛn]_\sigma[dɪks]_\sigma$
          veranda $[və]_\sigma['ræn]_\sigma[də]_\sigma$

The distinction is a matter of rhyme structure alone, as is illustrated by the target syllables of all the forms in (34), where the identity and number of onset consonants play no role in whether the syllable attracts or rejects stress. This again implies that the rhyme must be a unit which can be addressed by phonological rules.

Similar evidence can be found in the behaviour of the diminutive suffix in Dutch, in particular when it follows a noun ending in a sonorant consonant. We saw in (14c) and (15) of Chapter 1 that the form of the suffix in these cases depends on the nature of both the final consonant and the vowel preceding it, as illustrated again in (35):

(35) a. duimpje   DUIM+DIM   'thumb'
          maantje   MAAN+DIM   'moon'
          bijltje   BIJL+DIM   'axe'
          boertje   BOER+DIM   'farmer'
      b. kammetje   KAM+DIM   'comb'
          mannetje   MAN+DIM   'man'
          belletje   BEL+DIM   'bell'
          barretje   BAR+DIM   'bar'

The forms in (35a) contain a long vowel or diphthong followed by a sonorant consonant, and take a diminutive [tjə] (or [pjə] if the final consonant is labial), while those in (35b) contain a short vowel followed by a sonorant, and take a diminutive [ətjə]. Thus it is the shape of the rhyme as a whole which determines the choice of the appropriate form of the suffix. The onset, however, plays no role, as is shown by the forms in (36):

(36) a. aaltje   AAL+DIM   'eel'
         paaltje   PAAL+DIM   'pole'
         staaltje   STAAL+DIM   'specimen'
         maaltje   MAAL+DIM   'meal'
         baaltje   BAAL+DIM   'bale'
         kraaltje   KRAAL+DIM   'bead'
    b. arretje   AR+DIM   'sleigh'[17]
         palletje   PAL+DIM   'catch'
         stalletje   STAL+DIM   'stable'
         malletje   MAL+DIM   'mould'
         balletje   BAL+DIM   'ball'
         knalletje   KNAL+DIM   'bang'

We now consider a further possible level of constituent structure within the onset–rhyme view of the syllable, the internal structure of the rhyme.

3.4.1 Rhyme structure

In (31) the rhyme was represented as a flat constituent. However, as in the case of the syllable, we can find arguments for considering the rhyme to consist of two constituents, the **nucleus** and the **coda**, as illustrated in (37):

(37)   rhyme

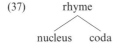

nucleus   coda

What evidence is there for claiming that the rhyme is not a flat structure, but has two immediate constituents as in (37)? We have already seen that certain syllables in languages may be stress-attracting, while others are not, and that this appears to be a function of the content of the rhyme – the onset is not relevant to such processes. In some languages, as in the English examples discussed in (27), this seems merely to be a question of the number of segments in the rhyme. The evidence of these forms suggests that the penultimate syllables of the forms *arena* and *agenda*, which are stressed, have something in common as opposed to the penultimate syllable of *America*, which rejects stress. From now on we will consider long vowels to be geminates, i.e. they

---

[17] Dutch has no noun *al*.

occupy two positions in the rhyme, and as such have exactly the same structure as diphthongs, which behave in the same way with respect to the stress rules of English (e.g. *angina* [æn]$_\sigma$[ʤaɪ]$_\sigma$[nə]$_\sigma$). Thus the distinction between **heavy** and **light** syllables in English (i.e. those which attract stress as opposed to those which do not) is simply a matter of the number of segments in the rhyme: heavy syllables contain two segments in the rhyme, as in (38a, b, c), while light syllables contain only one (38d):[18]

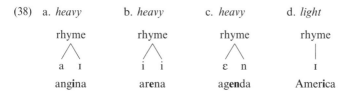

(38) a. *heavy*　　　b. *heavy*　　　c. *heavy*　　　d. *light*

The target rhyme for stress in each word (the penultimate) is given in boldface.

The data from English does not offer any clues as to whether the rhyme should have the internal structure in (37), then; all that seems to be relevant is whether the rhyme node has more than one daughter. However, not all languages draw the distinction between heavy and light syllables in the same way. In some languages, it is not only the number of segments in the rhyme, but also the type of segment, which plays a role. In Selkup, a West Siberian language, for example, a two-segment rhyme consisting of a long vowel is heavy, while a two-segment rhyme consisting of a short vowel followed by a consonant is light, as shown in (39) (from Halle and Clements 1983: 129):

(39) a. kɨ'pɔɔ　　　'tiny'
　　　　　qu'mooqɪ　　'two human beings'
　　　　b. 'amɨrna　　　'eats'
　　　　　'uucɨkkak　'I am working'

Stress falls on the rightmost heavy syllable in Selkup, or on the initial syllable if there is no heavy syllable. Thus in (39a), the syllables [pɔɔ] and [moo], like the corresponding syllables in (34a), function as heavy and are stressed. However, the penultimate syllables in (39b), [mɨr] and [cɨk], respectively, function as light, even though their rhymes contain two segments. Thus in Selkup, like English, a rhyme containing VV is heavy, but, unlike English, one containing VC is light. Evidence like this can be interpreted as suggesting that in (39b) the penultimate syllable is light because the vowel and consonant belong to different constituents within the rhyme – the nucleus and the coda, respectively

---

[18] We represent the long vowel in (38b) as a geminate, i.e. as /ii/, rather than as /iː/. In the remainder of this book, we will only use the geminate representation when the geminate status of a long vowel is relevant to the point at hand.

– and what is relevant in establishing the distinction between heavy and light in this language is the number of segments in the *nucleus*, not in the rhyme as a whole.

The distinction between the two types of languages with respect to what is referred to as **syllable weight** is summarised in (40), where we refer to the type of language instantiated by English as a **rhyme-weight language** and the Selkup type as a **nucleus-weight language** (cf. Hayes 1995):

(40) a. In rhyme-weight languages the nucleus plays no role in the distinction between heavy and light syllables: if the rhyme as a whole contains more than one element the syllable is heavy.

b. In nucleus-weight languages the structure of the nucleus node determines syllable weight: branching nuclei are heavy; non-branching nuclei are light.

In rhyme-weight languages we find the possibilities in (41):

(41) *Rhyme-weight languages*

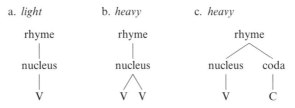

while nucleus-weight languages have those in (42):

(42) *Nucleus-weight languages*

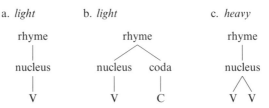

Although these are the most common types, other possibilities are found. For example, a language like Dutch appears to represent a third type, in which weight depends solely on whether or not a syllable is closed, i.e. on the presence of a syllable-final consonant, irrespective of whether the vowel is long or short, as is shown by the data in (43):[19]

---

[19] This analysis depends on the assumption that the Dutch vowel system is appropriately analysed in terms of long vs short, i.e. as involving a *quantitative* distinction, rather than in terms of tense vs lax, with a *qualitative* distinction. In the latter case, the difference between heavy and light would depend on a feature on the vowel, rather than on the number of elements involved (see also §3.6 below).

(43)   a.   kolibri   ['koː]ₒ[liː]ₒ[briː]ₒ   'humming bird'
           pagina   ['paː]ₒ[ɣiː]ₒ[naː]ₒ   'page'
       b.   agenda   [aː]ₒ['ɣɛn]ₒ[daː]ₒ   'diary'
           proportie   [proː]ₒ['por]ₒ[siː]ₒ   'proportion'

In Dutch, like English, a VC rhyme is apparently treated as heavy, so that a
form such as *'agenda is ill formed; however, unlike either English or Selkup,
a VV rhyme can be skipped, as in (43a), giving for example 'kolibri, rather
than *ko'libri. We might refer to this third type as **coda languages**, in which
the branching of the nucleus is apparently irrelevant, so that the distinction
between light and heavy syllables is as in (44):[20]

(44)   *Coda languages*

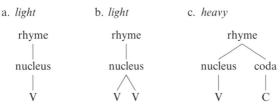

a. *light*   b. *light*   c. *heavy*

In the discussion above, we have been considering rhymes with at most
two segments. However, at first sight, it would appear that there are also
rhymes with more than two segments, either because they have two consonants in the coda, such as Dutch *balk* /bɑlk/ 'beam', or because they have a
complex nucleus and a consonant in the coda (English *pike* /paɪk/) or both
(English *wild* /waɪld/). We might suppose, then, that the structures in (45)
would be appropriate for such rhymes:

(45)   a.   b.   c.

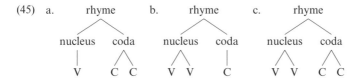

However, as we shall see, four-segmental rhymes, and even those containing
three segments, are very restricted, and where they do occur, this tends to be
in word-final, rather than in non-final, syllables. This in turn can be related

---

[20] It has also been claimed that there are languages in which the heavy–light distinction is sensitive to the
nature of the consonant in the rhyme. For example, a rhyme containing a vowel followed by a
sonorant consonant might be heavy, whereas one with a vowel followed by an obstruent would be
light (see (65) below).

to the more general fact that the constraints on **peripheral** – i.e. word-initial and word-final – syllables seem to differ in various ways from those on medial syllables. We now consider one aspect of this phenomenon.

3.4.2 *Syllabic prependices and appendices*

With respect to the syllabic behaviour of peripheral consonants, we can identify two classes, both of which are illustrated by Dutch and English. We consider the first type in this section, and return to the second type, involving 'extrasyllabic' consonants, in §3.4.4.

It appears to be the major class and manner features which provide the information relevant to the status of a segment within the syllable. In particular, the well-formedness of particular sequences of segments within a syllable is determined by their relative sonority (cf. §1.3.1), in such a way that, within the onset, less sonorous consonants precede more sonorous consonants, while, within the coda, the reverse holds. The most sonorous segment in the syllable, normally the vowel, forms the nucleus. Thus the sonority 'slope' within a syllable typically rises as we go from the initial consonant to the nucleus, and then falls until we reach the end of the syllable. Syllables like English *tramp* /træmp/ and *quilt* /kwɪlt/ and Dutch *plank* /plɑŋk/ 'shelf' are therefore 'canonical' in the sense that the order of segments obeys the sonority hierarchy (the obstruent precedes the sonorant consonant in the onset, and vice versa in the coda). Thus, elements within the syllable are subject to what is often referred to as the **sonority sequencing generalisation**.

In the forms we have been considering so far, we have seen examples of what appear to be branching onsets (English *tray*), branching nuclei (Dutch *ui* /œy/ 'onion') and branching codas (English *help*). Co-occurrence of branching constituents appears also to be possible (e.g. English *cry, old, tramp, flounce*). However, it is not difficult to find words in English and Dutch which appear to allow more than just two consonants in the onset and coda, at least in peripheral positions. Interestingly, in many such words we find violations of the sonority sequencing generalisation, in that we find examples of more sonorous consonants preceding less sonorous consonants at the beginning of a word, and vice versa at the end.

We start by considering what appear to be codas containing up to four or even five consonants. There are restrictions here on the type of consonants that can follow the 'normal' coda: they are almost always coronal, and furthermore they are primarily found in morphologically complex forms. All of this is illustrated by the Dutch forms in (46a), and the English forms in (46b):

(46) a. /ɛrɣst/   ergst   'most serious'
           /prɔmptst/   promptst   'most prompt'
           /mafst/   mafst   'daftest'
      b. /sɪksθs/   sixths
           /θrʌsts/   thrusts

One common strategy is to consider these segments and sequences (under-lined in (46)) not to be part of the syllable itself, i.e. the **core syllable**, but to form an **appendix**. Appendices, then, are considered to be outside the domain of normal syllabification processes.

In initial position we also find consonants which violate the sonority sequencing generalisation. As shown in (47a, b) for Dutch (and for the English translations), these occur in clusters consisting of /s/ followed by a voiceless obstruent (47a), with a further optional consonant (47b):

(47) a. /stɔk/   stok   'stick'
           /spɪn/   spin   'spider'
      b. /strɪp/   strip   'strip'
           /spleːt/   spleet   'split'

However, such sequences cannot appear at the beginning of medial syllables in Dutch. Rather, they are split between two syllables, as shown in (48a, b), unless the sequence is preceded by another consonant (48c):

(48) a. [pɑs]$_\sigma$[taː]$_\sigma$ pasta   'pasta'
           [hɑs]$_\sigma$[pəl]$_\sigma$ haspel   'reel'
      b. [ɑs]$_\sigma$[traː]$_\sigma$ astra   'astra'
           [ɛs]$_\sigma$[plaː]$_\sigma$[naː]$_\sigma$[də]$_\sigma$ esplanade 'esplanade'
      c. [hɑm]$_\sigma$[stər]$_\sigma$ hamster   'hamster'

The fact that the vowel is short/lax in the first syllable of the forms in (48) shows that the following obstruent must be syllabified in the rhyme of the first syllable; as we saw in §3.2, if the syllable were open, the vowel would be long/tense in Dutch.

For the English equivalents, however, we do not find unambiguous evi-dence of this kind for suggesting that the /s/ must be syllabified in the coda. We have already seen (in (23)) that plosives following initial /s/ are unaspirated in RP ([stəʊn] *stone* vs [tʰəʊn] *tone*). This holds whether or not the relevant cluster occurs medially (unless a strong enough morphological boundary in-tervenes: [dɪskɑːd] *discard* vs [ðɪs kʰɑːd] *this card*) and irrespective of stress (['mɪstə] *mister* vs [mɪ'steɪk] *mistake*). Similarly, post-plosive medial /r l j w/ do not show the devoicing associated with word-initial position (e.g. [pl̥eɪ] *play* vs [spleɪ] *splay* vs [dɪspleɪ] *display*). This would appear to suggest that the

/s/ belongs in the onset in both *splay* and *display*. However, in §3.8 we consider an approach in which the /s/ in these words is assigned to the coda of a preceding syllable; anticipating this discussion, we will for the moment merely assume that /s/ in English, as in Dutch, is syllabified in the coda of the first syllable in words such as *discard*, *display* and *mister*, and therefore that onsets are maximally binary.

One language which is frequently cited as having word-initial clusters which spectacularly violate the sonority sequencing generalisation is Polish (Rubach and Booij 1990: 122–3; Rowicka 1999: ch. 5). Polish allows a wide variety of initial clusters, both two-consonant clusters which appear to allow almost any combination of two consonants (49a) and clusters with more than two consonants (49b):

(49) a. ptak   'bird'   /pt-/
          scheda   'inheritance'   /sx-/
          skok   'jump'   /sk-/
          mnożyć   'multiply'   /mn-/
          lnu   'linen'   /ln-/
          rtęć   'mercury'   /rt-/
      b. pszczoła   'bee'   /pʃtʃ-/
          lśnić   'shine'   /lɕn-/
          bzdura   'nonsense'   /bzd-/

However, as in Dutch and English, the options for word-internal onsets in Polish are considerably restricted. Rubach and Booij assume that *any* peripheral consonant in Polish 'does not count from the point of view of the SSG [the sonority sequencing generalisation]'. Once this assumption is made, they claim, the number of exceptions to the SSG is dramatically reduced. Furthermore, assuming that initial peripheral consonants are not part of the onset means that there is no ambiguity in syllabifying a medial cluster like /rt/, which is found word-initially (*rtęć*). Because the initial /r/ is considered not to be part of the core syllable, a medial /rt/ cluster must be heterosyllabic: e.g. *karty* [kar]$_\sigma$[ti]$_\sigma$ 'cards'.

If, then, we assume that the consonants which violate the sonority sequencing generalisation in word-final position do not belong to the syllable, the same solution appears to be available for the initial consonants in (47). The consonant in question is not part of the onset of the syllable; rather, it forms a **prependix**.

On this view, the 'syllable' contains up to three parts, the obligatory core syllable and the optional prependix and appendix, as illustrated in (50), the representation of Dutch *striktst* 'strictest', where only the core syllable is dominated by the σ node:

(50)

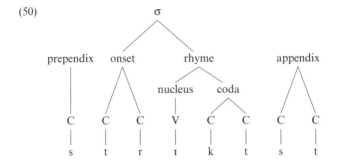

The structure of the core syllable is determined by the type of constraints discussed in the previous section. At this point we do not consider the question of the relationship of prependix and appendix to the rest of the prosodic structure, except to notice that various proposals have been put forward. One suggestion is that these elements are attached at the level of the prosodic word, so that the consonant is a constituent of the word, but not of the syllable.

Languages vary as to whether they allow prependices and appendices. Dutch clearly allows both possibilities, resulting in the highly complex sequence in (50). In the same way, the possibilities *within* the core syllable also vary, e.g. whether the onset may be branching or not, whether codas are permitted (i.e. whether syllables may be closed) and what combinations of segments are permitted. In other words, these are **parameters** which vary from one language to another, and which must be formulated in such a way that we can account for facts about 'preferred' syllable structure, such as that all languages have CV syllables, i.e. open syllables with a single consonant in the onset. This appears to be the basic type of core syllable. Some languages allow only CV syllables, while others admit various types of more complex structures. In terms of the onset–rhyme analysis of the syllable, we require a parameter which allows a language to choose to make onsets optional. This parameter must be formulated in such a way that languages which allow onsetless syllables also allow syllables with onsets – languages which prohibit onsets are not found. We formulate it as (51):

(51)   OBLIGATORY ONSET: **yes** *or* no

The fact that the setting 'yes' is in boldface in (51) indicates that this is the 'unmarked' (or default) setting. In studies on first language acquisition the unmarked setting is considered to be the one which the child assumes unless the data of the language being learned indicates that the marked setting is appropriate. We will not defend the various assumptions as to the relative markedness of the settings for the various parameters here, beyond saying that (51) reflects what appears to be the preferred minimal size for syllables. Notice that we might have formulated (51) as (52), which reflects this more directly:

(52)   BRANCHING SYLLABLE: **yes** *or* no

A further parameter concerns the number of consonants permitted in the onset. We formulate this as (53):

(53)   BRANCHING ONSET: yes *or* **no**

Languages which allow complex onsets seem to be more marked than those that do not; hence the unmarked setting as 'no'. Notice that there may be an interaction between the OBLIGATORY ONSET and BRANCHING ONSET parameters. If both are set to 'yes', we would have a language which would permit onsets with one or two consonants, but not empty onsets. If such languages are shown not to exist, then (53) is only required if (51) is set to 'no'.

Within the rhyme we will require similar parameters, formulated as in (54):

(54)   a.   BRANCHING RHYME: yes *or* **no**
       b.   BRANCHING NUCLEUS: yes *or* **no**

Notice that the markedness setting for the BRANCHING RHYME parameter implies that languages with codas are marked. This reflects a fundamental asymmetry between onsets and codas: the presence of the former is unmarked, the presence of the latter is marked. Stated differently, we expect syllables to be able to branch, but not the constituents within syllables. This in turn is reflected in the absence of a parameter regulating the branching of codas, which appears in (50) to be possible; we will see in §3.8 that there are powerful arguments to suggest that codas are never complex. If this is the case, then no BRANCHING CODA parameter is required.

Notice too that the unmarked value for the BRANCHING RHYME parameter may not be the same in all contexts, but may be dependent on the prosodic structure in question. Many languages require a stressed rhyme to be branching (English is typical in not allowing /ˈbɪ/, for example). A full account of parameter setting would have to take this into account.

We have already seen that there may be a dependency between the OBLIG-ATORY ONSET and BRANCHING ONSET parameters. A similar dependency holds between the complexity of the onset and the rhyme. It has been argued (e.g. Kaye and Lowenstamm 1984) that no language will allow complex onsets but not allow complex rhymes, i.e. will set the BRANCHING ONSET parameter to 'yes', but the BRANCHING RHYME parameter to 'no'.[21] On the assumption that the rhyme is the head of the syllable and the onset the dependent, a point of view which we will defend in §3.4.3, this can be accounted for by assuming that the dependent in any constituent cannot be more complex than its head. It has been suggested that this principle holds for a wide range of phonological constituents (see e.g. Dresher and van der Hulst 1998).

These parameters account for the core syllable. We will require further parameters to state whether prependices and/or appendices such as those in (50) are permitted in a language.

Finally, a set of parameters must be adopted which specify the permitted segmental content for each syllabic position. As we have already seen, the second position in the onset, for example, can generally only be filled by a sonorant consonant, which, as in English, may be restricted to a liquid or /j w/. Similarly, the second position in the nucleus can often only be filled by a limited set of vowels; in RP we find only high and central vowels, or the second half of a geminate. Codas generally only allow a subset of the consonants which can occur in onsets. Thus contrasts which are found in the onset are 'neutralised' in the coda, as we have seen with respect to final devoicing in Dutch – in onset position there is a contrast between voiced and voiceless obstruents which is not found in coda position. In terms of Harris's approach discussed in §2.6, the coda is a 'weak' position.

In §3.8 we discuss an approach to syllable structure in which parameters like these can be incorporated. In the meantime we turn our attention to the question of how syllabic structure is assigned.

3.4.3 *Syllabification*

It is generally assumed that lexical items, or underlying forms, need not be individually syllabified, i.e. syllabification is not distinctive. Rather, it is claimed to be by and large predictable on the basis of the feature content and linear order of segments, and, therefore, does not need to be specified underlyingly. Clearly, then, we need to have a set of principles which determine how strings of segments are assigned to the various syllabic constituents we have established above.

It might appear that we should simply start with the leftmost element in a string of segments. However, left-to-right assignment of segments to syllables would lead to problems with VCV sequences – the C would be assigned to the leftmost available constituent, the coda, whereas, by the maximal onset principle (§3.2), it should form the onset of the second syllable. We will

---

[21] This is not to say that a particular syllable may not have a CCV shape, of course; merely that if a language permits CCV, it also permits CCVV.

therefore assume that we first identify the syllabic elements; in other words, we start with the assignment of **syllabicity**, a procedure which we will refer to within onset–rhyme theory as **nucleus formation**. This involves assigning all sonority peaks (cf. the discussion in §3.1) to nuclei, as in (55) for English *albatross* /ælbətrɒs/ (we represent the nucleus by N):

(55)

We also require a process of **rhyme formation**. The rhyme is formed by creating a constituent of the nucleus and any following consonant which is not part of the onset of the next syllable (see below for onset formation). Within this constituent the nucleus is the head and the following segment is the dependent. As we saw in §2.5 with respect to the internal structure of the segment, head–dependent relations are invoked in linguistic structure when one of the elements of a constituent is in some sense more important than the other. In the case of the rhyme, the nucleus is clearly more important, in that it is the **obligatory** element of the rhyme: a rhyme must contain a nucleus, but need not contain any other segment. In the type of representation which we adopt here, the dependent is **adjoined** to the head, as in (56), the representation of the result of adjoining /t/ to /æ/ in the rhyme of the English monosyllabic word *at*:

(56)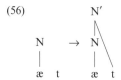

Thus /t/ is not the daughter of the node immediately dominating the nuclear vowel /æ/, but of a higher node, which bears the label N' (= Rhyme). This convention is used to indicate that the nucleus is the head of the rhyme: the constituent as a whole bears the label of its head. The path leading from the head to the topmost label is referred to as a **projection** or **projection line** – in this case the structure in (57) is the **nucleus projection**:[22]

(57)

---

[22] N' is often pronounced as 'N-bar'.

Rhyme formation thus picks out the postvocalic segments in (55) (if a well-formed rhyme is thus formed) and adjoins them to the nodes created by nucleus formation, to give (58):

(58)

However, (58) is incorrect in one respect. Although adjoining /t/ to the nucleus of the second syllable yields a well-formed rhyme, it should be part of the onset of the third syllable. We must therefore order a process of **onset formation** before rhyme formation. This ordering is in any case what we would expect, given the existence of the Maximal Onset Principle introduced in §3.2. By this principle, non-nuclear material is assigned to the onset unless an ill-formed syllable-initial cluster would be created; only then does rhyme formation apply.[23] Thus, after nucleus formation (50), any (non-final) segment constituting a sonority 'valley' (the reverse of a sonority peak; cf. (12)) is assigned to an onset. The relevant sonority valleys here are constituted by /b/ and /t/ (but not /l/ and /r/, which are more sonorous than at least one of their neighbours). Onset formation gives (59):

(59)

Notice that although /t/ is syllabified in the onset and /ɒ/ in the nucleus, the intervening /r/ has not yet been syllabified. In English and other languages, as we have seen, onsets may be complex. The process of onset formation in such languages can be followed by adjunction of a second consonant to the head of the onset, giving (60):[24]

---

[23] In addition, there are phonetic indications that the /t/ here belongs to the onset of the second syllable rather than the coda of the first. This is clear from the fact that the /r/ undergoes the devoicing typical of syllable-initial position; this takes place only following an initial voiceless stop in English (cf. *tress* /trɛs/ [tr̥ɛs]). As pointed out to us by Neil Smith, *albatross* /ælbətrɒs/ [ælbətr̥ɒs] contrasts in this respect with *Albert Ross* /ælbət rɒs/ [ælbətrɒs], in which, on morphological grounds, the /t/ is syllabified in the coda of the preceding syllable, and, as a result, there is no devoicing of the /r/.

[24] We assume here that within the onset – a consonantal constituent – the 'most consonantal' (i.e. least sonorous) consonant is the head, so that in the onset of the final syllable of *albatross*, /t/ is the head and /r/ the dependent. This is probably the most widely held position; for the view that the more sonorous segment is the head within *any* construction, see e.g. Anderson and Ewen (1987).

(60)

By convention, adjunction also assigns an extra level of structure even when there is no adjoined element, so that constituent structure is uniform. In other words, the head of the onset is identified by O'; the dependent in the onset is adjoined to the O' node. Thus /b/ in (60) is also labelled O', and, as head of the onset of the second syllable, has the same status with respect to its syllabic structure as /t/, the head of the onset of the final syllable.

Rhyme formation now follows onset formation, to give (61):

(61)

These processes are followed by **syllable formation**, which involves the grouping of a nucleus projection and a preceding onset projection, if there is one:

(62)

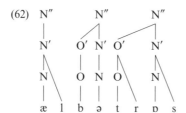

As in the case of rhyme formation, syllable formation involves the selection of the nucleus projection as the head of the syllable – the nucleus is the only obligatory element in the syllable. For the moment, we use the label N″ to characterise this, rather than the σ label which we have been using up to now. Notice that the status of the nucleus as head of the syllable is distinguished from its status as head of the rhyme by the extra prime: N″ vs N'.[25]

Although we have proposed rules of onset, nucleus, rhyme and syllable formation, we have as yet made no mention of a rule of coda formation. In view of the existence of syllables with apparently branching codas, such as English *tramp*, we might expect a rule which would select /p/ as the head of a coda constituent, to give the syllabic structure in (63):

---

[25] This notation is derived from that of X̄-syntax (Jackendoff 1977), applied to syllable structure by e.g. Kaye and Lowenstamm (1984) and Levin (1985). N″ is pronounced as 'N-double bar'.

(63)

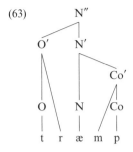

Although this is consistent with what we have been arguing so far, we have also noted that there are arguments to suggest that complex codas are in fact not possible and that there is therefore no need for a process of coda formation as such (cf. also our discussion of parameters in §3.4.2). However, we do assume that there is a coda *constituent*, even though this may not be complex, and consequently that rhyme formation also involves assigning a coda node to the dependent. This gives the final structure in (64) for *albatross*:

(64)

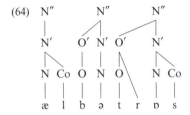

The processes outlined above provide an adequate account of syllabification in languages in which there is no motivation for a branching nucleus. However, our account must be refined to deal with languages which have a vowel-length distinction (i.e. in which the nucleus node may dominate either one or two Vs). Furthermore, there is evidence that for some languages, a postvocalic sonorant consonant should be incorporated in the nucleus, rather than forming the coda. This is appropriate, for example, for languages in which rhymes consisting of a long vowel or of a short vowel followed by a sonorant consonant are heavy, but where those consisting of a short vowel followed by an obstruent are light, as shown in (65):

(65) a. *heavy*   b. *light*
           VV   V
           VR   VO

(where R = sonorant consonant and O = obstruent). A number of cases of this sort are considered by Zec (1995a: §2.3). One such is the nucleus-weight language Kwakwala, also known as Kwakiutl (Boas 1947), which displays a

145

number of processes in which CVO syllables behave differently from CVR syllables. Stress, for example, falls on the leftmost heavy syllable, and on the final syllable if there is no heavy syllable in the word, to give the forms in (66):

(66) a. *heavy*　　　　　　　　　b. *light*
　　　'qaːsa　'to walk'　　　　　　bə'ha　'to cut'
　　　'dəlxa　'damp'　　　　　　　gas'xa　'to carry on fingers'

The forms in (66) follow the pattern in (65), such that /l/, a sonorant, makes the rhyme of the first syllable of ['dəlxa] heavy, while /s/, an obstruent, does not have the same effect in [gas'xa].

Rather than saying that syllable weight in these cases depends on whether the coda is filled by an obstruent or a sonorant, we might assume that the second element in the nucleus is subject to parametric variation: the degree of sonority which is required varies per language, such that certain languages demand that the second element of the nucleus be a full vowel, while others allow it to be a sonorant consonant. By assigning the sonorant consonant in such languages to the nucleus, rather than to the coda, we maintain the principle that syllable weight (or rather rhyme weight) is established on the basis of the number of segments within the various rhymal constituents, rather than allowing a situation in which the same rhymal configuration can be either heavy or light, with the distinction being made by whether a coda consonant is [+sonorant] or [−sonorant].[26]

Rhyme formation, then, involves the two processes in (67), which adjoin postvocalic material at different levels:

(67) a. Adjoin postvocalic segments of sufficient inherent sonority at N level.
　　　b. Adjoin any other postvocalic segments at N' level.

(67a) is illustrated by the Dutch word *bij* /bɛɪ/ 'bee' in (68a), where N now characterises a complex nucleus, and by the Kwakwala form in (68b), which contains a sonorant consonant in adjoined position:

(68) a. 　N　　　　b. 　N

　　　b　ɛ　ɪ　　　　d　ə　l

---

[26] As Harris (1994: 114) notes, 'to grant metrical processes access to melodic material . . . is to open the way for the generation of unattested systems in which stress assignment is sensitive to such dimensions as vowel height, backness or roundness'. However, it is not immediately clear whether there are *formal* grounds for allowing just those consonants which are [+sonorant] to occupy a nuclear position, even though it is clear that this is merely another aspect of the crucial role of sonority in syllabification.

However, although (68b) is appropriate for Kwakwala rhymes containing a short vowel followed by a sonorant consonant, the corresponding Dutch sequence in *bel* /bɛl/ 'bubble' will have the structure in (69a), where the sonorant consonant is adjoined to N′ rather than to N. We find the same structure for a sequence of vowel and obstruent, in both Dutch, as for *bek* /bɛk/ 'mouth' in (69b), and Kwakwala (69c):

(69)

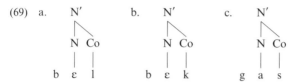

In what follows, we will employ a slightly simplified version of the representations that we have been using above. For clarity, we will return to the use of the labels σ and R, rather than N″ and N′. However, this is for convenience only; this relabelling does not affect the validity of the observations we have been making. In addition, our representations will not include the extra level of structure created by onset adjunction. Furthermore, we will not indicate the structure of complex onsets by the use of O′, but will simply use O alone. English *albatross* will therefore be represented as in (70):

(70)

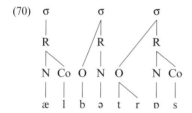

and Dutch *trein* 'train' as in (71):

(71)

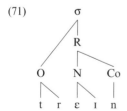

3.4.4 Extrasyllabicity and related matters

We have already seen that there are arguments for considering the prependix and appendix to be outside the syllable proper, so that we have now established a core syllable in which all constituents maximally display binary branching. However, as we anticipated earlier, there is a further set of arguments which suggest that even this simplified syllable structure can be further reduced.

These arguments concern consonants in the rhyme. We have already seen that peripheral final syllables allow appendices, which are primarily coronal, and whose presence typically violates the sonority sequencing generalisation. However, there is another set of 'extra' consonants in peripheral final syllables which we do not find in non-final syllables, as illustrated for Dutch in (72):

(72) a. *final syllables*
          VCC   balk   /bɑlk/   'beam'
      b. *non-final syllables*
          VC   balkon   /bɑlkɔn/ 'balcony'
          VCC   *balkpel

While the rhymes in final syllables of monomorphemic words can apparently contain VCC (72a), those in medial syllables cannot (with a few exceptions), as illustrated by (72b). In the acceptable form in (72b), *balkon*, the /k/ is syllabified in the onset of the second syllable, rather than in the rhyme of the first.[27] Notice that the final consonant in (72a) does not display the properties typical of appendices: it is not coronal, and the final cluster does not violate the sonority sequencing generalisation.

How can we give formal recognition to this observation? One common approach is to treat this extra consonant, like the appendix, as being outside the syllabic structure, i.e. as being **extrasyllabic**. Thus a word like Dutch *balk* might have the structure in (73), where the extrasyllabic consonant is indicated by ESP:

(73)

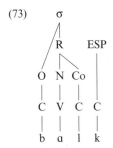

On this analysis, the core syllable is further reduced, to a structure with an optional onset, which may be branching, and a rhyme with an obligatory nucleus, which again may optionally branch, and may be followed by a single postnuclear consonant.

---

[27] Unsurprisingly, such sequences *are* permitted in compounds, such as *balkbrug* 'girder bridge'.

We have now arrived at the following structure for the core syllable and its various appendages:

(74)

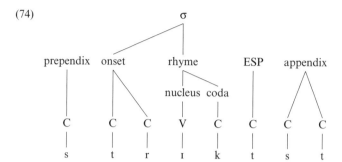

As in the case of the appendix and the prependix, we have to consider where the extrasyllabic consonant belongs in the prosodic structure. We do not discuss this question at this point, but will return to it in §3.8, where we consider in detail an approach that regards what we have interpreted here as an extrasyllabic consonant as forming the onset of a further (incomplete) syllable.

One category of rhyme which we have not yet considered is that involving a *branching* nucleus followed by two consonants (the second of which will be extrasyllabic, on the account just developed). Rhymes like these are found in English words such as *paint* /peɪnt/, *mild* /maɪld/ and *task* /tɑːsk/. Unsurprisingly, these rhymes are subject to severe restrictions – as well as occurring only peripherally in English, their composition is also restricted. Harris (1994: 77) notes, for example, that the coda consonant must be either a sonorant or a fricative, while what we have been calling the extrasyllabic consonant is nearly always coronal if the coda consonant is a sonorant. Furthermore, rhymes of this shape are very often lost in language change. For example, Lass (1984a: 257–8) notes that Old Icelandic, which had both long vowels and long consonants, permitted five rhyme structures in stressed syllables: VC, VVC, VCC, VV and what he calls 'overlong' or 'hypercharacterised' VVCC, as in (75) (the accent in the orthography denotes vowel length):

(75) a. fat   /fat/   'piece of clothing'
      b. fát   /faːt/   'confusion'
      c. fatt   /fatː/   'erect (NEUT)'
      d. fá   /faː/   'to take'
      e. fátt   /faːtː/   'few (NEUT)'

Later developments in most of the Scandinavian languages eliminated the overlong rhyme in (75e). Thus we find Swedish *fått* /fɔtː/, in which the vowel has shortened.

Syllables like these appear to have a structure containing three elements in the rhyme, as well as an extrasyllabic position, as shown in (76) for *paint*:

(76)

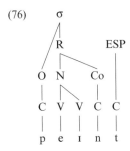

3.5 Mora theory

In our representation in (9) of the prosodic hierarchy, we observed that each constituent in the phonological phrase split into identical constituents at the immediately lower level, so that the phonological phrase consists of two phonological words, the phonological word consists of two feet, and the foot of two syllables. However, within the onset–rhyme theory of the syllable, the structure below the syllabic node no longer displays the property of splitting into identical daughter nodes – the syllable is made up of an onset and a rhyme, and the rhyme of a nucleus and a coda. This has been seen as a weakness in the onset–rhyme approach to syllable structure, especially in view of the fact that the distinction between heavy and light syllables has to be characterised as involving *either* branching of the nucleus *or* branching of the rhyme, rather than being given some uniform interpretation.

Alternative models have been proposed, in which attempts are made to provide a more direct characterisation of the notion of syllable weight. In one such approach, syllables are not divided into immediate constituents called onset and rhyme, but into 'weight units' or **moras**.[28] Light syllables contain only one mora (they are **monomoraic**); heavy syllables contain at least two (they are **bimoraic**). Thus in mora theory, unlike onset–rhyme theory, the immediate constituents of the syllable do belong to the same category: they are both moras.

In this approach, each mora contains one segment which contributes to the weight of a syllable, possibly together with a number of segments which do not contribute to the weight. As noted above, heavy syllables have two moras, while light syllables have only one. Thus, in a rhyme-weight language, in which CVC syllables are heavy, the vowel and the final consonant will be assigned to distinct moras. As we have seen, however, initial consonants do

---

[28] See particularly Hyman (1985), Hock (1986), Hayes (1989a).

not contribute to the weight of a syllable, and so the first consonant in a CVC syllable will not belong to a separate mora. In some versions of mora theory, initial consonants are assigned to the first mora of a syllable, i.e. the mora dominating the vowel. More commonly, however, initial consonants, and in general any prevocalic material, are characterised as being associated directly to the syllable node, i.e. an initial consonant is 'extramoraic'. This characterises the fact that such material never contributes to syllable weight. The difference between light and heavy syllables in rhyme-weight languages in mora theory is shown in (77), where, following Hayes (1989a), we assume that initial consonants are extramoraic (cf. (41), where representations of rhyme-weight languages within onset–rhyme theory are given):

(77)   *Rhyme-weight languages*

    a. *light*   b. *heavy*   c. *heavy*

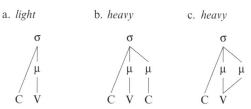

Here moras are represented as μ, and, as before, syllables as σ. In accordance with usual practice in mora theory, we assume that long vowels involve a single V specification, simultaneously associated with two moras, as in the case of the CVV syllable in (77c) (diphthongs would of course have two Vs, each associated with a mora).

In a nucleus-weight language, in which CVC syllables are light (cf. (42)), CVC syllables will be monomoraic, so that the final consonant does not associate with a separate mora, as in (78):

(78)   *Nucleus-weight languages*

    a. *light*   b. *light*   c. *heavy*

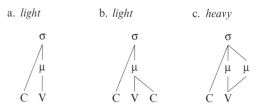

Although representations in mora theory look very different from those in onset–rhyme theory, there are perhaps more similarities than one might think at first sight. Both models are concerned with distinguishing 'weight-relevant' segments from those which do not affect syllable weight. In onset–rhyme theory, initial consonants form the onset, which is not relevant to weight, while in mora theory they can be seen as 'extramoraic'. The crucial difference is that this version of mora theory differs from onset–rhyme theory in not recognising an onset *constituent*:

(79) a.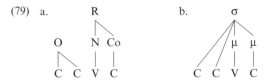

However, with respect to syllable-final consonants, as we have seen, the two models differ in a more obvious way. In mora theory, the number of moras determines whether a syllable is heavy or not, as can be seen in (77) and (78), where all heavy syllables have two moras and all light syllables one. In onset–rhyme theory, a heavy VC syllable in a rhyme-weight language (41) has exactly the same *structure* as a light VC syllable in a nucleus-weight language (42); the difference in weight does not follow from a difference in structure, but only by the setting of a parameter.

Overlong syllables, which, as we saw above, are typically peripheral, can be represented as trimoraic, as in (80):

(80)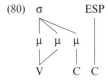

where we assume that the second consonant is extrasyllabic.

A phenomenon which can be given a natural representation in mora theory is that referred to as **compensatory lengthening**. One such process involves the deletion of a consonant between a vowel and another consonant, with resulting compensatory lengthening of the vowel. An example is found in the early history of English and other Germanic dialects, where a postvocalic nasal was deleted before a fricative. This process is responsible for alternations within the paradigms of certain irregular verbs in English, e.g. *think* vs *thought*, as well as the differences between various Germanic languages shown in (81):

(81)
Modern German		*Modern Dutch*		*Modern English*	
fünf	/fynf/	vijf	/vɛif/	five	/faɪv/
Mund	/mund/	mond	/mɔnd/	mouth	/maʊθ/
Gans	/gans/	gans	/ɣɑns/	goose	/guːs/

Modern German, in which the vowel is short and the nasal has been retained, most closely represents the original situation, Modern English shows the results of the loss of the nasal and the compensatory lengthening of the vowel, and Modern Dutch is hybrid with respect to this phenomenon.

In onset–rhyme theory, compensatory lengthening is more difficult to express than in mora theory. In both theories, the nasal is deleted, but the number of segments in the rhyme remains unchanged. Consider (82)–(84), where we show what is involved in both theories in the change from Proto-Germanic *fimf* 'five' to *fīf*:

(82)

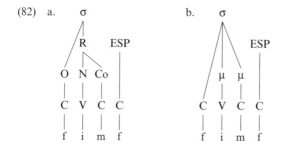

In onset–rhyme theory, as we have been presenting it up to now (but see §3.6 below), the nasal is delinked. Subsequently, the coda node is also delinked from the rhyme node, the C changes to a V, and becomes a daughter of the nucleus node, to give (83) (we ignore here the question of whether the extrasyllabic consonant can now be reassigned to the coda):

(83)

In mora theory, on the other hand, the process simply involves delinking of the nasal and the C node from the mora node, with reattachment of the mora node to the V node, as in (84):

(84)

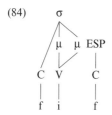

Certain of the advantages of the moraic account of this phenomenon can be countered in onset–rhyme theory by the introduction of a 'skeletal' tier, which we now consider in the context of the more general problem of the representation of segmental length, both consonantal and vocalic.

3.6 The representation of length

In our discussion of syllable structure we have been associating labels such as onset and rhyme or mora with C and V symbols functioning as abbreviations of segmental matrices (or, more correctly, feature trees such as (75) in Chapter 1). However, current approaches to phonological structure take a slightly different view of how this works. It is generally assumed that the **root** nodes of segments (see §1.4) associate to the 'terminal nodes' of the syllabic structure. In onset–rhyme theory these terminal elements are said to occupy a **skeleton** or **skeletal tier**. (85) gives a representation incorporating the skeleton for the English word *beacon* /biːkən/, where skeletal points are represented by 'x':

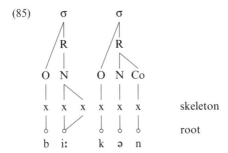

On this view, the representation of a long (or geminate) segment involves simply a single root node associated to two skeletal positions, whereas for short segments there is a one-to-one relationship between the skeleton and the root tier, as in (86):

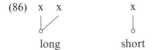

Such statements form part of a characterisation of the segment types allowed by an individual language. (86), then, characterises a language which makes a phonological distinction between long and short vowels. Exactly the same approach would characterise the phonemic contrast between long and short consonants in a language such as Italian, evidenced in minimal pairs such as *papa* /papa/ [papa] 'pope' and *pappa* /pappa/ [papːa] 'daddy':

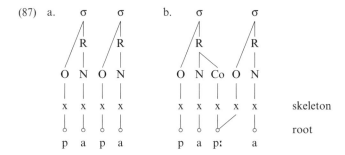

Here the single root node is shared between two syllables; the geminate consonant /pː/ is simultaneously the coda of the first syllable and the onset of the second.

In addition to structures involving two skeletal positions associated to a single root node, the reverse is also found. Complex segments such as affricates (cf. §1.4) function as single segments with respect to the syllable, and therefore require only one skeletal position, but are segmentally complex. An affricate consists of a stop part and a fricative part, and therefore has two root nodes, so that *church* /tʃɜːtʃ/ will have the representation in (88) (where we ignore the syllabic structure above the skeleton):

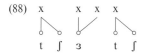

(88)

Underlying this account of skeletal positions, which originates with Clements and Keyser (1983), is the notion that skeletal positions are 'timing units' in the syllable. Because long monophthongs have the duration of two segments, they have two timing slots, but only one segmental tree – there is only a single articulation involved – while affricates show the reverse: they have the duration of a single segment, but involve two articulations.[29] For practical purposes, we can consider the notion of timing unit to be equivalent to that of 'segment'; the number of skeletal positions in a word is the same as the number of segments.

Do we also require a skeletal level of representation in moraic theory, or can moras be associated directly to the root node, as in (89), which would be the moraic equivalents of (87)?

---

[29] The analysis of complex segments is considerably more complicated than is here suggested. Although we have represented affricates as involving two distinct segmental trees, with two root nodes, van de Weijer argues that such two-rooted representations are more appropriate for consonants involving double articulations such as /p͡t/. Affricates, he suggests, involve complexity *within* the segmental tree, and contain both a [stop] and a [continuant] feature. For a discussion of these issues, see van de Weijer (1994).

(89) a.   σ   σ   b.   σ   σ

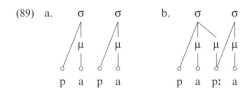

p   a   p   a   p   a   pː   a

Here the intervocalic geminate in (89b) is simultaneously associated to the
second syllable node and to a mora dominated by the first syllable node. As
such, it is formally distinct from a single intervocalic consonant, which is not
immediately dominated by a mora. However, the lack of a skeletal tier in
(89) raises the question of how geminate consonants might be distinguished
lexically from single consonants in moraic theory. As we have seen, syllabic
structure is not present lexically, but is assigned by rule on the basis of the
factors discussed above, such as relative sonority. Thus, if geminate consonants have only a single root node in their representation, we must find some
other means of distinguishing them underlyingly from single consonants. This
might be achieved by assuming that a geminate consonant is always lexically
associated with a mora; i.e. the difference between a geminate and a single
consonant is the fact that the geminate always contributes to the weight of
the syllable. The representation of the single consonant is shown in (90a) and
that of the geminate in (b):

(90) a.   b. μ
                         |
          o   o
          p   pː

On this analysis, the presence of a geminate consonant means that the
preceding syllable must be bimoraic. Therefore, as pointed out by Lahiri and
Koreman (1988) and Tranel (1991), a syllable closed by a geminate should
always be heavy. However, Tranel (1991) notes that in at least some cases,
this prediction is not borne out. Consider again the nucleus-weight language
Selkup (cf. (39)):

(91) a.   qu'moːqɪ   'two human beings'
      b.   'amɪrna   'eats'
      c.   'uːcɪkkak   'I am working'

Stress in Selkup falls on the last heavy syllable, where VV but not VC counts
as heavy, or on the first syllable of the word. Thus stress in (91a) falls on the
penultimate, which is heavy, but in (b) on the antepenultimate, as the penultimate contains VC, and is therefore light. (91c), which contains a geminate
consonant, behaves like (b) in having antepenultimate stress; the syllable

containing the geminate must therefore be light. This is not a problem for onset–rhyme theory, where, as shown in (92), (b) and (c) share the same structure:

(92) a.

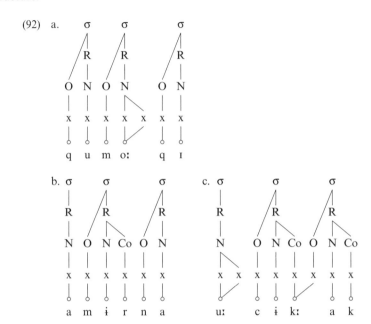

The /r/ in /amɨrna/ has the same status with respect to the skeleton (coda of the second syllable) as the first part of the geminate /k/ in /uːcɨkkak/, and so neither contributes to the weight of the syllable. In other words, as we might expect, both count as VC rhymes.

A representation in terms of mora theory which does not incorporate a skeletal tier appears to be unable to characterise /amɨrna/ as having the same structure as /uːcɨkkak/, as shown in (93):

(93) a.

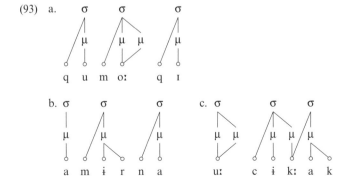

In the absence of the skeleton, the penultimate syllable of (93c) is now wrongly characterised as having the same moraic structure as that of (a), and so is incorrectly predicted to take stress on the penultimate.

Thus, like onset–rhyme theory, mora theory apparently needs to incorporate skeletal positions in syllabic representations, so that geminates will have one of the representations in (94), rather than that in (89b):

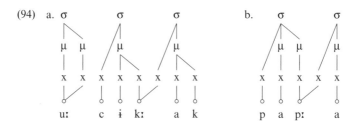

Whether or not the left half of the geminate contributes to weight is determined by whether the language in question treats VC as light or heavy. Selkup (94a) treats VC as light, so that although /kː/ occupies two skeletal positions, its first position does not project a mora, as opposed to Italian (94b), where the first position of /pː/ does. In general, whether or not a coda contributes to weight is determined by what is often referred to as the 'weight by position' rule, i.e. 'the rule or principle of syllabification that assigns a mora to a postvocalic consonant within the syllable' (Hayes 1995: 52). On this account, then, a rhyme closed by a geminate behaves in exactly the same way as one closed by a consonant cluster, and so geminates need bear no special marking in the lexicon.

A similar problem for mora theory is identified by Lahiri and Koreman (1988), in their account of the stress system of Dutch. They consider Dutch to have a contrast between long and short vowels, i.e. to have a quantitative distinction in the vowel system, rather than between tense and lax vowels (a qualitative distinction; cf. the discussion in §1.3.3 above). Long vowels occur in open syllables only (except word-finally, where there may be a closing consonant), while short vowels can only occur in closed syllables. Thus, in onset–rhyme theory, we have two types of rhyme, VV and VC. As we saw in §3.4.1, stress in Dutch is weight-sensitive, but, contrary to the expected pattern, VC syllables are heavy and VV syllables are light, as illustrated by the forms in (95), where the target syllable for stress is the penultimate:

(95) a. [deː'tɛktɔr]   detector   'detector'
    [wɪl'hɛlmus]   Wilhelmus   (name)
  b. ['moːniːtɔr]   monitor   'monitor'
    ['fɛstiːval]   festival   'festival'

The VV penultimate syllables in (95b) reject stress, which shifts to the ante-penultimate. Lahiri and Koreman point out that this state of affairs is inexpressible if mora theory does no incorporate a skeleton, since long vowels are represented as bimoraic. The heaviness of closed syllables is in itself unproblematical (weight by position), but there is no way of characterising these as heavy while at the same time excluding VV:

(96)   a. σ   b. σ

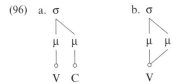

Lahiri and Koreman propose that for Dutch, as in the case of Selkup above, we need to incorporate the skeleton in mora theory, such that Dutch long vowels are monomoraic, but are associated with two skeletal positions:

(97)   a. σ   b. σ

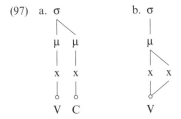

It seems, then, that there is a body of evidence to suggest that syllable structure must incorporate a skeletal tier, both in onset–rhyme theory and in mora theory.

3.7   The independence of syllabic positions

We have been assuming that syllable structure is assigned to the strings of root nodes which are underlyingly present, although in specific cases, such as the representation of long vowels and complex segments, some syllabification information must be specified underlyingly, as we saw in §3.5. Lexically, then, we have strings of segmental trees without any syllabic organisation. The creation of syllabic structure presupposes the existence of segmental structure.

However, there are various phenomena in the languages of the world which suggest that syllabification and syllable structure are not as straightforward as this might suggest. Thus we find cases in which segmental material appears to be underlyingly present, but is only realised if it finds itself in an appropriate position in the syllabic structure. One frequently discussed case involves the realisation of /r/ in English.

3.7.1 *lrl in English*

We can distinguish three different groups of 'dialects' of English as far as the behaviour of 'final' *r* is concerned. Let us refer to these as the 'fully rhotic' dialects, the 'fully non-rhotic' dialects and the 'intrusive [r]' dialects.[30] The fully rhotic dialects, such as Scots, realise postvocalic /r/ under all circumstances:

(98)   rotor   [rotər]
           queer   [kwiːr]
           queerer [kwiːrər]
           hurry   [hʌrɪ][31]

Fully non-rhotic dialects, such as some varieties of RP, only realise /r/ if it can be syllabified into the onset of a following syllable, as in (99):[32]

(99)   rotor   [ɹəʊtə]
           queer   [kwɪə]
           queerer [kwɪəɹə]
           hurry   [hʌɹɪ]

Thus the initial /r/ in *rotor* is realised, but the final one is not, while the intervocalic /r/ in *queerer* and *hurry* is syllabified into the onset of the second syllable, and so is realised (cf. *queer*, where the /r/ does not surface). Notice that the presence of a word boundary does not inhibit the realisation of the /r/, as shown by a phrase such as *queer and quaint* [kwɪəɹənkweɪnt]. /r/ realised in this context is said to be 'linking'.

The third group, the 'intrusive [r]' dialects, have the same realisations as in (99), but also realise [ɹ] in a further context. Thus 'fully non-rhotic' RP speakers have linking [ɹ] only in contexts in which there is an <r> in the orthography, while 'intrusive [r]' speakers insert the consonant between *any* vowel-final word[33] and a following vowel-initial word (i.e. when two vowels are in hiatus), irrespective of the orthography, giving pronunciations such as [kɒməɹəŋkəʊlən] for *comma and colon*, which for speakers of 'fully non-rhotic' dialects, would be [kɒməəŋkəʊlən], without the [ɹ].

In the 'intrusive' dialect, the insertion of the [ɹ] is totally predictable from the phonetic context, and so we do not have to specify it underlyingly. Rather, we simply require a rule which forbids empty onsets intervocalically in foot-

---

[30] This division is a simplification of the actual situation, but will serve to illustrate the point we wish to make here. Unsurprisingly, many speakers fall between the dialects identified above. For a discussion of the dialect situation in English, see Wells (1982).

[31] We are not concerned here with the phonetic details of the realisation in Scots English of /r/, which may vary from a trilled [r] through an alveolar tap [ɾ] to some kind of approximant [ɹ] or [ɻ], depending partly on its position in the word (see Wells 1982: 410–11). The only relevant factor here is whether or not the consonant is present phonetically.

[32] RP /r/ is realised as [ɹ] in all relevant contexts.

[33] The word-final vowel must not be high, however, and for some speakers can only be low.

internal position; if there is no segmental material available, then [ɹ] is inserted. In this case, then, syllabic structure is at least partly independent of segmental material, to the extent that each syllable *must* have an onset.

Fully non-rhotic speakers, on the other hand, must have different underlying representations for words which yield linking [ɹ] and those which do not. Thus, although *comma* [kɒmə] and *bomber* [bɒmə] have the same shape in isolation, the speaker must 'know' that *comma and colon* has no [ɹ], while *bomber and fighter* [bɒməɹənfaɪtə] does. Thus we must assume that *bomber* has an underlying /r/, to give /bɒmər/. 'Intrusive [r]' speakers, however, treat the two forms identically, and therefore can have identical underlying representations, i.e. /kɒmə/ and /bɒmə/.

How, then, does syllabification operate for speakers of the fully non-rhotic dialects, who apparently have underlying /r/ which is not realised in final position, as in [bɒmə] from underlying /bɒmər/? We return to this after our discussion of a related phenomenon, liaison in French.

3.7.2   Liaison

French displays two phenomena, liaison and *h-aspiré*, which have interesting repercussions for our analysis of syllable structure. We consider first liaison.[34]

In some respects, liaison is very similar to the linking-[ɹ] phenomenon of RP English. Both result from the loss of word-final consonants at an earlier stage of the language. We find Modern French forms such as those in (100), which, reflecting the earlier pronunciation, have a final consonant in the orthographic representations, which, however, is no longer realised phonetically:

(100)   petit   [pəti]   'small'
        gros   [gʀo]   'large'
        un   [ɛ̃]   'one, a'

In these words, the final consonant is not realised phonetically at the end of a phrase or if it is followed by a word beginning with a consonant, as in (101a). However, if the consonant is followed by a vowel-initial or glide-initial word, it *is* realised (101b):

(101)   a.   petit livre   [pəti livʀ]   'small book'
             gros camion   [gʀo kamjõ]   'large truck'
             un pouce   [ɛ̃ pus]   'a thumb'
        b.   petit ami   [pətit ami]   'small friend'
             petit oiseau   [pətit wazo]   'small bird'
             gros arbre   [gʀoz aʀbʀ]   'large tree'
             un enfant   [ɛ̃n ɑ̃fɑ̃]   'a child'

---

[34] For a full discussion of liaison, see Tranel (1987: ch. 11). See also Selkirk (1972), Clements and Keyser (1983).

The realisation of the final consonant in some contexts (preceding vowels and glides) is the phenomenon referred to as liaison. Unlike linking [ɹ] in RP, a range of consonants is involved in liaison, as illustrated above for [t], [z] and [n]. Whether or not liaison actually occurs in the appropriate phonetic context is governed by a number of factors which need not concern us here, but which are morphological, syntactic and stylistic in nature (see Tranel 1987).

How can we account for liaison in a theory of syllable structure? Notice first of all that, whatever our treatment of [ɹ]-insertion in fully non-rhotic dialects of RP, our account for liaison must be different; there is no way of predicting – from the phonetic context alone – which consonant will be realised. For example, there is nothing in the phonetic context to lead us to expect [t] in [pətit wazo] 'small bird', but [z] in [groz wazo] 'big birds'. Rather, we must propose an account in which the final consonant is initially present, but is deleted in the appropriate context.

If the facts of liaison were as straightforward as we have just suggested, this would be as far as we would need to go. We would simply say that the phonological form of *petit* was /pətit/ and that of *gros* /groz/, and that French had a rule which deleted final consonants in the appropriate environments. However, the facts are considerably more complex.

Notice first that not *all* consonants in French can serve as linking consonants in liaison. By far the most common are those in (101), i.e. the coronals [t n z], with [ʀ p g] also being found in a restricted number of cases (e.g. *au premier étage* [opʀømjɛʀetaʒ] 'on the first floor', *beaucoup aimé* [bokupɛme] 'much loved', *un long été* [ɛ̃lõgete] 'a long summer'). Other consonants are not found in liaison processes. More importantly – indeed, crucially for rejecting the idea that French has a rule deleting 'final' consonants in general – there are many words in which final consonants *are* realised, as shown in (102):

(102) a. cher garçon [ʃɛʀ gaʀsõ] 'dear boy'
            cher livre   [ʃɛʀ livʀ]   'dear book'
            avec ça   [avɛk sa]   'with that'
      b. cher ami   [ʃɛʀ ami]   'dear friend'
            cher oiseau [ʃɛʀ wazo]   'dear bird'
            avec eux   [avɛk ø]   'with them'

These consonants are not deleted under any circumstances; they behave like the liaison consonants in surfacing before vowels and glides (102b), but, unlike them, also before consonants (102a). Clements and Keyser note 'minimal' pairs such as *donc* 'therefore', which is always [dõk], and *dont* 'whose', which is [dõt] in liaison contexts, but [dõ] elsewhere. We must therefore distinguish between the two types of consonants in our phonological representation, to ensure that liaison only affects the relevant set of words in French.

Let us assume for the moment that the liaison facts force us to say that phonological sequences are underlyingly syllabified in French. On this assumption, the final consonant of non-alternating words such as *avec* and *donc* will, as in the regular case, be syllabified in the rhyme, as in (103):

(103)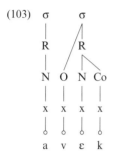

The final consonant will be phonetically realised even if the onset of the following syllable is not empty, as in (104a), *avec ça*:

(104)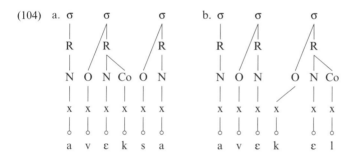

In (104b), *avec elle*, the final consonant 'resyllabifies' phonetically to allow the empty onset to be filled, giving [a.vɛ.kɛl], where we denote syllable boundaries with a dot. This again demonstrates the relevance of the Maximal Onset Principle (cf. §3.2); even though the final /k/ is first syllabified in the rhyme, on this analysis it shifts to the following onset when possible, even if that onset belongs to a different word. In general, French seems to avoids empty onsets within the phonological phrase – i.e. the domain of syllabification in French is the phonological phrase.

How do we prevent liaison consonants from being realised when they are followed by a consonant, while ensuring that they are realised when a vowel follows? We assume the following *surface* representations for *petit garçon* and *petit ami*:

(105) a.

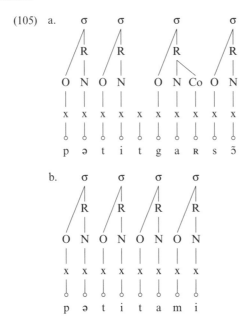

In (105a) the final /t/ of *petit* is not associated to any syllabic constituent, while in (b) it forms the onset of the third syllable of the sequence. Thus, on the surface, the final consonant is only syllabified, and therefore realised, if the following onset is empty.

What, then, is the *underlying* representation of a word like *petit*? Recall that we must be able to identify the segmental content of the consonant, as we need to know how it surfaces in liaison contexts. One possible strategy would be to say that the underlying representations directly encode whether a final consonant is incorporated in the syllabic structure of a word, so that the final /t/ of *petit* is underlyingly not syllabified, as in (106):[35]

(106)

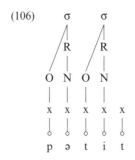

---

[35] We are assuming here that the linear order of segments is determined by the ordering of skeletal positions. This means that the root node of the final consonant is associated to a skeletal position – otherwise it would not be ordered with respect to the other elements in the string.

Contrast this with the representation for *avec* in (103), where the final consonant *is* underlyingly syllabified. Thus the skeletal position of the final consonant in *petit* is not dominated by any node. In the case of *petit garçon*, the /t/ remains unsyllabified, and is therefore not realised phonetically – it does not form part of the syllabic structure. In other words, the /t/ is not **licensed** in this word. The concept of licensing is used in determining whether or not a particular segment can be phonetically realised; in this case there is no node available in the syllabic structure to which the final underlying /t/ of *petit* can associate, and so it is phonetically not present.[36]

However, underlyingly unsyllabified consonants in French can be 'rescued' by the presence of a following onsetless syllable. Because a word like *ami* has no onset, and, as we have seen, French avoids empty onsets where possible within the phonological phrase, the lack of an onset licenses the final /t/ of *petit* in *petit ami*, giving the surface representation in (107):

(107)

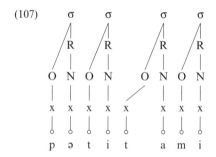

The final /t/ of *petit* is now associated to the empty onset of the first syllable of *ami*.

However, the account of liaison which we have just given, although adequate in the sense that the correct phonetic representations can be generated, is bedevilled by a problem. As we have already seen in this chapter (§3.4.3), syllabification is normally predictable from the linear order of segments. Our rules of onset, rhyme and nucleus formation were meant to reflect this. It seems undesirable to abandon this claim – which is seen as being generally true of languages – merely to account for one type of phenomenon in a particular language. Furthermore, the analysis we have given does not identify the appropriate category of segments as being 'abnormal'. In general in languages, as we have seen, segments are underlyingly not syllabified, and are, of course, phonetically realised. However, in the analysis we have given, the 'normal' category, i.e. the fixed final consonant in a word such as *avec*, is syllabified underlyingly, while the 'exceptional' category, a final consonant

---

[36] See for discussions of licensing Itô (1986), Goldsmith (1990).

undergoing liaison, for example the [t] in *petit*, is underlyingly not syllabified. Clearly, then, the account we have given is not optimal.

An alternative analysis is available, however, one which makes use of a concept similar to that of extrasyllabicity, which we introduced in §3.4.4. In this analysis, final liaison consonants are simply marked in the lexicon as being extrasyllabic, i.e. as being 'invisible' to the normal syllabification algorithm of French:

(108) a. x x x x <x>   b. x x x x
          | | | | | | | | |
          o o o o o   o o o o
          p ə t i t   a v ɛ k

where extrasyllabicity is denoted by < >.

Notice that the motivation for marking liaison consonants as extrasyllabic is different from the cases which we considered earlier in §3.4.4 with respect to extrasyllabicity. There we found that a consonant was extrasyllabic because its presence violated the constraints on syllable structure in the language in question. Here, however, there is no such violation involved: the pronunciation [pətit] would be well formed in French even if no empty onset followed (and, indeed, is a possible realisation of the feminine form *petite*, as in *la petite bonne* [lapətitbɔn]). Rather, it is an idiosyncratic fact about the set of words with liaison consonants that these consonants behave as if they were invisible for syllabification, and so it is appropriate to mark just these consonants as being exceptional. < > in (108) can therefore be viewed as a diacritic marker whose presence is not predictable from any phonological aspect of the segment involved.

We assume that the extrasyllabicity marking is not visible at the phonetic level when the final consonant is licensed by a following vowel-initial word, so that, as before, the final /t/ of *petit*, for example, can associate to the empty onset of *ami*.

The extrasyllabicity analysis also appears appropriate for 'fully non-rhotic' speakers of RP English, i.e. those who display linking [ɹ], but not intrusive [ɹ]. For these speakers, the final /r/ can be marked as extrasyllabic, being realised only when the following onset is empty, so that the underlying representation of *rotor* will be:

(109) x x x x x <x>
       | | | | | |
       o o o o o o
       r ə ʊ t ə r

3.7.3 *h-aspiré*

French displays another phenomenon relevant to the relationship between segments and syllabic structure, involving words beginning with what is normally referred to as an *h-aspiré*.

We have already seen that vowel-initial words in French trigger liaison; they are also involved in a number of other phenomena, such as the loss of the vowel in the definite article. Compare the consonant-initial words in (110a) with the vowel-initial and glide-initial words in (b):

(110) a. le pouce   [lø pus]   'the thumb'
           la main   [la mɛ̃]   'the hand'
       b. l'arbre   [laʀbʀ]   'the tree'
           l'étoile   [letwal]   'the star'
           l'oiseau   [lwazo]   'the bird'

It would appear that the vowel is elided in the same environment as that in which liaison is triggered. However, consider the forms in (111), all with an initial orthographic *h*:

(111) a. le hibou   [lø ibu]   'the owl'
           la hache   [la aʃ]   'the axe'
       b. l'hirondelle [liʀɔ̃dɛl]   'the swallow'
           l'humidité   [lymidite] 'the humidity'

The vowel-initial words in (111b) behave as we would expect from (110b); they trigger elision of the vowel in the definite article. However, those in (a), although also pronounced with an initial vowel (e.g. [ibu]), are resistant to the processes which normally affect vowel-initial words. The forms in (a) are the *h-aspiré* words.

In the case of *h-aspiré* words, we appear to have an initial consonant, which, although it is never realised phonetically, is nevertheless in some sense 'present' on the surface, in order to block elision from applying. Rather than having a consonant which is fully specified but unsyllabified, as in the case of liaison consonants, then, we have a skeletal position which is underlyingly present, but has no segmental content, as in (112a), and is therefore syllabified, as in (112b), the representation for *le hibou*:

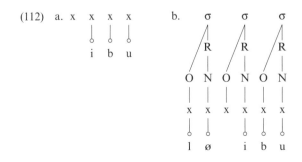

The onset of the first syllable of *hibou* is associated to a skeletal position, and so, for the purposes of elision, the word has an onset, thus preventing loss of the vowel. On the other hand, a word like *hirondelle* has no onset, like 'normal' vowel-initial words, and so elision is triggered.

Interestingly, there are a few vowel-initial words without orthographic *h* (113a) which also behave like *h-aspiré* words, as well as a number of glide-initial items ((113c); cf. the forms in (b), which permit elision):

(113) a. le onze août   [lø ɔ̃z u]   'August 11th'
       b. l'oiseau   [lwazo]   'the bird'
           l'huile   [lɥil]   'the oil'
       c. le yaourt   [lø jauʀt]   'the yoghurt'
           le huit avril [lø ɥit avʀil] 'April 8th'
           le ouistiti   [lø wistiti]   'the marmoset'

The form in (113a), *onze*, must be treated like *hibou* in (111a), i.e. with a segmentally empty syllabic position. Those in (113c) apparently treat the initial glide as being a consonant, and so elision is blocked. However, in (113b), the surface glide does not block elision.[37] This means either that we must consider the glide to be syllabified not in the onset, but in the nucleus (this is the solution adopted by Tranel 1987: 174), or that we should allow complex onsets when the second element is a glide. French does in fact allow such onsets within morphemes (e.g. *lui* [lɥi] 'him', *loi* [lwɑ] 'law'), and so the best surface representations of the various forms are perhaps those in (114):

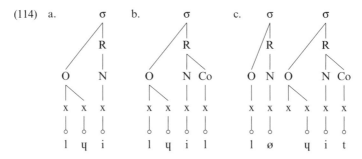

In (a) and (b) the semi-vowel [ɥ] is part of the complex onset whose head is [l], which is underlyingly present in (a) and becomes part of the onset in (b) as a result of elision. In (c), on the other hand, elision is blocked because the underlyingly complex onset has a head, which, however, has no segmental content (cf. *hibou* in (111a)).

By and large, liaison and *h-aspiré* interact in the expected way, such that words with *h-aspiré* block liaison, to give *petit hibou* [pəti ibu] 'small owl', for

---

[37] Notice that there do not appear to be examples of /j/-initial words which permit elision.

example.[38] Because the onset of the first syllable of *hibou* is associated to a skeletal position, the final unsyllabified /t/ of *petit* cannot be associated to it (liaison in French cannot form complex onsets, unless the second element is a glide, as discussed above – cf. *petit rêve* *[pətitʀɛv] 'small dream' – rather, its function is to prevent onsetless syllables). Because this onset is not associated to any segmental material, it too cannot be realised. On the other hand, *petit hymne* 'small hymn' will behave just like *petit ami* 'small friend' ([pətitimn] and [pətitami]); there is no skeletal position associated to the onset of *hymne*, which is underlyingly vowel-initial, like *ami*.

3.7.4   Compensatory lengthening and related processes

We turn now to a slightly different type of phenomenon, but again one in which we can make appeal to the concept of empty syllabic positions. A common type of argument for having a particular tier in phonological representation involves its independence from other aspects of the phonological structure. In particular, we can identify phenomena involving **stability effects**, in which some aspect of a segment is deleted, while some other aspect is apparently still present in the phonological representation. In such cases, the two aspects involved form independent parts of the structure. Thus, we saw in §1.4 with respect to tonal representations that there are cases where tone-bearing units are deleted, but the tones to which they were associated are 'left behind', and associate to a neighbouring tone-bearing unit. Tone is therefore appropriately represented on a separate tier.

Similar phenomena can be found to support the view that skeletal positions are elements on a distinct phonological tier. One such phenomenon involves compensatory lengthening, an example of which we introduced in §3.5. The term is used to describe the lengthening of a segment to preserve the number of elements on the skeletal tier, generally when some process has operated – or sometimes has failed to operate – in order to associate segmental material by other means to the skeletal node in question.

One such case, from Tiberian Hebrew, is cited by Lowenstamm and Kaye (1986: 104). Consider the nouns in (115):

(115) a.   seefer   'book'
            geʃem   'rain'
       b.   ʔiiʃ   'man'
            ʕaam   'people'
            haar   'mountain'

---

[38] Here, as elsewhere, we are ignoring various other optional phonetic processes, such as the one which typically deletes the schwa in *petit*, giving, for example, [pti ibu].

Tiberian Hebrew has a process in which the definite article /ha/ is attached to the beginning of the noun. When this happens, the initial consonant of the noun normally becomes a geminate, as in (116):

    (116)   hasseefer   'the book'
             haggeʃem 'the rain'

In (117) we provide a representation with both the skeletal and the root tier for [haggeʃem]:

    (117) x x x x x x x x

             h a   g e ʃ e m

However, the forms in (115b) behave differently. The initial consonants in these words form part of a set, /ʔ ʕ h r ħ/, which never geminate in Hebrew. We might expect, then, that the article would simply be attached to the noun, with no further change, to give [haʔiiʃ] and [hahaar], for example. However, the actual forms are:

    (118)   haaʔiiʃ   'the man'
             haaʕaam 'the people'
             haahaar   'the mountain'

in which the vowel of the definite article is lengthened, rather than the initial consonant of the noun. We can attribute this to the fact that the process in question demands a 'template' in which there must be three skeletal slots preceding the noun. This demand is normally satisfied by the gemination of the initial consonant; however, if that consonant belongs to the set which cannot undergo gemination, one skeletal slot is left without segmental content, as in (119):

    (119) x x x x x x x

             h a   ʔ i i ʃ

To satisfy the template, compensatory lengthening of the vowel takes place, by associating the vowel to the empty skeletal position:

    (120) x x x x x x x

             h a   ʔ i i ʃ

Phenomena like these suggest that syllabic positions can exist (albeit in this case temporarily) without segmental information, and provide strong evidence for assuming that syllabic positions form an independent part of phonological representation.

Other examples of compensatory lengthening display a more complex state of affairs. For example, Steriade (1982) and Wetzels (1986) discuss compensatory lengthening in the East Ionic dialect of Ancient Greek, in which a postconsonantal /w/ was lost, with concomitant lengthening of a vowel:

(121)   odwos   > o:dos   'threshold'
        kalwos > ka:los   'beautiful'
        ksenwos > kse:nos   'stranger'

The deleted /w/ in (121) is not adjacent to the vowel which lengthens. Deletion of /w/ is shown in (122):

(122)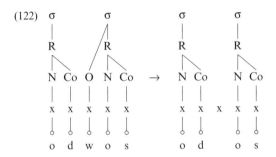

After the deletion of /w/ the second syllable becomes onsetless. To provide an onset for this syllable, the preceding consonant moves from final position of the first syllable into the onset position of the second syllable:

(123)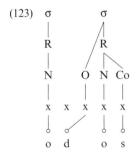

This in turn triggers compensatory lengthening of the vowel, as in (124):

(124)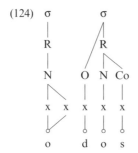

The skeletal positions again behave independently from the content of the segment, thus justifying their presence in the syllabic structure.

Such compensatory processes also appear to be relevant to sequences larger than the syllable. Although these are strictly speaking outwith the domain of this chapter, we devote some space to a consideration of some relevant examples here. One such involves a process in the history of English known as Middle English Open Syllable Lengthening (MEOSL). MEOSL, as the name suggests, is traditionally viewed as involving the lengthening of a vowel in an open syllable, i.e. in a stressed syllable followed by a single consonant followed by a vowel, i.e. schwa. Examples are given in (125) (from Lass 1992: 48):

(125) /wikə/ > [weːkə] 'week'
      /wudə/ > [woːdə] 'wood'
      /berə/ > [bɛːrə] 'to bear'
      /nosə/ > [nɔːzə] 'nose'
      /samə/ > [saːmə] 'same'

The traditional interpretation appears to have nothing to do with the notion of compensation – nothing is lost as a result of the change in (125). However, one view of the change, first proposed by Minkova (1991), is that the lengthening is not triggered by the fact that the vowel is in an open syllable, but rather by the loss of the final schwa.[39] In other words, the equivalence is not between, for example, [wudə] and [woːdə], but between [wudə] and [woːd]. On this interpretation, the lengthening of the first vowel compensates for the loss of the second. This can again be argued to be the result of pressure to maintain the number of elements on the skeletal tier: a sequence of two syllables with short vowels is in some sense equivalent to a single syllable with a long vowel, or, alternatively, two light syllables are here treated as having the same weight as one heavy. The process can be characterised as in (126):

---

[39] But see for arguments against this reinterpretation, Lahiri and Dresher (ms).

(126)

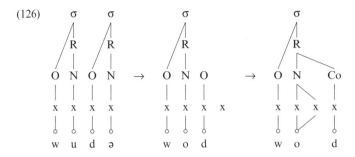

A similar account could be proposed to explain the different realisations of the diminutive morpheme in Dutch following a noun ending in a sonorant consonant. Recall from §1.3.1 that following a monosyllabic noun with a rhyme consisting of a long vowel followed by a sonorant consonant, such as *maan* /maːn/ 'moon', the form of the diminutive suffix is [tjə], but if the vowel is short, as in *man* /mɑn/ 'man', a vowel is inserted, to give [mɑnətjə]. As in the case of MEOSL, this can be viewed as compensatory, although in this case we are dealing with compensatory epenthesis rather than compensatory lengthening. In both cases, though, there appears to be a **template** defined in terms of elements on the skeletal tier which has to be satisfied by associating segmental material with all the skeletal elements.

Similar factors can be involved in the deletion of segmental material. For example, in the history of English, a process known as High Vowel Deletion deletes the vowels /i/ and /u/ when they follow a heavy syllable (VC, VV) but not a light syllable (V) (see Lass 1984a: §4.3.2). This leads to Old English forms like those in (127) (vowel length is indicated by a macron):

(127)
		singular	plural	
	a.	scip	scipu	'ship'
		lim	limu	'limb'
	b.	word	word	'word'
		land	land	'land'
		bān	bān	'bone'
		sweord	sweord	'sword'

These nouns all belong to the same class, the *a*-stem neuter nouns, and would be expected to form their plural in the same way, i.e. by suffixation of /u/. However, /u/ can only be attached to a light syllable (a), while a heavy syllable (b) rejects the suffix. It appears then that, just as in the case of diminutive formation in Dutch, this morphological process places a constraint on the output. In terms of the skeletal tier, only three slots are permitted in the relevant part of the plural template. In moraic terms, these slots are dominated by two moras. If all the slots are already filled by the segmental material from the stem, the suffix cannot surface; otherwise, it does:

(128) a.   μ   μ   b.   μ   μ   c.   μ   μ
             | | | | | |
          x x x x   x x x x   x x x x
          | | | | | | | | ○ | ⟍ | ○
          ○ ○ ○ ○   ○ ○ ○ ○   ○   ○
          ʃ i p + u   w o r d + u   b   a   n + u

If the suffix cannot be attached to a skeletal position, it is simply not realised.

3.8 Licensing and government

In (74) we proposed a structure for the syllable which consisted of the 'core' syllable (made up of the onset, rhyme, nucleus and coda) and a number of optional constituents: a prependix, an extrasyllabic position and an appendix. We observed that although this appears to be a highly complex structure, this complexity was largely due to the fact that languages allow a far greater range of possibilities at word edges than they do word-internally. Thus extra consonants can occur at the left or right periphery of words, leading to initial and final clusters that we do not find word-internally as syllable-initial or syllable-final clusters, respectively. However, we have not yet discussed the exact status of the constituents which we have identified as falling outside the core syllable, 'what they are' and how they are integrated into the prosodic structure.

It is obviously desirable to have a theory of syllable structure in which the number of possibilities is restricted as far as possible, consistent with what we actually find. Our representation in (74) is an attempt to do this, in that what does not form part of the core syllable is viewed as having a peripheral status in the syllable. Let us continue this approach by considering what the maximal complexity of the constituents within the core syllable might be.

Recall that in the analysis discussed above the onset constituent within the core syllable is maximally binary – in an apparent three-consonant onset, the first consonant is assigned to a prependix outside the core syllable. However, the rhyme constituent does not appear at first sight to display this property; the existence of what are sometimes referred to as **superheavy** (VVC) rhymes, as in English *pike*, suggests that both the rhyme node and its daughter, the nucleus, can branch in the same syllable. This is confirmed by the fact that we also find VVCC sequences, as in English *paint*; we saw in (76) that the /t/

occupies an extrasyllabic position, but that it seemed appropriate to syllabify the /n/ within the rhyme, yielding (129):

(129)   R   ESP

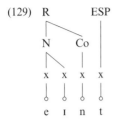

Nevertheless, some phonologists have claimed that even this structure should not be permitted within the syllable. Rather, on this view *all* syllabic constituents are maximally binary, so that a branching nucleus cannot be followed by a coda consonant. This claim is particularly associated with an approach to syllable structure that we discuss in this section, an approach usually referred to as **government phonology** (e.g. Kaye *et al.* 1985, 1990; Charette 1991; Harris 1994; Brockhaus 1995; Ritter 1995).

Notice that if we adopt the hypothesis that the rhyme is maximally binary, it is not just superheavy rhymes followed by an extrasyllabic constituent, such as that in *paint*, which must be accounted for in some other way. Word-final superheavies, such as the rhymes of English *rhyme* /raɪm/ and *pike* /paɪk/, are then also ill formed, as in (130), where both the Rhyme node and the Nucleus node branch:

(130)   R

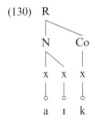

If we accept the claim that the rhyme is maximally binary, so that structures such as (129) for *paint* and (130) for *pike* are ill formed, how can these forms be accounted for?

One possibility might be to extend the notion of extrasyllabicity further than we have been doing up to now, so that any consonant following a branching nucleus would be extrasyllabic. This would give a structure like (131a) for *pike*, while *paint* would presumably have two extrasyllabic consonants, as in (131b):

(131) a.

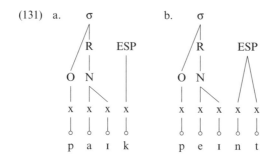

However, there do not at first sight appear to be independent reasons for treating these consonants as extrasyllabic, other than a desire to restrict all syllabic constituents to a maximum of two daughters. Why, then, should we want to claim that a structure with a branching nucleus within a branching rhyme is ill formed in any case?

As we have already noted, strings of the type under discussion, superheavies, are typically restricted to word-final position, as illustrated by the Dutch forms in (132). Those in (132a) are well formed, while the strings in (132b), with the same superheavy syllables in non-word-final position, are ill formed:

(132) a. kameel /kaːmeːl/ 'camel'
           bordeel /bɔrdeːl/ 'brothel'
       b. *meelka /meːlkaː/
           *deelbor /deːlbɔr/[40]

Given that these superheavy syllables are typically restricted to final position, an appeal to the notion of extrasyllabicity does not seem out of place. In other words, the final consonant of a superheavy syllable falls outside the core syllable proper.

However, at this point we should ask why constraints of this type exist. In other words, what is it about final position (indeed any 'edge' position) that allows so many of the 'normal' restrictions on syllable structure to be relaxed? We approach this question by considering some of the basic claims made within the model of government phonology.

Government phonology provides a much more restrictive view of the syllable than other theories of syllable structure. As we have seen, central to the model is the claim that *all* syllabic constituents are maximally binary. This claim, then, holds not just of the onset, but also of the rhyme, as we have suggested above. However, up to this point we have been merely *stipulating* that all

---

[40] The forms in (132b) would be well formed if they were compounds, i.e. if a boundary intervened between the two syllables, e.g. *keelpijn* 'sore throat'. However, this does not affect the point being made.

branching is maximally binary. In government phonology, this principle is not a stipulation, but follows from the notion of **licensing**, which, as we shall see, gives us a formal means of excluding structures which apparently violate binary branching.

This concept of licensing is similar, but not identical to, that discussed in §3.7.2. In government phonology, the dependent within any domain must be **licensed** by the presence of the head. Within a syllabic constituent such as the onset or the nucleus, licensing relations are from left to right, i.e. constituents are **head-initial**, so that in (133a), /t/ licenses /r/ within the onset, and /e/ licenses /ɪ/ within the nucleus, while in (133b), /f/ licenses /l/ within the onset, and /æ/ licenses /p/ within the rhyme:

(133) a.   b.

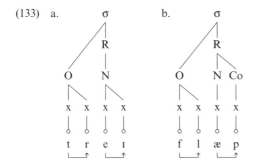

We indicate licensing as in (133).

Crucially, one further restriction on licensing is proposed: it holds only between strictly adjacent skeletal positions (the **locality** condition; Harris 1994: 156). Thus in (133b) /f/ licenses the adjacent skeletal position /l/, and /æ/ licenses /p/, as we have seen. Consider now potential superheavy rhymes such as those of *band* and *pike*:

(134) a.   b.

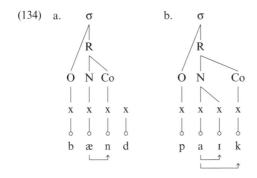

In (134a), the /d/ cannot be syllabified in the first syllable, as the /n/ occupies the coda position. In (134b), we have a head-initial branching nucleus node, so that the first vowel licenses the second. However, we also have a head-initial branching rhyme node. The head (the first vowel) should therefore license the other skeletal position in the rhyme, /k/. These two skeletal positions are not strictly adjacent (the second vowel intervenes), and so the structure is ill formed.

This version of government phonology, then, allows only the syllabic structures in (135):

(135) a. O   b. R   c. R

The three constituents, onset, rhyme and nucleus, are the only ones found in government phonology. Although we have included a coda node in (135c), this is not in accord with standard practice in government phonology. As we have seen, a coda can never be complex, and so it is argued that there is no need to have a constituent corresponding to it. The 'coda' position is generally referred to in government phonology as the **rhymal adjunct**; in what follows, however, we will continue to employ the term 'coda'.[41] Government phonology also claims that there is no constituent corresponding to the traditional notion of the syllable, in that phonological processes have no need to refer to this node. In addition, there are no constraints holding between onset and rhyme which would lead us to consider the syllable to be some kind of phonological domain (recall the discussion of the motivation for the onset–rhyme division in §3.4). Nevertheless, it is argued, onsets and rhymes always occur together; we do not find an onset without a following rhyme, and vice versa. Again, in the remainder of this chapter, we will continue to use the term 'syllable' informally.

All this means that phonological sequences in government phonology have the following general shape:

(136)

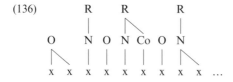

---

[41] In any case, it is not immediately clear that the fact that a particular category cannot branch, i.e. cannot be made up of two smaller units, necessarily means that it should not form a constituent, i.e. be part of a larger unit.

We have already seen that any dependent must be licensed by a head. If it is not so licensed, it cannot be realised. If we now return to the representation of a word like *pike*, the /k/ is apparently not licensed by any head:

(137)

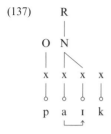

Recall that the vowel is not the licensor of a constituent containing /k/, as this would violate strict adjacency. How, then, can the /k/ be licensed?

Consider the following two principles, as formulated by Harris (1994: 160) (cf. also Kaye 1990: 311):[42]

(138) a. *Onset licensing*
          An onset head position must be licensed by a nuclear position.
       b. *Coda licensing*
          A rhymal adjunct position must be licensed by an onset position.

This type of licensing differs from the examples of constituent licensing which we saw above. Here the licensing relationship is *between* two constituents, rather than within constituents, as in the case of the onset, rhyme and nucleus above. **Interconstituent licensing** differs in one very important respect from constituent licensing; it goes from right to left, rather than from left to right.

The principle of onset licensing (138a) is intuitively a straightforward one: an onset is only an onset by virtue of the fact that it is followed by a nucleus. (This is why theories which recognise a syllabic constituent typically characterise the nucleus as the head and the onset as the dependent; cf. (63) above.) Thus a word like English *try* will have the licensing relations shown in (139):

(139)

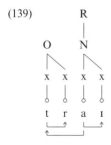

---

[42] Notice the term 'coda licensing' is used, in spite of the absence of a coda constituent in most versions of government phonology.

By left-to-right constituent licensing, /a/ licenses the non-head position in the nucleus, filled by /ɪ/; by right-to-left interconstituent licensing, it licenses the head position of the onset, filled by /t/, which, by left-to-right constituent licensing, itself licenses the non-head position in the onset, filled by /r/.

Although onset licensing appears to correspond to a traditionally accepted idea – that onsets are in some sense 'less important' than nuclei, coda licensing appears to embody a much more revolutionary concept. (138b) states that a coda consonant is licensed by the following onset, i.e. the head of the following constituent.

Government phonologists argue that this reflects the fact that there are very severe restrictions on the segmental material that can occupy the coda position. For example, Harris (1994: §2.4.4) shows that the sonority sequencing generalisation can be extended to give (140):

> (140)   In an optimal coda–onset cluster, the first consonant is no less sonorous than the second.

This, of course, is the mirror image of the sonority sequencing generalisation when applied to onsets, where the first consonant is generally less sonorous than the second. In other words, coda–onset sequences typically display rising sonority; the two elements of an onset constituent display falling sonority. Thus we find well-formed coda–onset sequences in monomorphemic items such as English *candy*, *custard*, *kilter*, *perfume*, etc., but not **cadny*, **cutsard*, **kitler*, **pefrume*. Furthermore, as Harris notes, languages may display restrictions on the well-formed clusters which can occur; frequently only the sequence sonorant–obstruent is permitted.

There are also other further respects in which the coda is influenced by the following onset. Thus we saw in Chapter 1 that in an English nasal coda + stop onset sequence, the nasal had to be homorganic with the stop, to give *camber*, *canter*, *canker* ([ŋk]), etc.

This behaviour leads Harris to subcategorise the various examples of licensing (both constituent and interconstituent) into two sub-types. In the case of onsets, nuclei and coda–onset sequences (often referred to as 'interludes'), he argues, we have to do with **governing domains**, in which there is a **government** relation between the two segments, i.e. between the head and the dependent. Government, then, is a sub-type of licensing. Within these governing domains, 'quite particular phonotactic restrictions are . . . in force'. In other words, the range of possibilities in the dependent position is at least partially determined by the head. We have already seen examples of this in the coda–onset domain. In the onset domain, as we have also seen, rising sonority must be respected, there is often a minimal 'sonority distance' required (i.e.

the dependent must not be too close in terms of sonority to the head) and there may be restrictions involving homorganicity (English does not allow */tl-/, for example). Within the nucleus, the second vowel is either identical to the first (long vowels) or, in the case of a diphthong, must often be one of a restricted set. RP English is typical in this respect in only allowing /ɪ ʊ ə/ as the second element of a diphthong. On the basis of these facts, Harris (1994: 168) characterises the structures in (141) as being governing domains:

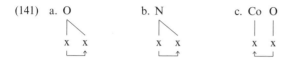

(141) a. O   b. N   c. Co O

Thus the head of an onset can be simultaneously the governor in two domains, as shown in (141a) and (c).

Such phonotactic restrictions do not hold between the elements of the other licensing domains, however. As we showed above, there are typically no restrictions between the content of an onset and the following rhyme. Similarly, the *content* of the coda is independent of the nucleus, although there may, of course, be restrictions associated with syllable weight. Thus the two domains in (142) are licensing domains, but not governing domains:

(142) a.   R   b. R

In the light of these considerations, a word like *brandy* will have the structure in (143):

(143)

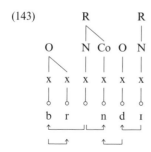

non-governing licensing domains
governing domains

It will be noticed that the /n/ is licensed twice, once by the nucleus of the first syllable, and once by the onset of the second syllable, but is governed only by the onset of the second syllable, from which it gets its specification for place of articulation.

How can this theory account for syllables which apparently have more than two elements in the rhyme? We saw in (137) that *pike* has a branching nucleus, so that the final /k/ cannot be syllabified into the rhyme, because there is no following onset. However, government phonology argues that this consonant in fact displays none of the typical properties of a coda consonant. Normal coda consonants, as we have just seen, are highly restricted in their occurrence; peripheral final consonants, on the other hand, are free in their occurrence: there are few or no restrictions on which consonants can occur in this position. As Harris (1994: 72) observes: 'If the word-final consonant of a V(V)C or VCC cluster were syllabified in coda position, it would be reasonable to expect it to display the same kind of distributional characteristics as morpheme-internal coda consonants. In fact, it does not. If anything, it behaves just like a morpheme-internal onset.'

This point of view gains further support from a consideration of word-final superheavy VCC syllables, such as *band*. As we have seen in (134), the /d/ cannot be syllabified into the rhyme here. Up to now, we have been arguing that it must be extrasyllabic, but we are now in a position to make a much more specific claim. The relationship between the nasal and the final stop in *band, camp, rank*, etc., is exactly the same as that between the nasal and the stop in *brandy, camber, conker*, etc. Homorganicity is required in both cases. In words like *brandy* we associated this requirement with the fact that the nasal was the non-head in a governing domain of which the head was the onset of the following syllable, filled by the stop. Government phonology argues that exactly the same analysis is appropriate for *band*, i.e. the /d/ is considered not to be 'extrasyllabic', but to form the onset of a following syllable. Similarly, in *pike* the /k/, which shows all the distributional properties of an onset, is syllabified accordingly, to give (144):

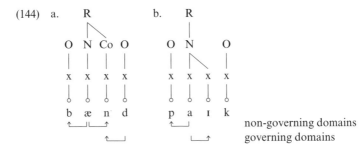

However, the representations in (144) are still ill formed, in that the onset consonant must be licensed by a following nucleus, as determined by onset licensing. An *empty* nucleus must be assigned, to give the structures in (145):

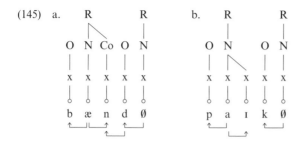

Government phonology claims that this approach also allows an account of the fact that English *kept* /kɛpt/ has a short vowel, while *keep* /kiːp/ has a long vowel. Kaye (1990) attributes this difference to the effects of the coda licensing principle given as (138b). In *keep* the /p/ cannot be syllabified into the coda of the first syllable, because there is no following onset to license it. Therefore, it must itself form the onset. In *kept*, however, the onset /t/ licenses the coda consonant /p/, so that the /p/ can be syllabified into the rhyme of the first syllable. Because the /p/ is in the rhyme, the vowel must shorten, thus avoiding a rhymal structure VVC, which, as we have seen, is ill formed. *Kept*, then, has the same structure as *band* in (145a), and *keep* the same as *pike* in (145b).[43]

Further evidence for treating word-final postvocalic consonants as onsets can be found from various phonological regularities which treat word-internal rhymes and word-final rhymes alike, but only if the final consonant of the word-final rhyme is ignored. This again suggests that this final consonant is in fact the onset of a syllable with an empty nucleus. Thus, as we saw in §3.4.1, the English Main Stress Rule, as originally formulated by Chomsky and Halle (1968), places main stress on the penultimate syllable of a noun, unless that syllable is not heavy (VC or VV). Thus we find *agenda* with a heavy (VC) penult, but *America*, with a light penult (V), which therefore rejects stress. However, for verbs, the target syllable for stress is the final one, rather than the penultimate, so that *maintain* and *collapse* have final stress, whereas the final syllable of *astonish* rejects stress. Here, apparently, the distinction between heavy and light is VCC/VVC vs VC, rather than VC/VV vs V. If the

---

[43] This analysis holds for 'root-level' suffixation, in which the root + suffix are considered to be a single phonological domain, and therefore subject to the normal phonotactic restrictions on syllabic constituency. Suffixation may also occur at 'word level', in which case the sequence of root and suffix is considered to form two domains, so that otherwise ill-formed sequences are tolerated. The fact that the past tense of *seep* is [siːpt], not *[sɛpt], shows that here word-level suffixation is involved.

final consonant is ignored, of course, then our definition of light and heavy syllables in English is the same for both nouns and verbs, as we would expect. In the government approach, word-final consonants are onsets, and so the relevant syllables have the same shape as their non-word-final counterparts.

We have seen that government phonologists argue that branching within syllabic constituents is maximally binary. However, although the evidence for interpreting the final consonant in VVC and VCC rhymes as the onset of a following syllable is clear, it is difficult to see that *both* consonants in a VVCC rhyme such as that of *sound* or of *flounder* should be assigned to a following onset. The relationship between the /n/ and the /d/ here is the same as in words such as *band* and *brandy*, where we treated the nasal as a coda (more correctly, a rhymal adjunct). This leads Harris (1994: §2.4.4) to allow structures in which both the rhyme node and the nucleus node branch, but only for superheavy rhymes such as that in *flounder*. This is shown in (146):

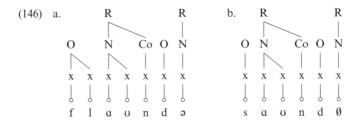

Harris notes that codas in superheavy rhymes are subject to restrictions which are much more severe than in heavy syllables. He notes that the following holds for English superheavies:

(147) a. The coda position is restricted to a sonorant or a fricative (e.g. *colt, poultry, paste, pastry*).
b. A coda sonorant is unable to support a distinctive place contrast.
c. In the case of (b), the favoured place category determined by the following onset consonant is coronal.

These restrictions, then, can be argued to stem from the complexity of the syllabic structure required to characterise superheavy rhymes.

3.8.1 *Empty positions*

It is evident from the above that the strategy adopted by government phonology means that 'syllables' containing rhymes with more segments than are permitted by the various principles discussed above are treated as sequences of at least two onsets and rhymes, with the resulting presence of empty positions. Much the same approach is utilised for the analysis of what we referred to as prependices in §3.4.2. These are again interpreted as belonging to a different onset/rhyme sequence, as in (148), the representation for German *Spruch* /ʃprʊx/ 'motto' proposed by Brockhaus (1999) (see also Kaye 1996):

(148)

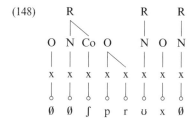

Here the initial /ʃ/ is assigned to the coda position of a syllable preceding the branching onset /pr/.

It is clear that the principles adopted by government phonology lead to a sharp reduction in the types of 'syllables' that are recognised in the model, and, as such, is to be preferred over less restrictive accounts. However, this comes at the cost of the introduction of what at first sight appears to be a very powerful, and apparently unrestricted, theoretical device, the empty position.

Is the motivation for the introduction of empty positions merely theory-internal, or are there indications to be found that they correspond to anything outside the model? An obvious sign of the latter state of affairs would be if we can find alternations between the empty position and some realisation.

One such example involves word-internal clusters, and therefore provides evidence for the recognition of empty positions in word-internal as well as word-peripheral contexts. The English word *empty* /ɛmptɪ/ will have the following representation in government phonology (we indicate only those licensing domains which are relevant):

(149)

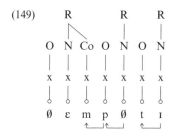

Here the /p/ cannot be assigned to the rhyme of the first syllable, which already contains a rhymal adjunct (/m/). Rather, the /p/ functions as the onset of the second syllable, which licenses the /m/ in the coda of the first syllable, by the coda licensing principle in (138b). Now the /t/ cannot be syllabified into the onset of the second syllable, as /pt/ is an ill-formed onset in English. As a result, we must propose an empty nucleus in the second syllable, which licenses the /p/ in the onset, by (138a). Finally, /t/ is syllabified into the onset of the third syllable, where it is licensed by the /ɪ/, rather than into the coda of the second syllable.

Interestingly, one possible realisation of *empty* is [ɛmpətɪ], where the normally empty position is filled by the default vowel, the schwa, thus providing some degree of independent evidence for the postulation of the empty nucleus.[44] There are other phenomena, too, in which similar realisations are found. We have already observed that intervocalic heterosyllabic clusters typically show falling sonority: e.g. *al.pa*, but not *ap.la*, whereas onset clusters typically consist of less sonorous followed by more sonorous consonants, so that English *play*, *brown* and *throat* are well formed, while *lpay*, *rbown* and *rthoat* are not. By constituent government, a coda is governed, and hence licensed, by the following onset; but if the second consonant is more sonorous than the first both consonants are syllabified into the onset.[45] However, this is not possible in a language which does not allow branching onsets, but does allow intervocalic sequences of two consonants displaying rising sonority. In such a case, the two consonants must be assigned to successive onsets, with an intervening empty rhyme:

(150)

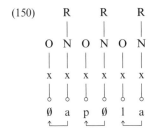

where, by onset licensing (138a), the onset of each syllable is licensed by the following nucleus.

Support for structures like (150) can be found in the fact that vowel–zero alternations are much more common between the members of ill-formed medial clusters (i.e. those with rising sonority) than of well-formed clusters. Thus we do not find, for example, English [faɪndɪŋ] *finding* alternating with *[faɪnədɪŋ], but we do, as Harris (1994: 192) points out, find alternations such

---

[44] The schwa here is normally interpreted as the realisation of the neutral feature @ (cf. §2.5).

[45] Recall from §2.6 that in the version of government phonology discussed by Harris (1994: ch. 4) the notion of sonority is replaced by one of segmental complexity. We do not consider this further here, except to remark that there is a fairly direct inverse relation between complexity and sonority: more sonorant consonants are less complex than less sonorant ones (see also Harris 1990). This in turn leads to a more general constraint on the government relation (Harris 1994: 170), such that the head in any construction is never more complex than the segment which it governs.

as [fɪdlɪŋ]/[fɪdəlɪŋ] *fiddling* corresponding to [fɪdəl] *fiddle* (cf. also words such as *athlete*, with the realisations [æθliːt] and [æθəliːt]).

Harris analyses the *fiddle/fiddling* type of case by assuming that the representation of *fiddle* contains three syllables:

(151)

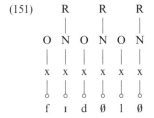

while *fiddling* will have the representation in (152):

(152)

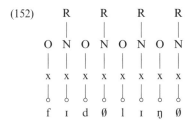

In (151), the empty nucleus of the second syllable *must* be filled by segmental material, i.e. schwa, while in (152) this is optional. We return presently to the question of why this should be.

Similar evidence can be cited to support the existence of **empty onset positions**. We find cases parallel to the alternation in *empty*, but this time involving the onset, typically in cases of hiatus. Compare the English and Dutch forms for *mayonnaise*, viz. /meɪəneɪz/ and /maːjoːnɛːzə/ (or its common abbreviation /maːjoː/). In the Dutch form the onset is filled by a glide, while English permits the onset to remain empty.

Some languages indeed reject empty onsets altogether at the phonetic level; German, for example, is generally claimed to insert a glottal stop wherever the onset is phonologically empty, so that a word like *Ende* /ɛndə/ 'end' is realised as [ʔɛndə]:

(153)

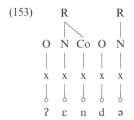

Analyses like these raise a general question which we have not yet addressed. How do we constrain the occurrence of empty positions in the syllable? In other words, why does the second syllable of (151) (/fɪdØlØ/) *require* that the underlyingly empty position be filled phonetically, while the empty position of the second syllable of (152) (/fɪdØlɪŋØ/) may remain empty? More generally, what is to stop us proposing surface representations like (154)?

(154)

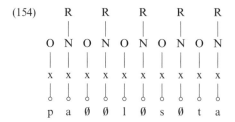

The relevant constraint here is that an empty nucleus must be followed by a filled nucleus, or, more precisely, by a nucleus that is 'audible'; we will see below that 'being audible' does not necessarily mean that features are actually associated to the skeletal position. Whether or not a language permits a *final* empty nucleus is a matter of whether it allows what in other models are referred to as word-final coda consonants. Languages which do allow word-final consonants have final empty nuclei which license the consonant in the onset (cf. the representation of *pike* in (145b)), while those which allow only 'open syllables' do not allow final empty nuclei. This is a matter of parameter setting, and must be specified for each language.

In formal terms, a *non-final* empty nucleus must be licensed by a following nucleus, under what is referred to as **proper government**. The proper governor, i.e. the second of two nuclei, must not itself be empty. This principle, then, explains why the second syllable of *fiddle* in (151) must be realised with [ə]; the final nucleus is itself empty, and so cannot license a preceding empty nucleus. On the other hand, the nucleus of the third syllable in *fiddling* (/fɪdØlɪŋØ/) in (152) is filled, so that the empty nucleus in the second syllable is properly governed, and therefore need not be filled.

Notice that the principle is not that a rhyme with segmental content *must* be preceded by a rhyme that is empty. Rather, what the theory demands is that if an empty rhyme occurs it must be followed by a rhyme that is filled. Kaye *et al.* (1990: 219) formalise the principle governing the phonetic interpretation of empty positions as the **Empty Category Principle**, formulated as (155):[46]

---

[46] For a reinterpretation of the ECP, see Rowicka (1999).

(155)   *Empty Category Principle* (ECP)
A position may be uninterpreted phonetically if it is properly governed.

They discuss various examples of vowel–zero alternations in Moroccan Arabic which illustrate this principle:

(156)   a.   tan kti̵b   'I write'
        b.   tan ki̵tbuː   'we write'

In (156), the vowel [i̵], a high central vowel, is the phonetic realisation of an empty nucleus.

Compare now (157a) and (b), the initial structures for (156a) and (b):

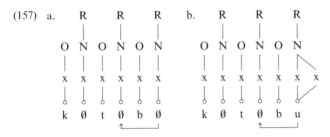

The empty nucleus of the second syllable of (157a) must be given phonetic interpretation, as it precedes another empty nucleus, just as in the case of *fiddle*. However, the plural form involves suffixation of /uː/, so that the empty nucleus of the second syllable is properly governed by a filled nucleus, and therefore need not be realised. This yields the forms [kØti̵bØ] and [kØtØbuː], respectively. The singular form is now well formed, as the nucleus of the second syllable is filled, and can therefore properly govern the nucleus of the first syllable, as in (158a). However, the plural form is still ill formed, because the empty nucleus of the second syllable cannot properly govern the empty nucleus of the first, which must therefore receive phonetic content:

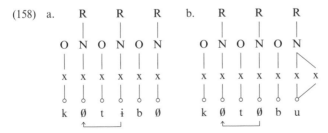

The first nucleus of (b) is now filled by [i̵], to give the surface form [ki̵tbu]. The constraint on empty positions plays a role in accounting for many paradigmatic alternations of this sort.

The ECP may be overridden by other factors. Charette (1990) discusses apparent schwa-deletion processes in French, such as that illustrated by the alternations in (159):

(159) semaine [səmɛn] ~ [sØmɛn] 'week'
       ennemi   [ɛnəmi] ~ [ɛnØmi] 'enemy'

The alternations here are in accord with the ECP, with all the empty positions being properly governed by a following filled nucleus. However, the form in (160) does not show the same alternation:

(160) secret [səkʀɛ] ~ *[sØkʀɛ] 'secret'

Here proper government appears to be obeyed, as indicated in (161):

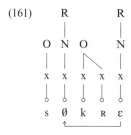

(161)

Charette attributes the failure to allow the empty position in (161) to surface to the fact that a 'governing domain' intervenes, i.e. a domain containing a governing segment, in this case the head of the complex onset. Thus the presence of an onset cluster means that the ECP does not apply in *secret*, whereas it does apply in *semaine*, allowing the first nucleus not to be realised.

Let us consider finally a further case involving vowel–zero alternations, this time from the phonology of Dutch. Dutch has what is traditionally described as an optional process of schwa epenthesis between a liquid and a – in traditional terms tautosyllabic – consonant:

(162) help   [hɛlp] ~ [hɛləp]   'help'
       worp   [wɔrp] ~ [wɔrəp]   'throw'
       balk   [bɑlk] ~ [bɑlək]   'beam'
       snurk [snœrk] ~ [snœrək] 'snore'

However, if the final consonant is a coronal obstruent, the schwa is not found:

(163) vilt   [vɪlt]   ~ *[vɪlət]   'felt'
      hard   [hɑrt]   ~ *[hɑrət]   'heart'
      hars   [hɑrs]   ~ *[hɑrəs]   'resin'
      arts   [ɑrts]   ~ *[ɑrəts]   'doctor'

How can we account for this in government terms? The forms in (162), which permit the vowel–zero alternation, must have a structure in which both the final consonants are onsets:

(164)

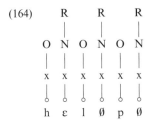

This structure provides an empty position – the nucleus of the second syllable – which can be filled by segmental material under proper government. However, it is not clear how government phonology would account for the realisation without schwa, which would apparently involve a violation of the ECP, as two successive nuclei would then remain empty.[47] One possibility is that the /l/ in *help* is reinterpreted as the nucleus of the second syllable, as in (165):

(165)

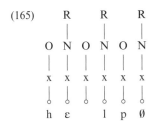

The phonetic plausibility of this is confirmed by the speech of one of the authors, for whom postvocalic /l/ is vocalised.

The forms involving final coronals appear to require a different representation. Observe that we are dealing here with homorganicity between the two consonants.[48] Recall that homorganicity between a sonorant and a following consonant is a classic situation in coda licensing; the place of articulation of, say, a nasal and a following stop is not independent. We suggest that *vilt* has the representation in (166):

[47] This difficulty does not arise when suffixation is involved: a form like *helpen* 'to help' has a filled final nucleus, which means that both the realisations [hɛlØpə] and [hɛləpə] are in accord with the ECP.
[48] We are assuming here that /r/ in Dutch is at least phonologically coronal.

(166)

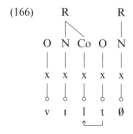

i.e. the structure contains only two syllables, with no empty position between the /l/ and the /t/, and therefore no possibility of an alternation with a form with an epenthetic schwa. Thus /l/ is licensed by /t/, the onset of the second syllable.

Interestingly, if the liquid is followed by a sonorant consonant, the form with schwa always seems to be possible, irrespective of whether the sonorant is coronal, as shown in (167):

(167) helm [hɛlm] ~ [hɛləm] 'helmet'
       arm   [ɑrm] ~ [ɑrəm]   'arm'
       kern [kɛrn] ~ [kɛrən] 'kernel'

This may reflect the presence of a 'minimal sonority distance' constraint in Dutch, as proposed by Harris as a language-particular restriction on the elements which are involved in some governing relationship. In turn, this can be associated with a more traditional notion, the **syllable contact law** (e.g. Vennemann 1988: 40), which, in government terms, states that not only do coda–onset domains involve falling sonority, but the sonority distance between them should be as great as possible. Thus the optimal coda–onset sequence is a highly sonorant consonant followed by a plosive. In the case of Dutch, an onset can license a homorganic sonorant coda only if there is sufficient sonority distance between them (however this is to be measured; in Harris's approach this is formulated in terms of relative complexity). Liquids and nasals are very close in terms of sonority, and so, even if the two consonants are homorganic, the second one cannot license the first, and so the syllabification must be as in (164), with an empty nucleus intervening between the two (onset) consonants, thereby allowing schwa 'insertion'.

This analysis is supported by the fact that, although Dutch allows the final sequence [rn] (*kern*), it does not permit either [rl] or [ln]. This suggests that the sonority distance between these consonants is too small to allow the second to license the first, and so they can only occur with an intervening vowel. This is illustrated by the forms in (168), where we contrast Dutch forms with their cognates in English and German, which do not display this restriction:[49]

(168) *Dutch*   *German*   *English*
      Karel [kaːrəl]   Karl [karl]   Charles [ʧɑrlz]
      kerel [keːrəl]   Kerl [kerl]   churl   [ʧɜrl]

Thus the different sonority distances between the members of the pairs [rl], [rn] and [rt] is reflected by their behaviour in Dutch: [rl] never forms a licensing domain, [rn] does so optionally and [rt] always involves coda licensing.

3.9 Summary

In this chapter we have considered phonological structure above the level of the segment. After briefly indicating in §3.1 that we can establish a prosodic hierarchical structure which corresponds to sentences, motivated among other things by phonological processes which have the various layers of this hierarchy as their domain of application, we focused in §3.2 on the first layer in this structure, the syllable. The need for a syllabic domain in phonological representations was motivated intuitively (by appealing to the awareness that native speakers have of syllabification) but also, and more firmly, in terms of restrictions on well-formedness (phonotactic constraints) and processes that refer to the syllabic domain or to its edges. In §§3.4–3.5 we reviewed a number of theories which differ in their view of the internal structure of the syllable. We concentrated particularly on two approaches, onset–rhyme theory and mora theory. The way in which strings of segments can be organised in syllables was examined in detail within the context of the former theory, and we also addressed the issue of how to represent cross-linguistic differences in syllabic organisation in terms of the setting of a number of parameters. Having established that syllable structure forms part of the phonological representation, we proceeded to investigate the relation between the terminal position of the syllable structure and the featural structures that represent the content of segments, and showed that this relation is autosegmental. This allowed us to show in §3.6 that a particular set of features can associate to more than one syllabic position, giving us a representation of phonological length. A further consequence of syllabic positions and segmental content being independent of each other is that one can exist without the other. In

---

[49] We are assuming here dialects of English which are rhotic, and dialects of German in which the /r/ is not vocalised. Notice that in Scots English, for example, [ə] is possible in these forms, as in the realisations [ʧɑrəlz] and [ʧʌrəl].

§3.7 we discussed various examples of this phenomenon. §3.8 was concerned with an interpretation of onset–rhyme theory within the theory of government phonology, in which the occurrence of syllabic positions is subject to their contracting appropriate licensing and government relations. Within this approach to phonological structure, we discussed further aspects of syllabic organisation and syllable-based processes such as vowel–zero alternations. In this model, syllabic positions crucially enter into a head–dependency relation, which plays an active role in characterising constraints and processes.

3.10 Further reading

Phenomena that involve the relevance of phonological properties to strings of segments (§3.1) are widely discussed in Firthian phonology (cf. §1.5) and in autosegmental phonology. The spreading of nasality and other features over larger domains is considered in van der Hulst and Smith (1982a). A variety of cases involving spreading of nasality are analysed in Piggott (1988) and Piggott and van der Hulst (1997). On *Raddoppiamento Sintattico*, see e.g. Napoli and Nespor (1979), Nespor and Vogel (1982), Kaisse (1985) and Loporcaro (1996). The prosodic hierarchy is discussed by Nespor and Vogel (1986) and Selkirk (1984a, 1995). On sonority, see Hankamer and Aissen (1974), Farmer (1979), Kiparsky (1981), Dogil (1988), Clements (1990), Ohala (1992), K. D. Rice (1992), Zec (1994, 1995a) and Basbøll (1999). Proposals for 'strength hierarchies', in which the notion of strength is related to sonority, are made by Lass (1971) and Foley (1977).

Anderson (1969), Vennemann (1972), Anderson and Jones (1974), Hooper (1976), Kahn (1976), Selkirk (1982) and Blevins (1995) provide arguments for the need to incorporate syllable structure in phonological representations (§3.2). See also the papers in Bell and Hooper (1978). Awedyk (1975) provides a history of the concept of the syllable. For views on syllable structure (§3.3), see Steriade (1982), Clements and Keyser (1983), Harris (1983), van der Hulst (1984), Levin (1985), van der Hulst and Ritter (1999).

Onset–rhyme theory (§3.4) and rhyme structure (§3.4.1) are discussed in Fudge (1969, 1987), Cairns and Feinstein (1982), Lapointe and Feinstein (1982), Selkirk (1982), Davis (1985, 1990), Kaye *et al.* (1985) and Dell (1995). For proposals involving syllable appendices (§3.4.2), see Fudge (1969). Blevins (1995) provides an overview of syllable typology parameters. On syllabification (§3.4.3), see Pulgram (1970), Kahn (1976), McCarthy (1979), Selkirk (1982, 1984b), Steriade (1982), Dell and Elmedlaoui (1985), Anderson (1987), Clements (1990), Archangeli (1991) and Noske (1992). On ambisyllabicity, see van der Hulst (1985), Borowsky (1986) and Rubach (1996). Jones (1976) analyses a number of processes of consonant deletion and epenthesis in the history of English as involving the creation of ambisyllabicity within the foot. See also Jones (1989).

Discussions of mora theory (§3.5) can be found in Hyman (1985, 1992), Hock (1986), Hayes (1989a), Kubozono (1989), Tranel (1991), Pulleyblank (1994) and Zec (1995b).

On the representation of length, syllable weight, syllable quantity and the need for a representation incorporating the skeletal tier (§3.6), see Newman (1972), McCarthy (1979), Árnason (1980), Steriade (1982), Anderson (1984), Hyman (1985), Schein and Steriade (1986), Hayward (1988), Lahiri and Koreman (1988), Tranel (1991), Davis (1994), Hayes (1994), Broselow (1995), Piggott (1995), Broselow *et al.* (1997) and Rosenthall and van der Hulst (1999).

The notion that syllabic positions can persist independently of segmental content (§3.7) is presented in Clements and Keyser (1983). English /r/ (§3.7.1) is discussed in Wells (1982), Harris (1994: ch. 5) and McMahon *et al.* (1994). For discussions of liaison in French (§3.7.2), see Klausenburger (1978), Piggott and Singh (1985), Durand (1986b), Tranel (1987: ch. 11) and Charette (1991). Klausenburger (1977), Clements and Keyser (1983) and Tranel (1995) give accounts of *h-aspiré* (§3.7.3). On compensatory lengthening (§3.7.4), see the papers in Wetzels and Sezer (1986), as well as the papers by De Chene and Anderson (1979), Hock (1986), Hayes (1989a), Schmidt (1992) and Bickmore (1995).

On licensing in phonology (§3.8), see Itô (1986), Goldsmith (1989, 1990), Steriade (1995, 1996), Piggott (1997). For a treatment within Optimality Theory, see Itô *et al.* (1995). Licensing within a government-based model is dealt with by Kaye (1990) and Harris (1994, 1997). Kaye *et al.* (1985, 1990), Charette (1991), Brockhaus (1995), van der Hulst and Ritter (1999) and Rowicka (1999) are other works dealing with government in phonology. On empty positions, see Anderson (1982) and Giegerich (1981, 1985), as well as many of the works in government phonology cited above.

The acquisition of syllable structure is dealt with in Ingram (1978), Fikkert (1994) and Macken (1995). For a historical perspective, see Árnason (1980), Murray and Vennemann (1983), Lass (1987: ch. 3), Vennemann (1988), Jacobs (1989), Ritt (1994) and Kiparsky (1995). On the application of the notion of the syllable to sign language phonology, see Wilbur (1990, 1993), Perlmutter (1992), Brentari (1995, 1999).

There is an extensive literature on the interface between syntax and phonology with respect to prosodic structure; see for example the papers in Inkelas and Zec (1990), as well as Inkelas and Zec (1995) and Selkirk (1995).

4
Feet and words

4.1 Introduction: stress and accent

In dictionary entries we often find a symbol, adjacent to or above one of the letters of a word, to indicate the location of what is usually referred to as 'stress'. If a phonetic or phonemic transcription is given in addition to the orthographic form, the symbol is often a small vertical line, placed before the stressed syllable, as in (1a), or an accent on the vowel, as in (1b) (in this book we have been using the system in (1a), and will continue to do so in this chapter):

(1) a. /ˈdʌndʒən/   dungeon   b. /dʌ́ndʒən/
         /ˈmɛθədɪzəm/   methodism   /mɛ́θədɪzəm/
         /rɪˈbeljən/   rebellion   /rɪbéljən/

This is of course meant to provide information about the correct pronunciation of the word. Thus the syllable following the vertical line in (1a) is pronounced in such a way that it is perceptually more 'prominent' or 'salient' than the other syllables. In a language like English, this syllable is normally characterised as being stressed. The exact phonetic correlates of stress are notoriously difficult to establish.[1] For the moment let us simply assume that prominence is achieved by enhancing various phonetic properties, e.g. duration, amplitude and pitch.

However, there are other languages – of which Japanese is an often quoted example (see e.g. McCawley 1968, Haraguchi 1977) – in which the primary indicator of relative prominence is pitch alone, with other phonetic properties playing a much less important role. Such languages are often referred to as having **pitch accent**, while languages like English are called **stress-accent** languages. In the remainder of this chapter we will use the term **accent**, rather than stress, to characterise the abstract property of 'prominence', as indicated in (2):

---

[1] For detailed discussion, see e.g. Sluijter (1995), van Heuven and Sluijter (1996), Dogil (1999).

(2) *abstract*   accent
     property   (prominence)

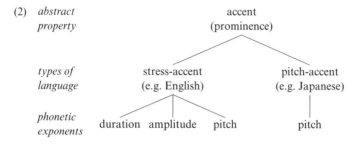

     types of   stress-accent   pitch-accent
     language   (e.g. English)   (e.g. Japanese)

     phonetic   duration amplitude   pitch   pitch
     exponents

In what follows we will not be concerned with the phonetic cues (or phonetic exponents) that signal the accent to the listener, whether these be in a pitch-accent or a stress-accent language.

The information provided by the symbol indicating the position of the accent is relevant to the pronunciation of all syllables of the word, even those that do not bear accent. In English, unaccented syllables are typically pronounced with a lax manner of articulation, leading to vowel reduction. Indeed, in English, the least accented syllables usually contain schwa, the most reduced vowel, which is never found in accented syllables (cf. the discussion in §1.3.2). Thus, even though the accent symbol is associated with a particular syllable, it gives information about the accentuation of the entire word.[2] Each accent, then, signals the presence of one accentual **domain**. In many languages, this domain corresponds to the notion of 'word', so that between any two accents there must always be a word boundary. Accents may thus play a role in parsing sentences into words. In fact, in languages where the location of accent is on a fixed syllable in the word (e.g. the first one, as in Icelandic, Hungarian or Czech), the exact boundary between words can be uniquely determined. Thus, accent can have what is called a **demarcative** function.

The placement of accent may be predictable according to certain rules in the language, or it may be a non-predictable property of individual words, i.e. it has to be specified in the lexical representations of the morpheme or morphemes making up a particular word. Languages thus vary according to whether accent is rule-governed or lexical. Polish, for example, is generally considered to be a language in which the placement of accent is largely predictable, regularly falling on the penultimate syllable, as illustrated by the forms in (3) (from Halle and Vergnaud 1987a: 57):

(3) hipo'potam   NOM SG   'hippopotamus'
     hipopo'tam-a   GEN SG
     hipopotam-'ami   INSTR PL

---

[2] This property of accent is often called **culminativity**, i.e. 'each word or phrase has a single strongest syllable bearing the main stress' (Hayes 1995: 24).

Thus the addition of the suffix forces the accent to move from its original position in the unsuffixed stem to the penultimate syllable, even though this syllable may itself be part of the suffix, as in the disyllabic instrumental plural suffix *-ami*. Polish accent placement, then, is predictable on the basis of the position of the syllable in the word. On the other hand, Russian appears to need to have accent specified lexically for nearly all of the morphemes in the language, given the existence of pairs of words differing only in the placement of accent (cf. Revithiadou 1999: ch. 3):[3]

(4) 'glaski   'eyes (DIM)'   vs   glas'ki   'peepholes'
     'muka   'torture'   vs   mu'ka   'flour'

In many languages in which accent placement is predictable, it is the segmental make-up of the syllables which is relevant, as well as the position of a syllable in a word; thus heavy syllables (cf. the discussion in §3.4.1) are more likely to bear accent than light ones. In some languages, the accentual rules first seek out a heavy syllable, and only if they fail to find one in the relevant domain will accent be assigned to a syllable in a particular position in that domain (we return to this in §4.4.6).

Returning to our dictionary, we find that words consisting of a single syllable are usually not provided with an accent symbol; cf. e.g. disyllabic /ˈbraɪdɡruːm/ *bridegroom*, with an accent symbol, and monosyllabic /braɪd/ *bride*, without. Clearly, though, the single syllable of *bride* can bear accent, cf. (5a) and (b):

(5) a.   The 'bride a'greed.
     b.   The 'bridegroom a'greed.

In both cases the syllable /braɪd/ is accented.

To the user of the dictionary this causes no problems, since, in monosyllabic words such as these, the accent falls on the only syllable.[4] Notice that the fact that a monosyllable can bear accent suggests that 'being accented' is not purely a relative notion. This is confirmed by the fact that monosyllabic words in English can be divided into two categories, those in which the vowel is never reduced, and those which are typically – often obligatorily – pronounced with a reduced vowel, e.g. schwa. As we might expect, the words

---

[3] The situation in Russian is not as straightforward as we are suggesting here; various aspects of accentuation in the language are in fact rule-governed, especially in situations where the number of lexically determined accents in a single accentual domain is either none or two. See §4.3.1 for further discussion of this. Nevertheless, the basic characterisation of Russian as involving 'free' accent is generally accepted.

[4] In some languages, however, accented monosyllabic lexical items are not permitted. These languages demand that a phonological word be minimally disyllabic. We consider this phenomenon in §4.4.

which have full vowels are typically accented. This is the class often referred to as **lexical words**, e.g. nouns, adjectives and verbs. On the other hand, the words which normally occur only with reduced vowels are not generally accented, and belong to the closed class of **grammatical words**, such as determiners (e.g. /ðə/ *the*), pronouns (e.g. /ðəm/ *them*) and prepositions (e.g. /ət/ *at*, /tə/, /tʊ/ *to*).[5]

Any utterance, then, consists of a sequence of accented and non-accented syllables. In probably all languages, utterances have an **intonational melody** (Bolinger 1978), created by the way in which the pitch changes during the utterance. The manner in which the pitch movements that make up this melody are lined up with the words in the utterance provides information as to which parts of the utterance are 'important'. In addition, intonation contours also provide cues to the overall syntactic and semantic structure of utterances, i.e. the grouping of words into meaningful 'chunks'.

In English, perceptual salience is given to the important parts of an utterance by lining up the accented syllables of certain words with specific pitch targets or pitch movements. That is, an accented syllable may be realised on a higher pitch than the syllables surrounding it, so that the listener can easily identify it, or a constituent (a word or phrase) of which it forms part, as important. Such syllables are said to bear **pitch peaks**. Consider for example the sentence *Britten composed a lengthy symphony* /'brɪtən kəm'pəʊzd ə 'leŋθɪ 'sɪmfənɪ/. We might represent the structure of this sentence as in (6):

(6)   H
                             |
      Britten composed [A LENGTHY SYMPHONY]

Here the pitch peak, represented by H (for high tone), is associated with the first syllable of *symphony*.

Let us assume that the above utterance is an answer to the question *What did Britten compose?* The important constituent of the utterance is in this case *a lengthy symphony*. This constituent is **in focus** (indicated in (6) by capitalisation), and the pitch peak is lined up with the accented syllable in the constituent. Unaccented syllables are not normally candidates for bearing a pitch peak; for example, the second syllable of *symphony* (/fə/) in (6) could not bear a peak.

Note that there may be more than one accented syllable in an utterance which can potentially form the pitch peak. For example, if we align the H tone in *Britten composed a lengthy symphony* with the accented syllable of the

---

[5] For a discussion of the use of such reduced or **weak** forms in RP, see e.g. Collins and Mees (1996: §3.4).

word *lengthy*, the utterance would be more likely to be an answer to a question such as *What kind of symphony did Britten compose?* In the answer to this question, the constituent in focus is *lengthy*, as in (7) (as indicated, *a lengthy symphony* is still a constituent within the utterance, even though it is not in focus):

(7)
          H
          |

Britten composed [a [LENGTHY] symphony]

The rules governing the location of intonational pitch peaks in English are highly complex, and we will not discuss them here.[6] However, it is clear that, just as a lexical word contains one word accent, so a phrase contains one **phrasal accent**. Thus, a particular syllable may be accented with reference to several inclusive domains, as shown in (8), *Britten was a British composer* /ˈbrɪtən wəz ə ˈbrɪtɪʃ kəmˈpəʊzə/ (a possible answer to the question *Who was Benjamin Britten?*):

(8)
                 H   tone
                 |
    ×   ×   phrasal accent
    ×   ×   ×   word accent
[[Britten [was [A BRITISH COMPOSER]]]]

(We use × to denote the presence of an accent at the relevant level.) Here the first syllable of *Britten* and the second syllable of *composer* bear both word accents and phrasal accents – they are the heads of their respective phrasal constitutes. In addition, the second syllable of *composer* also bears the pitch peak of the entire utterance. The first syllable of *British*, however, has only word accent.

In (8) it is not possible to associate a high tone with either of the words that belong to closed classes (*was* and *a*), in order to show that the phrases of which they are part (*was a British composer* and *a British composer*, respectively) are in focus. Such words can only bear pitch peaks if they are themselves placed in focus, normally in some kind of contrastive context, as in (9):

(9)   H   H
       | |

I said [[A] lengthy symphony], not [[THE] lengthy symphony]

In this case, the unaccented word is not properly contained in a focused constituent, but rather itself forms a focused constituent. Notice that in such

---

[6] See e.g. Fuchs (1976), Gussenhoven (1984), Baart (1987), Selkirk (1984a, 1995) and Ladd (1996) for extensive discussion of these issues.

200

cases the word is pronounced with a full vowel, rather than in its normal weak form.

This strategy can also be used to place normally unaccented syllables in polysyllabic words in focus, yielding utterances such as *I didn't say Ham*[LET], *but Ham*[BURG]. Again the focused syllable will be pronounced with a full vowel, e.g. /hæm'lɛt/, not */hæm'lət/.

Up to now we have been assuming that only one syllable in polysyllabic words can be accented. However, this is clearly not the case; in many dictionaries a second symbol is used to indicate what is referred to as **secondary** or **non-primary** accent, as in (10a). Indeed, when words are sufficiently long, more than one non-primary accent can be found, as in (10b):

(10) a. /ˈhʌrəˌkeɪn/   hurricane
          /ˈtɛləˌfəʊn/   telephone
          /ˈkɒmpənˌseɪt/   compensate
          /ˌkɒmpənˈseɪʃən/   compensation
          /ˌɪnstrəˈmɛntəl/   instrumental
      b. /ˌɪnstrəˌmɛnˈtælɪtɪ/ instrumentality
          /ˌæpəˌlætʃɪˈkəʊlə/   Apalachicola

The indication of non-primary accents shows that not all syllables lacking the primary accent are felt to be equal in salience. In English, for example, syllables marked with a non-primary accent symbol typically do not display reduction to schwa. Rather, like primary accented vowels, they have a full-vowel quality.[7] Nevertheless, such syllables are less salient than primary accented syllables. Furthermore, they normally cannot be associated with pitch peaks, so that (11) is not possible:

(11)   H
                                        |
        *Britten composed [A LENGTHY ˌORAˈTORIO]

Although it is possible to distinguish degrees of non-primary accents, many lexicographical works do not distinguish between, for example, secondary accent and tertiary accent. However, Gimson, in his introduction to Jones (1977), observes: 'Many long polysyllabic words or compounds have two secondary stresses preceding the primary, e.g. "cross-examination, decontamination, mispronunciation, intercontinental", etc. Of the two secondary stresses, the first is the stronger . . . I have chosen to use ' for the first secondary, e.g. "cross-examination" /ˈkrɒsɪgˌzæmɪˈneɪʃn/ with the convention that

---

[7] Some words have alternative realisations, such as *hurricane*, whose final syllable may either bear secondary accent (/ˈhʌrəˌkeɪn/) or be unaccented (/ˈhʌrəkən/). The quality of the vowel depends on whether the syllable bears accent.

the first sign ' is subsidiary to the second ' (1977: xxiii)'. At least the distinction between primary and secondary accent is represented in most dictionaries.

In our discussion so far, we have suggested that the presence of an accent signals the presence of some domain. Thus a primary accent signals the word domain and a phrasal accent signals the phrasal domain, as shown in (8) above. Given this understanding of the notion accent, secondary accents must be properties of a domain that is smaller than the word. This non-primary accent domain is the **foot**, which we introduced in our discussion of the prosodic hierarchy in §3.1, and whose existence we will defend in §4.2. Words, then, may consist of more than one foot, so that *oratorio*, for example, has two foot accents, but only a single word accent, as in (12):

(12)   ×   word accent
     × ×   foot accent
     oratorio

The introduction of the foot allows us to extend the notation of (8) as in (13), for the phrase *a lengthy oratorio* /ə ˈlɛŋθɪ ˌɒrəˈtɔːrɪəʊ/:

(13)
```
                      H           tone
                      |
    ( ·           ×      )        phrasal accent
    (×    ) ( ·    ×      )        word accent
    (×   · ) (×   · ) (×   ·   · )  foot accent
    σ   σ   σ   σ   σ   σ   σ   σ
    ə  lɛŋ θɪ   ɒ  rə tɔː  rɪ  əʊ
```

At the lowest level syllables are gathered up into feet, by procedures which we consider in detail in the remainder of this chapter. This gives the three feet *lengthy*, *ora-* and *-torio* in (13). From now on we indicate the unaccented syllables in a foot with a dot, and the accented syllable with ×. Notice that the initial syllable of the phrase, *a*, remains unfooted, and is therefore not marked with a dot. This is typical of **clitics**, i.e. unaccented grammatical words which normally occur in their weak form, and which are not incorporated into the foot structure.[8] The feet are organised into phonological words; each word bears one word accent. At this level, we mark those foot accents which are not selected as word accents with dots. In general, then, × indicates the head of any domain; · its dependent sister or sisters. Finally, the words are combined to form the single phrase in (13). There being only one phrase, the phrasal accent also bears the pitch peak. The hierarchical structure in

---

[8] This is a simplification: clitics and, more generally, syllables with unaccentable vowels must ultimately be incorporated into the prosodic structure, either at the foot level or at higher levels (cf. Itô and Mester 1992; Peperkamp 1995; Nespor 1999).

(13) is referred to as a **bracketed metrical grid** (cf. Halle and Vergnaud 1987a; Hayes 1987, 1995). As we have already pointed out, each domain – foot, word and phrase – is characterised by a *single* accent, i.e. there is a single syllable which is 'stronger' than the others. This is the principle of culminativity mentioned in note 2 above.

We should notice that bracketed metrical grids are formally equivalent to tree structures incorporating headship, of the type which we used to characterise syllable structure in Chapter 3. The tree in (14) is equivalent to the grid in (13):

(14)

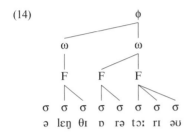

We use here the symbols for foot, word and phrase introduced in (9) in Chapter 3. In what follows, however, we will represent accent in terms of the grid.

4.2   Feet

The term **foot** is familiar from the study of the metre of traditional verse-forms. Verse of this sort makes use of a number of different foot types, among which the **trochee** and the **iamb** are the most familiar, and, indeed, the simplest. These two metrical foot types involve alternations between accented and unaccented syllables; syllables are thus grouped into pairs, and therefore form **binary** feet. Trochaic and iambic feet differ in their **prominence** or **salience** patterns; in trochaic feet, the first syllable is more prominent than the second, while in iambic feet the opposite relation holds. This is shown in (15), which uses the notation of Kiparsky (1977) and Hayes (1983):

(15)   a.   *Trochaic*

     s   w   s   w   s   w   s   w   s   w   s   w
     (σ   σ)(σ   σ)(σ   σ)(σ   σ)(σ   σ)(σ   σ)

    b.   *Iambic*

     w   s   w   s   w   s   w   s   w   s   w   s
     (σ   σ)(σ   σ)(σ   σ)(σ   σ)(σ   σ)(σ   σ)

Here 'w' denotes the weak syllable of a constituent, and 's' the strong syllable. Thus the trochaic pattern can be represented as in (16a) (from Longfellow's poem 'The Song of Hiawatha'), and the 'prototypical iambic pentameter' (from Shakespeare's *Richard III*; Kiparsky 1977: 189) as in (16b) (where ´ marks a strong syllable, and ˘ a weak syllable):

(16) a.   s   w   s   w   s w   s   w
      (Ón thĕ) (shóre stŏod) (Hí-ă)-(wá-thă)
      s   w   s   w   s   w   s   w
      (Túrned ănd) (wáved hĭs) (hánd ăt) (pár-tĭng)
    b.   w s   w   s   w   s   w   s   w   s
      (Thĕ lí)-(ŏn dý)-(ĭng thrúst)-(ĕth fórth) (hĭs páw)

In verse traditions such as these, the number of syllables in a foot is usually fixed; in the case of trochaic and iambic patterns, there is exactly one accented and one unaccented syllable. In patterns with more than two syllables, the foot will still have only one *accented* syllable – as we have seen, the foot domain is defined as containing one accented syllable – but more than one unaccented syllable. Thus a **dactylic** pattern is shown in (17):

(17)   *Dactylic*
      s   w   w   s   w   w   s   w   w   s   w   w
      (σ   σ   σ) (σ   σ   σ) (σ   σ   σ) (σ   σ   σ)

This pattern is illustrated in (18) (from Ralph Hodgson's 'Eve'):

(18)   s   w   w   s   w   w
      (Éve wĭth hĕr) (bás-kĕt wăs)
      s   w   w   s   w   w
      (Déep ĭn thĕ) (bélls ănd grăss)

These verse patterns involve what Hayes (1995: 372) refers to as **eurhythmicity**. Eurhythmic patterns are those in which accents 'are spaced not too closely and not too far apart'. More generally, the optimal eurhythmic pattern is one in which the accented syllables are equally spaced.[9]

This pattern is clearly achieved if the number of unaccented syllables between the accented syllables remains constant (one in the case of iambic and trochaic patterns; two in the case of dactylic patterns). However, this is not a prerequisite – the distance between the accented syllables can remain constant, even though the number of intervening unaccented syllables varies. In this view of verse structure, the foot is essentially interpreted as a unit of **timing**: a line of metrical verse consists of a fixed number of feet, with the

---

[9] It is possible to suggest that such rhythmic considerations determine the occurrence of what we referred to as 'secondary accents' in §4.1. That is, after primary accent has been assigned in a word, any remaining sequence of unaccented syllables, if it is sufficiently long, will be assigned a 'rhythmic pattern', thus avoiding what are sometimes referred to as a rhythmic 'lapse' (a sequence of too many unaccented syllables; see e.g. Selkirk 1984a; Nespor and Vogel 1989; Visch 1989).

accented syllables being roughly **isochronous** – i.e. they tend to recur at roughly equal intervals of time. The concept of the foot in verse is thus more or less equivalent to that of the bar or measure in music, with the accented syllable being equivalent to the first (strong) beat of the bar. Abercrombie (1965: 22), for example, provides the following scansion:

(19)   w   w   s   ww   s   w   w   s   w   s
       'Tĭs thĕ (míd-dlĕ ŏf) (níght bў thĕ) (cás-tlĕ) (clóck)

We ignore here the first two syllables, which on this analysis do not form a foot, but rather belong to the final foot of the previous line, if present. Notice that the number of unaccented syllables in the four complete feet varies from zero to two. Nevertheless, the accented syllables occur at regular intervals of time – they are more or less equally spaced.

The rhythm of this type of verse, then, depends on the structure of verse-feet, rather than on simply counting the number of syllables, which would be a possible strategy for the type of verse in (16).[10] But there are other metrical phenomena which are clearly foot-related. Germanic alliterative verse, for example, involves alliteration between stressed syllables, i.e. between the onsets of the first syllables of feet, as evidenced by the following extract from the Old English epic poem *Beowulf* (lines 4–7):

(20)   Oft 'Scyld 'Scēfing 'sceaþena 'þreatum,
       'monegum 'mǣgþum 'meodo-setla of'tēah;
       'egsode 'Eorle, syððan 'ǣrest 'wearð
       'fēasceaft 'funden; hē þæs 'frōfre ge'bād.[11]

where the initial syllable of the first three feet of each line must alliterate (in the first line on /ʃ/ (perhaps /sc/) <sc>, in the second on /m/, in the third on an empty onset and in the fourth on /f/).

Within this essentially verse-based approach to the foot, it is often argued that the temporal organisation of verse extends to the rhythmic organisation of spoken language (e.g. Abercrombie 1964). In a language like English, then, any of the structures in (21) would be permissible (we use the bracketed grid notation of (13) above):

---

[10] Indeed, Abercrombie notes that Samuel Taylor Coleridge, in his preface to his poem 'Christabel' in 1816, from which (19) is taken, observes: 'The metre of "Christabel" is . . . founded on a new principle: namely, that of counting in each line the accents, not the syllables . . . in each line the accents will be found to be only four.'

[11] Scyld Scefing often deprived his enemies,
many tribes of men, of their mead-benches,
He terrified his foes; yet he, as a boy,
had been found a waif; fate made amends for that.
                    (from *Beowulf*, translated by K. Crossley-Holland (1968). London: Macmillan)

(21) a. (× ·)   b. (× · ·)
     σ σ   σ σ σ

   c. (× · · ·)   d. (× · · · ·)
     σ σ σ σ   σ σ σ σ σ

where the different types of foot are instantiated by the forms in (22):

(22) a. silly   b. syllable   c. sedentary   d. generalising

This approach is motivated by the claim that English is a 'stress-timed' language, i.e. one in which the 'rhythmic pulse' or the 'beat' of the language is determined by the timing relationship between *accented* syllables. That is, each accented syllable coincides with an isochronous beat – the distance between them is roughly the same. Stress-timed languages such as English are often contrasted with 'syllable-timed' languages such as French, in which isochrony is attributed not to stressed syllables, but to syllables in general. Thus, in a syllable-timed language, 'each syllable is aligned with a . . . beat in the metrical grid' (Selkirk 1984a: 41). One way of interpreting this is to say that every syllable forms a rhythmic foot by itself, on the assumption that the foot is the basic unit of rhythm. Even in syllable-timed languages, however, it has been argued that the foot may be branching: thus Selkirk (1978) argues that the foot in French consists either of one syllable, as just outlined, or of two, but only if the second syllable contains [ə]. Thus foot structure in French can be illustrated by (23), for *mon petit garçon* /mɔ̃ pəti gaʀsɔ̃/ 'my little boy':[12]

(23) (× ·) (×) (×) (×)   foot accent
     σ σ σ σ σ
     mɔ̃ pə ti gaʀ sɔ̃

Thus only two foot structures are possible in French: unary and binary.

The approach just outlined appears to allow for a wide range of foot types, ranging from the unary feet in (23) to **unbounded** feet containing a large number of syllables, such as (22d). However, the unbounded structure in (22d) ignores the secondary accent on the fourth syllable of '*genera,lising*, which might better be represented as containing two feet, as in (24) (cf. also (13) above):

(24) (× · ·) (× ·)   foot accent
     σ σ σ σ σ
     ge ne ra li sing

---

[12] The distinction drawn here between stress-timed and syllable-timed languages is not uncontroversial, and is certainly not as simple as suggested here (see e.g. Dauer 1983; Nespor and Vogel 1989).

The two feet in (24) together form a word, in which the first accented syllable is the more prominent, as shown in (25):

(25) (×   ·   )   word accent
      (×   · ·) (× ·)   foot accent
      σ   σ   σ   σ   σ
      ge ne ra li sing

How, though, do we know which syllable in a foot will bear the accent, and, indeed, which of the accented syllables will be the most prominent, i.e. primary?

Notice that all the foot types which we have considered so far display one common property: the accented syllable occurs at one of the **edges** of the foot. In the case of trochaic and iambic patterns, this is trivial, of course – the accented syllable *must* be at an edge: it is the first of two in the case of a trochaic foot and the second of two in the case of an iambic foot. In larger feet, however, this still holds. Thus the accented syllable in a dactylic foot (s w w) is at the left edge. Typically though, we do not find foot types such as w s w, in which the accented syllable is in the middle of the foot.[13]

Moreover, primary accents, as we shall see, also prefer to occur at the edge of a word. In general, then, the strong element of any constituent prefers to be **peripheral**, as pointed out by Liberman (1975). This also mirrors principles of versification, in which, again, initial and/or final feet tend to be the most prominent in the line. Liberman suggests that the edge preference of primary accent and the alternating character of non-primary accents follow naturally if we assume that assigning accent involves first grouping syllables into feet and then assigning primary status to the accent of the leftmost or rightmost foot within the domain in question.

4.3   Fixed accent and free accent systems

We return now to the difference between the two types of accent systems discussed briefly in §4.1, those in which the accent apparently falls on a particular syllable in the word, i.e. **fixed accent systems**, as opposed to those in which the placement of accent is not predictable from the syllabic structure of the word, i.e. **free accent systems**. In particular, we will be considering the status of English with respect to this distinction. Why is it, one may ask, that accents are indicated on a word-by-word basis in English dictionaries? This would appear to suggest that English is not a language with fixed accent, unlike for example Polish (which we saw in (3) appears to be a language

---

[13] We should note, however, that appeal has sometimes been made to the w s w foot type, the **amphibrach**, notably by Halle and Vergnaud (1987a), in their analysis of Cayuvava, which we consider in §4.4.5.

Feet and words

which has accent fixed on the penultimate), Finnish (fixed initial accent) or Tübatulabal (a language spoken in Southern California which has fixed final accent). In all these languages, the location of accent is predictable by reference to (distance from) one of the word-edges.

The large number of possible accent patterns in English, illustrated in (26), suggests at first sight that it is a language more like Russian, i.e. one in which accent is free:

> (26) 'abstract (ADJ, NOUN)   'marma,lade
>   ab'stract (VERB)   se'rene
>   ca'sino   ,Apalachi'cola

This range of possible patterns means that English dictionaries, as we have already observed, tend to mark the accents in each word. However, we will show below that the placement of stress in many English words is in fact predictable, so that it does not provide an example of a free accent system. Indeed, the terms fixed vs free accent refer to extreme situations that are probably not encountered in any language in an absolute sense. Anderson (1984) observes that Avar, a northeast Caucasian language, provides an example of a system in which 'stress can only occur on one of the first two syllables of the word, but beyond this it is unpredictable', as shown in (27) (data from Ebeling 1966: 59):

> (27) 'hoːɾo 'threshing floor'   hoːɾo 'honey'
>   'q'adal 'wall (GEN SG)'   q'a'dal 'wall (NOM PL)'

That is, accent is 'fixed' in the sense that it must occur within the 'window' formed by the first two syllables, but is 'free' in the sense that there is no way of predicting which of these syllables will bear the accent in any particular word (although, as Anderson observes, 'some grammatical categories are associated with stress on a particular syllable', so that the difference in the patterns for the genitive singular and nominative plural forms for 'wall' in (27) can be attributed to predictable morphological factors).

Similarly, there is probably no fixed-accent language in which the accent is located in accordance with a rule that refers to word-edge and nothing else in *all* the words (simple and complex) of the language. In this respect, let us consider Polish, an example of a fixed-accent language, in a little more detail. Although Polish has regular penultimate accent (28a), we find morphologically simple words that have antepenultimate accent (28b) and also some that have final accent (28c):

> (28) a. regular *penultimate*   mar'molad 'marmalade (GEN PL)'
>   wi'osna   'spring'

b.	irregular	*antepenultimate*	uni'wersitet	'university'
			gra'matyka	'grammar'
c.	irregular	*final*	re'żim	'regime'
			me'nu	'menu'

Exceptions such as those as in (28b, c) (which in Polish are often loanwords) can only be dealt with by providing their lexical representations with an indication of which syllable is accented; the regular cases bear no such indication.

However, more interesting are those cases in which apparent exceptions themselves form a subsystem of some kind, so that a language may be said to have more than one regular pattern. This is often determined by some non-accentual property, very often membership of a specific word class (just as in Avar above), such that nouns behave differently from verbs, for example. Thus, morphological properties often interfere with the basic accentual principles of a language. Some of the apparent irregularity in English is caused by factors such as these, as we shall now show.

Chomsky and Halle (1968) provide the first extensive generative analysis of accent in English, and we consider the principles of their analysis briefly here. On the basis of the forms in (29), we might conclude that English takes primary accent on the final syllable:

(29) a. ap'pear   sur'mise
          col'lapse u'surp
      b. su'preme   re'mote
          ro'bust   ab'surd

However, the words in (30) appear to contradict this claim:

(30) a'rena   an'gina
      sy'nopsis fi'asco

Chomsky and Halle observe that this difference is due to the different morphological categories of the words involved: those in (29a) are verbs and those in (29b) adjectives, while the words in (30) are nouns. Thus stress falls on the final syllable if the word is a morphologically simple verb or adjective, but on the penultimate if it is a noun.

Another way in which morphology yields apparent counterexamples to the stress patterns of a language involves affixation. For example, we have just seen that the adjectives in (29b) behave like verbs in taking accent on the final syllable. However, as Chomsky and Halle (1968: 81) point out, the adjectives in (31) apparently deviate from this pattern:

(31) ˌanec'dotal   ˌuni'versal
      mo'mentous   de'sirous

However, these items are morphologically complex:

(32)   ANECDOTE+AL   UNIVERSE+AL
         MOMENT+OUS   DESIRE+OUS

Whatever the accentual pattern of the word from which the adjective is derived, the primary accent falls on the syllable immediately preceding the derivational suffix.[14]

Other suffixes are 'accent-neutral'; they have no effect on the stress pattern of the word to which they attach:

(33) a. di'vinely   DIVINE+LY
          'vulgarly   VULGAR+LY
     b. ma'rinehood MARINE+HOOD
          'adulthood   ADULT+HOOD[15]
     c. e'xactness   EXACT+NESS
          'wanton   WANTON+NESS

Whatever the details, it is apparent that English is not a free-accent language. Rather, there are a number of interacting principles which determine the accentual pattern, one of which, the internal structure of the 'target' syllable, we consider below in §4.4.2. Moreover, even though English has words containing a large number of syllables, the syllable which bears the primary accent is virtually always one of the final three:

(34) ˌApalachiˈcola[16]   ˌarchiˈpelago
     ˌWinnipeˈsaukee aˈsparagus
     ˌConstantiˈnople geˈranium

Notice again that the suffixation of accent-neutral affixes may override this restriction:

(35) a. 'desperately   DESPERATE+LY
     b. 'bachelorhood   BACHELOR+HOOD
     c. ad'venturousness ADVENTURE+OUS+NESS

Morphology can play a role even in languages such as Russian, which, as we have seen, is considered to have a free-accent system. A language like

---

[14] We return in §4.4.2 to the reasons for the antepenultimate accent in words such as *maximal* and *rigorous*. This has to do with the weight of the rhyme of the target syllable for accent (the penultimate, in these cases).

[15] For speakers whose pronunciation is /əˈdʌlt/, stress on the derived noun remains on the second syllable: /əˈdʌlthʊd/.

[16] The reader may wonder why we choose to illustrate our argument with such apparently exotic English words. A perusal of the literature on accent would quickly yield a large number of such items. This appears to be a consequence of the fact that it is difficult to find *morphemes* in English consisting of so many syllables; 'native' polysyllabic English words tend to be compounds or contain prefixes and/or suffixes, e.g. *excommunication*.

Russian is a **lexical accent language**, as accentuation has to be marked in the lexicon. However, even in such free systems we find regularities in morphologically complex words: when morphemes are combined to form words, rules will decide which syllable will receive the primary (i.e. word) accent. Revithiadou (1999) observes data such as the following:[17]

(36)		NOM SG		NOM PL		
	a.	golova	[gɑlɑˈvɑ]	golovy	[ˈgɔlɑvɨ]	'head'
	b.	rabota	[rɑˈbɔtɑ]	raboty	[rɑˈbɔtɨ]	'work'
	c.	gora	[gɑˈrɑ]	gory	[gɑˈrɨ]	'mountain'

It will be seen that the relationship between the accentual patterns of the singular and plural forms of these three Russian nouns is different in each case. This can be explained by assuming that morphemes differ in Russian in being lexically either marked or unmarked for accent. That is, although Russian is a free-accent language, not every morpheme is lexically accented. Furthermore, certain morphemes may be lexically marked as being 'unaccentable' – they reject accent wherever possible. The various morphemes in (36) can be assigned the following lexical accentual properties:

(37)	a.	*unmarked*	golov-	/gɔlɔv/	'head'
			-y	/ɨ/	'FEM NOM PL'
	b.	*marked*			
		accented	raˈbot-	/rɑˈbɔt/	'work'
			-ˈa	/ˈɑ/	'FEM NOM SG'
		unaccentable	gor-	/gɔr/	'mountain'

If an unmarked stem combines with an accented suffix, or an accented stem with an unmarked suffix, then the accent is realised on the lexically accented syllable, giving e.g. *goloˈva* and *raˈboty*. Similarly, if an unaccentable stem (e.g. *gor-*) combines with an unmarked suffix, the suffix retains its accent, giving e.g. *goˈra*, to avoid violating the 'unaccentable' specification of the stem. That is, if there is only one lexically specified accent in a sequence of morphemes, that accent will be realised, as we might expect. If, however, both stem and suffix are accented, then the sequence has *two* lexically marked accents, as in *raˈbot + ˈa*. Under these circumstances, one accent is omitted, to give the realisation *raˈbota*. What happens if there are *no* lexical accents in a particular sequence? If two unmarked morphemes combine, the realisation of accent appears to be governed by a general rule stipulating that the default accent is word-initial, so that *golov + y* yields *ˈgolovy*. Thus even a free-accent language such as Russian is subject to certain accentuation rules.

---

[17] Underlying /ɔ/ in Russian is realised as [ɑ] in unaccented syllables.

Returning now to English, we have distinguished two types of affix: **accent-neutral**, such as -*ly*, and what we might call **integrating** affixes, which are integrated into the domain to which they are attached, and thus considered to be part of that domain for the purposes of accent assignment. However, we can draw a further distinction within the set of integrating affixes. These may be either what we might call **accent-attracting** affixes, such as -*al* (38a), or **accent-bearing** affixes, such as -*ese* (38b):

(38) a. 'anecdote   ,anec'dotal
          'incident   ,inci'dental
          'universe   ,uni'versal
      b. 'journal   ,journa'lese
          Tai'wan   ,Taiwa'nese[18]
          'Java   ,Java'nese

Dutch has a set of prefixes which are accented when combined with verbs, as shown in (39):

(39) a. 'voeren   'to lead'   'opvoeren   'to perform'
          'lossen   'to unload'   'oplossen   'to solve'
      b. 'staan   'to stand'   'uitstaan   'to put up with'
          ran'geren 'to shunt'   'uitrangeren 'to put out to grass'
      c. 'keren   'to turn'   'omkeren   'to turn over'
          'kopen   'to buy'   'omkopen   'to bribe'

Thus these prefixes are accent-bearing, and must be lexically marked as such; they override the accentual pattern of the original morpheme. However, they in turn must yield to the demands of certain other suffixes, as shown in (40), where the forms in (39) are combined with the adjectival suffix -*baar* '-able':

(40) a. op'voerbaar   'performable'
          op'losbaar   'soluble'
      b. onuit'staanbaar   'unbearable'
          uitran'geerbaar   'able to be put out to grass'
      c. om'keerbaar   'able to be turned over'
          om'koopbaar   'bribable'

The suffix -*baar* attracts accent to the immediately preceding syllable, and obliterates the lexical accent of the prefixes in (40).

Having discussed affixation, we now turn to compounding. Members of compounds behave like independent domains for accent in many languages, although they may fuse into a single domain. In English, for example,

---

[18] The shift of the original accent of *Taiwan* to the first syllable is the result of a process which is independent of the fact that -*ese* is an accent-bearing affix (see §4.3.1 for further discussion).

compounds behave differently from phrases with respect to their accentuation: whereas phrases in English typically have a w s pattern, compounds show the reverse, s w. This results in accentual 'minimal pairs', familiar from the literature on accentuation, such as *a black 'board* 'a board which is black' vs *a 'blackboard* 'a board for writing on with chalk'; cf. *'greenfly* vs *green 'fly*, *'White House* vs *white 'house*, etc. In terms of the representation in (13), we need to add an extra grid layer to represent the compound accent, as in (41), the representation for *White House politics* /ˌwaɪt haʊs ˈpɒlɪtɪks/:

(41)
(·		×		)	phrasal accent
(×	·)	(×		)	compound accent
(×)	(×)	(×		·)	word accent
(×)	(×)	(×	·)	(×)	foot accent
σ	σ	σ	σ	σ	
waɪt	haʊs	pɒ	lɪ	tɪks	

(Notice that the first syllable of *politics*, which is not a compound, is vacuously assigned an accent by the compound accent rule.)

The various phenomena which we have been considering – e.g. the preference for accents to fall at the edge of domains and the interaction between morphological structure and accent – have to be accounted for in some kind of formal theory of accent. Before we move on to this, though, let us consider the role of non-primary accents.

4.3.1 Non-primary accent

To what extent do the generalisations relating to the placement of primary accents apply to non-primary accents as well? As in the case of the primary accent, the position of the non-primary accent in many languages is rule-based. The simplest case is that in which these accents form an alternating pattern moving away from the primary accent. An example of a language with a system like this is Warao, spoken in Venezuela. Osborne (1966: 115) observes that in Warao 'alternate syllables are stressed with a weaker secondary stress, counting back from the strongly stressed syllable'. This is illustrated by the forms in (42):

(42)
koˈranu	'drink it!'
ˌkonaˈruae	'carried away'
yiˌwaraˈnae	'he finished it'
ˌnahoˌroaˌhakuˈtai	'the one who ate'
eˌnahoˌroaˌhakuˈtai	'the one who caused him to eat'

In a system such as this, the syllables preceding the primary accent are gathered up into trochaic binary feet, with the first syllable of each foot being assigned a secondary accent. If there is an odd number of syllables in the word, the initial syllable remains unfooted. This gives the following structure for *enahoroahakutai*:

```
(43)   ( ·      ·        ·     ×   )          word accent
       (× ·) (× ·) (× ·) (× ·)                foot accent
        σ  σ  σ  σ  σ  σ  σ  σ  σ
        e  na ho ro a  ha ku ta i
```

Just as with primary accents, the placement of non-primary accents may be affected by morphological structure. In English compounds of the type *blackboard* and *petrol station*, the syllable of the second morpheme, which lexically bears primary accent, is realised with secondary accent when it forms a compound, as in (44), *petrol station* /ˈpɛtrəl ˌsteɪʃən/:

```
(44)  (×        ·    )             compound accent
      (×    ) (×    )              word accent
      (× ·) (× ·)                  foot accent
       σ  σ  σ  σ
       pɛ trəl steɪ ʃən
```

Thus, the location of non-primary accent in these compounds is dependent on the location of the primary accent in the units that they are composed of. This is generally also the case when words combine to form a phrase, which in English yields a w s pattern, as in ˌNew ˈYork, ˌhard-ˈboiled, ˌRugby ˈUnion and ˌweight-ˈsensitive. However, if such phrases are themselves part of compounds, we often encounter sequences which violate the principles of eurhythmicity discussed in §4.2, for example because two accented syllables are 'too close' after compounding, as illustrated by forms such as *New York pizza*, *hard-boiled egg*, *Rugby Union president* and *weight-sensitive stressing* in (45):

```
(45)  ˌNew York ˈpizza
      ˌhard-boiled ˈegg
      ˌRugby Union ˈpresident
      ˌweight-sensitive ˈstressing
```

Consider the bracketed grid corresponding to *New York pizza* /njuː jɔːk piːtsə/:

```
(46)  (     ·    ×    )             phrasal accent
      ( ·   ×) (×    )              phrasal accent
      (×) (×) (×    )               word accent
      (×) (×) (× ·)                 foot accent
       σ  σ  σ  σ
       njuː jɔːk piː tsə
```

(Notice that the complete phrase is made up of two smaller phrases, *New York* and *pizza*, so that phrasal accents are assigned twice.) At the word-accent level the two rhythmic 'beats' corresponding to the primary word accents on *York* and *pizza* are adjacent, giving /njuː ˌjɔːk ˈpiːtsə/, and thus display a **rhythmic clash**. Under these circumstances English allows the secondary stress to move to the first element of the phrase, by a process known as **stress shift**, to give the grid in (47):

(47)   (·   ×   )   phrasal accent
  (×   ·) (×   )   phrasal accent and stress shift
  (×) (×) (×   )   word accent
  (×) (×) (×   ·)   foot accent
   σ   σ   σ   σ
  njuː jɔːk piː tsə

in which the strong and weak syllables display an alternating pattern.

This process is not restricted to phrases of which the first element is a compound. If the first element is a word in which a secondary accent precedes a primary accent, then it will also be available for stress shift, as shown in (48):

(48)   ˌJapaˈnese   *but*   ˌJapanese ˈsushi
  ˌMississˈsippi   ˌMississippi ˈmadrigals
  ˌsevenˈteen   ˌseventeen ˈsisters

Again we see that the original primary accent shifts to the place of the original secondary accent, and becomes subordinated to the primary accent of the righthand element of the whole phrase.

We will not pursue the details of stress shift here.[19] Rather, we turn to some examples from morphology which, like the compounding phenomena discussed above, demonstrate that primary accents of morphemes which lose their status as primary as a result of their being embedded may still be recognisable in surface realisations. Chomsky and Halle (1968: 116) consider the case of the two nouns *compensation* and *condensation*, which apparently have the same prosodic structure. Their morphological structures differ, however: the underlying representations of the verbs from which the nouns are derived is presumably as given in (49):

(49)   a. (×   ·)   b.   (×)   word accent
   (×   ·) (×)   (×) (×)   foot accent
   σ   σ   σ   σ   σ
  com pen sate   con dense

---

[19] There is an enormous literature on this phenomenon, much of which is concerned with the appropriate representation of stress shift. See e.g. Liberman and Prince (1977), Prince (1983), Hayes (1984a), Selkirk (1984a), Giegerich (1985) and, for an overview, Visch (1989).

'*Compen,sate* has primary accent on the initial and secondary accent on the final syllable; *con'dense* has primary accent on the final syllable. The vowel in the first syllable of *condense* is at least potentially not reduced to schwa, and therefore forms a foot. When suffixation of *-ation* or *-ion* takes place, primary accent moves to the first syllable of *-ation*, which is an accent-bearing suffix. As a result, the initial syllable of *condense* acquires secondary accent. We might assume, then, that the two words would have identical grid structures, as in (50):

```
(50)  a. ( ·      ×    )     b. ( ·      ×    )    word accent
         (×  · ) (×   · )       (×  · ) (×   · )   foot accent
          σ  σ   σ   σ           σ   σ   σ   σ
         com pen sa  tion      con den sa  tion
```

However, Chomsky and Halle observe that in many dialects of English the pronunciation of these two words differs in one crucial respect: whereas the second syllable of *compensation* contains a reduced schwa-type vowel, that of *condensation* has a full vowel. Thus in RP, the two words would be realised as /ˌkɒmpənˈseɪʃən/ and /ˌkɒndenˈseɪʃən/, respectively. Chomsky and Halle associate this difference with the fact that the second syllable of *condensation* originally bore a primary accent; the presence of the full vowel in the derived noun reflects its 'history'.

It might be possible to represent this syllable as bearing tertiary accent, as in (51):

```
(51)  a. ( ·      ×    )     b. ( ·      ×    )     primary accent
         (×   ) (×    )         (×  · ) (×    )     secondary accent
         (×  · ) (×   · )       (×) (×) (×   · )    tertiary accent
          σ  σ   σ   σ           σ   σ   σ   σ
         com pen sa  tion      con den sa  tion
```

However, it is a moot point whether it is possible to distinguish more than two levels of accent, and we take no position on this matter here. Nevertheless, the discussion above has clearly shown that accents may be 'persistent'.[20]

4.4 Metrical theory

In §4.2 above, we suggested that accents prefer to occur at the edge of a foot, and that primary accents prefer to occur at the edge of a word. Nevertheless, we have also seen that there are languages such as Polish in which primary accent regularly falls on a non-peripheral syllable. In the case of Polish this is

---

[20] In traditional derivational phonology, this persistence is captured in terms of **cyclicity**: accent rules may apply cyclically to successive morphological domains. See e.g. Cole (1995) for a discussion of the cycle in phonology.

the penultimate syllable, but the full array of attested systems shows a wide range of possibilities, as shown in (52) (drawn partly from the inventory given by Hayes 1995):

(52) *initial*   *postinitial*
      Finnish   Dakota
      Maranungku   Southern Paiute

      final   *penultimate*   *antepenultimate*
      Tübatulabal   Polish   Macedonian
      French   Warao

Hyman (1977) identifies more cases of penultimate than initial primary stress, with final stress coming third. Postinitial and antepenultimate patterns are rare, and post-postinitial virtually unknown.

Initial and final accent could be accounted for by primary accent rules which identify the edges of the accentual domain. Such rules would construct the elementary metrical grids as in (53), i.e. grids with no internal bracketing:

(53) a. $(\times \quad \cdot \quad \cdot \quad \cdot \quad \cdot)$ b. $(\cdot \quad \cdot \quad \cdot \quad \cdot \quad \times)$
         $\sigma \quad \sigma \quad \sigma \quad \sigma \quad \sigma$ $\sigma \quad \sigma \quad \sigma \quad \sigma \quad \sigma$

But what about postinitial, penultimate and antepenultimate accent?

Notice first that there is an asymmetry between left-edge accent and right-edge accent. Whereas the latter seems to be able to reach the third syllable from the edge (as in Macedonian), post-postinitial accent is virtually never attested. Even though only a few examples of fixed antepenultimate accent have been recorded, it is frequently found in the exceptional vocabulary of languages which otherwise have fixed penultimate accent. A theory of accent placement must account not only for this asymmetry, but also for the fact that fixed patterns other than those in (53) are never found. If primary accent placement were unrestricted, in the sense that any syllable at some fixed distance from the word-edge could be reached, we would expect to find languages having accent on the fourth syllable from either the left or right edge, or even in the 'middle'.

We therefore need a mechanism for determining primary accent placement that excludes such non-occurring cases. This means that a system which simply allows us to indicate any syllable as potentially accentable is inadequate. For example, such a theory fails to account for the fact that words can have only one primary accent: there is nothing in the theory to prevent us from assigning an accent mark to the first *and* last syllables in (53), or indeed to every syllable in the word. The theory of accent placement proposed in Chomsky and Halle (1968) has much the same drawback. In their model, any vowel bears a segmental feature [±accent] (in their terms [±stress]), which is formally identical to other segmental features such as [±round] and [±sonorant]. Here, too, there is no formal reason not to mark *all* the syllables in a word as [+accent], which would be in conflict with the culminative nature of accent.

A model which allows any syllable in a word to be accented also fails to account for the ways in which accent can exhibit its edge preference (i.e. its demarcative property; cf. §4.1). The grids in (53) are for the 'optimal' initial and final patterns; it seems just as easy to construct the grids in (54a–c) for the less common postinitial, penultimate and antepenultimate patterns, and indeed those in (54d–e) for the – at best – marginal post-postinitial pattern, and the apparently impossible pre-antepenultimate pattern:

(54) a. *postinitial*   b. *penultimate*

    (· × · · ·)   (· · · × ·)
     σ σ σ σ σ   σ σ σ σ σ

  c. *antepenultimate*

    (· · · × · ·)
     σ σ σ σ σ σ

  d. *post-postinitial*   e. *pre-antepenultimate*

    (· · × · · ·)   (· · · · × · · ·)
     σ σ σ σ σ σ   σ σ σ σ σ σ σ σ

Clearly, any theory which simply allows us to pick out any syllable within a word as accented fails to provide insight into the phenomena we have been considering, and so is inadequate as a theory of primary accent placement. Its inadequacy is emphasised when we consider further non-primary accents.

We have already seen that the distribution of non-primary accents is rule-based and non-random. Accentual patterns tend to show alternations between accented and non-accented syllables. Thus, as we saw in §4.3.1, accents on adjacent syllables (**clashes**) are avoided where possible, for example by stress-shift processes such as that of English. Equally, languages tend to avoid stretches of more than two unaccented syllables (**lapses**). At the lowest level of rhythmic organisation, then, languages have binary rhythmic patterns (55a) or ternary rhythmic patterns (55b), but not quaternary rhythm (55c):

(55) a. (× ·) (× ·) (× ·) (× ·) (× ...
        σ σ σ σ σ σ σ σ σ

    b. (× · ·) (× · ·) (× · ·) ...
         σ σ σ σ σ σ σ σ σ

    c. * (× · · ·) (× · · ·) (× ...
          σ σ σ σ σ σ σ σ σ

In the previous section we suggested that rhythmic non-primary accents can be regarded as properties of a domain that is smaller than the word, which we called the foot. It would seem, then, that we must construct a set of algorithms for assigning foot structure. These form the central core of what is known as metrical theory, and we will turn to this in the next section. We will show that, although the languages of the world appear to display a great variety of accentual patterns, metrical theory requires only two rules for the placement of primary accent, one which places accent on the leftmost foot accent in a particular domain (56a), and one which places accent on the rightmost foot accent (56b):

(56) *Primary accent rules*

    a.   ×

        × → × / __)   foot accent

    b.   ×

        × → × / (__   foot accent

4.4.1 Metrical structures

In this section we examine how the various observations on word and foot structure in the previous sections can be formalised within metrical theory. Let us start by considering again the English word *Apalachicola*, introduced in §4.1. The six syllables of this word are organised into three trochaic feet, as in (57):

(57) (× ·)(× ·)(× ·)   foot accent

      σ σ σ σ σ σ

      æ pə læ tʃɪ kɛʊ lə

How do we generate the structure in (57)? The metrical structure assigned to any word is the result of the setting of a number of **parameters**, which specify the choices available to a language with respect to some property. With respect to *Apalachicola*, which has initial primary accent and a rightward alternating rhythmic pattern, the two parameters in (58) determine the foot structure:

(58) *foot structure*

      i.   left-headed (i.e. the leftmost syllable of the foot is accented)

      ii.   assigned from right to left

(58.i) specifies that the foot structure of (57) is trochaic, i.e. it is the first syllable of the foot which is accented. Notice that (58.i) is formulated in terms of headedness; metrical theory makes use of headed tree structures, represented as bracketed grids. As in our account of syllable structure, headed trees embody the claim that each constituent contains just one 'central' unit, the **head**, and in addition one or more non-heads, the **dependents**. As we have seen, the notion of head is central to the kind of structures that linguists posit in syntax, morphology and phonology.[21]

The use of headed structures, and more specifically the notion that each accent forms a head, guarantees that every domain has precisely one accent. In this way, we derive the property of culminativity of accent. The additional property that heads in metrical structure can only be located at edges of constituents expresses the demarcative function of accent (cf. §4.1).

(58.ii) specifies that the six syllables of *Apalachicola* are organised into feet, starting from the right. However, since the word *Apalachicola* has an even number of syllables, it does not itself provide evidence for (58.ii); left-to-right assignment would yield the same structure, given that we have specified the feet as trochaic. However, words with an odd number of syllables provide the necessary evidence, as is shown by a word such as *Mo₁nonga'hela*, which has the foot structure in (59a). If feet had been assigned from the left, we would have the incorrect structure in (59b):

(59) a. $(\times \quad \cdot)(\times \quad \cdot)$ b. * $(\times \quad \cdot)(\times \quad \cdot)$ foot accent
           σ σ σ σ σ   σ σ σ σ σ
           mə nɔŋ gə hiː lə   mɔ nɔŋ gæ hiː lə

Notice that the first syllable in (59a) is left unfooted, i.e. it is not parsed, but is 'stranded' (as before, unparsed syllables are not marked with a dot). Allowing stranded syllables implies that we do not require foot parsing to be exhaustive, i.e. that not all syllables have to be assigned to a foot. Such stranded syllables are sometimes characterised as forming a **degenerate** foot, but the question of how they are incorporated into metrical structure is a matter of some controversy, which we return to in §4.4.4.

After the assignment of foot structure by (58), *Apalachicola* will be assigned word accent by the parameter setting in (60):

(60) *word structure*
       right-headed (i.e. the rightmost foot accent receives primary accent)

This gives the word structure in (61):

(61) $(\cdot \qquad \cdot \qquad \times \quad)$ word accent
       $(\times \quad \cdot)(\times \quad \cdot)(\times \quad \cdot)$ foot accent
       σ σ σ σ σ σ
       æ pə læ tʃɪ kɛʊ lə

In (61) we adopt a ternary structure at word-accent level; we assume that the first two feet are both 'weak', i.e. depend on the foot containing the primary accent, but that neither is stronger than the other.

---

[21] See Anderson and Ewen (1987), Halle and Vergnaud (1987a), Dresher and van der Hulst (1995, 1998) for discussions of the notion 'head' in phonological structure.

It is clear that the adoption of the parameter settings in (58) and (60) allows us to generate the correct accentual pattern for *Apalachicola*. It is easy to see that if we had chosen the opposite value for each of the parameters, we would have produced the incorrect structure in (62):

```
(62)  (    ×        ·        · )      word accent
      ( ·   ×) ( ·   ×) ( ·   ×)      foot accent
        σ   σ   σ   σ   σ   σ
        ə  pæ  lə  ʧɪ  kə  læ
```

The structure in (62) would result from the application of a rule stating that the primary accent falls on the second syllable and secondary accents on every other syllable following the primary accent, yielding **A'pala,chico,la*.

More importantly, however, it is claimed that these settings are appropriate for English in general. That is, while (58) and (60) represent the choices for English, other languages differ in their settings for each of the parameters in (63), which gives the full set developed so far:

(63) a. *foot structure*
      i. HEADSHIP: left-headed (LH) *or* right-headed (RH)
      ii. DIRECTIONALITY: assigned from left to right (L→R) *or* right to left (R→L)
  b. *word structure*
      HEADSHIP: left-headed (LH) *or* right-headed (RH)

These parameters are in principle independent of each other. The parametric approach to accent was first proposed by Halle and Vergnaud (1978) and further developed and richly exemplified in Hayes (1981, 1995). One of its achievements has been to analyse the variety of attested accentual patterns in terms of a small set of parameters such as those in (63).

It is clear that, given the three binary parameters in (63), we might generate eight different types of accentual systems. The foot structure parameters give four possibilities; combined with the word headship parameter – left-headed or right-headed – this allows us to generate the eight systems in (64):

(64) a. Word (LH), Foot (LH, L→R)
    b. Word (LH), Foot (RH, L→R)
    c. Word (RH), Foot (LH, R→L)
    d. Word (RH), Foot (RH, R→L)
    e. Word (LH), Foot (LH, R→L)
    f. Word (LH), Foot (RH, R→L)
    g. Word (RH), Foot (LH, L→R)
    h. Word (RH), Foot (RH, L→R)

However, although there are eight possible patterns, (64a–d) are significantly more common than those in (64e–h). (65) shows the structures generated by the four common patterns:

(65)   *odd number*   *even number*
                        of syllables   *of syllables*

   a. word (LH)   (×   ·   )   (×   ·   ·   )

      foot   (× ·)(× ·)   (× ·)(× ·)(× ·)

     (LH, L→R) σ σ σ σ σ   σ σ σ σ σ σ

   b. word (LH)   (×   ·)   (×   ·   ·)

      foot   (· ×)(· ×)   (· ×)(· ×)(· ×)

     (RH, L→R) σ σ σ σ σ   σ σ σ σ σ σ

   c. word (RH)   (·   ×)   (·   ·   ×)

      foot   (× ·)(× ·)   (× ·)(× ·)(× ·)

     (LH, R→L) σ σ σ σ σ   σ σ σ σ σ σ

   d. word (RH)   (·   ×)   (·   ·   ×)

      foot   (· ×)(· ×)   (· ×)(· ×)(· ×)

     (RH, R→L) σ σ σ σ σ   σ σ σ σ σ σ

Kager (1995) gives examples of each of these systems: (65a) is that of Hungarian (see Kerek 1971), (65b) that of Araucanian (Echeverría and Contreras 1965), (65c) that of Warao (Osborne 1966) and (65d) that of Weri (Boxwell and Boxwell 1966).

We can observe a correlation in (65) between directionality and primary accent location. (a) and (b) display left-to-right parsing, with primary accent falling on the leftmost foot; in (c) and (d) we have right-to-left parsing, with primary accent falling on the rightmost foot. This appears to be typical of accentual systems, such that the head of the word is the foot which is closest to the edge from which the parsing begins. As noted by van der Hulst (1984), the systems in (66), in which this correlation is not found, are much less common, although they do occur:

(66)   *odd number*   *even number*
                        of syllables   *of syllables*

   a. word (RH)   (·   ×)   (·   ·   ×)

      foot   (× ·)(× ·)   (× ·)(× ·)(× ·)

     (LH, L→R) σ σ σ σ σ   σ σ σ σ σ σ

   b. word (RH)   (·   ×)   (·   ·   ×)

      foot   (· ×)(· ×)   (· ×)(· ×)(· ×)

     (RH, L→R) σ σ σ σ σ   σ σ σ σ σ σ

c. word (LH)   (×   ·   )   (×   ·   ·   )
   foot   (× ·)(× ·)   (× ·)(× ·)(× ·)
   (LH, R→L)   σ σ σ σ σ   σ σ σ σ σ σ

d. word (LH)   (×   ·)   (×   ·   ·)
   foot   (· ×)(· ×)   (· ×)(· ×)(· ×)
   (RH, R→L)   σ σ σ σ σ   σ σ σ σ σ σ

Note that in systems of this kind the exact location of the primary accent is dependent on the number of syllables that the word is composed of.

The systems we have been considering are those involving trochaic and iambic feet only. We return in §4.4.5 to the analysis of dactylic feet, which we introduced in §4.2 above.

4.4.2 Weight-sensitivity

In our discussion of accent assignment, we have so far been ignoring the internal structure of the syllables which go to make up feet. However, we saw in §3.4.1 that in certain languages we can distinguish between 'heavy' and 'light' syllables. Under the appropriate circumstances, heavy syllables are capable of bearing accent, while light syllables are not. For example, Churchward (1940: 75) gives the following forms from Rotuman (an Austronesian language spoken on Rotuma, an island north of Fiji):

(67) a. 'taka   'to lie'   b. kara'raː 'to snore'
          hunu'nuka 'to gasp'   ma'roː   'to win'

The forms in (67) exemplify the Rotuman rule of accent placement in (68):

(68) Primary accent falls on the final syllable if this syllable contains a long
      vowel, otherwise it falls on the penultimate syllable.

Similarly, Yapese (Hayes 1981: 65–6) has the rule in (69):

(69) Primary accent falls on the penultimate syllable if the final is closed and
      the penultimate is open, otherwise it falls on the final syllable.

Accent rules that are sensitive to the structure of the syllables are often said to be quantity-sensitive, a term which suggests that the accent rule is primarily sensitive to length distinctions. However, as shown by (69), and as discussed in §3.4.1, the distinction between heavy and light syllables may also involve factors such as whether the syllable is open or closed. We will see below that quantity and closure are probably independent factors in the determination of weight, and that there are other accent-attracting properties which may also play a role. Hence we adopt here the more abstract term

weight-sensitive. Generally, only the two weight categories identified in §3.4.1 play a role in accent assignment: syllables are either heavy or light.

How, then, can our theory of foot assignment be enriched such that weight-sensitive systems can be accommodated? It is clear that systems are weight-sensitive whenever certain syllables (i.e. those that are heavy) are unable to occupy the dependent position in the foot, with the result that they always end up as the head of the foot.

Let us assume the **weight-sensitivity** parameter in (70):

> (70) WEIGHT-SENSITIVITY: heavy syllables are unable to occupy the dependent position in a foot.

which can be set to 'yes' or 'no'. If the weight parameter is set to 'yes', then we must also establish what constitutes a heavy syllable in the language in question; i.e. are we dealing with a rhyme-weight language or a nucleus-weight language, as discussed in §3.4.1?

The introduction of the weight parameter means that we now have the set of parameters in (71):

> (71) a. *foot structure*
>   i. HEADSHIP: left-headed (LH) *or* right-headed (RH)
>   ii. DIRECTIONALITY: assigned from left to right (L→R) *or* right to left (R→L)
>   iii. WEIGHT-SENSITIVITY: yes *or* no
>
>   b. *word structure*
>   HEADSHIP: left-headed (LH) *or* right-headed (RH)

The addition of the weight-sensitivity parameter obviously doubles the number of different types of accent systems that can be generated. One such system is shown in (72):

> (72) a. *foot structure:* LH, R→L, weight-sensitive
>   b. *word structure:* RH

Let us consider the system defined by (72). If we consider only the rightmost foot in the word, then there are four possible configurations, as shown in (73), where σ̄ represents a heavy syllable and σ̆ a light syllable:

> (73) a. σ̄ σ̆   b. σ̆ σ̆   c. σ̆ σ̄   d. σ̄ σ̄

(73a) and (b) present no problem, since we can simply assign the final two syllables to a binary trochaic foot without violating the weight parameter, which prevents a heavy syllable from occurring in the dependent foot position. This gives the grids in (74):

(74)   a. (×   ·)   b. (×   ·)   foot accent
          ŏ   ŏ   ŏ   ŏ

Recall that the weight parameter bars heavy syllables from dependent position, but does not bar light syllables from head position, so that (74b) is well
formed. However, we cannot construct a trochaic foot over the two word-
final syllables (73c) and (d), because the final heavy syllable would then end
up in the weak position of the foot. What we can do, however, is assign a
monosyllabic foot to the final syllable only, giving the following representations for (73c) and (d):

(75)   a.   (×)   b.   (×)   foot accent
            ŏ   ō   ō   ō

In (c) and (d), the heavy syllable forms a foot by itself. The structures in (75)
are appropriate for a system which has primary accent on the final syllable if
this is heavy and on the penultimate syllable otherwise, i.e. the type represented by Rotuman in (68).

As we saw in (69), Yapese represents a second type of weight-sensitive
system. In such systems, primary accent also falls on the final syllable in the
(73b) case, i.e. if the last two syllables are both light. The simplest way of
analysing such systems appears to be to assume that foot structure is iambic,
rather than trochaic, i.e. that the parameter setting is as in (76):

(76)   a.   *foot structure:*   RH, R→L, weight-sensitive
          b.   *word structure:*   RH

This yields the foot structures in (77):

(77)   a. (×)   b. (·   ×)   c.   (×)   d.   (×)   foot accent
          ō   ŏ   ŏ   ŏ   ŏ   ō   ō   ō

Notice that in (77a) we have not assigned the final light syllable to a foot. We
assume that this reflects the following condition on foot structure:

(78)   *Condition on foot size*
       In weight-sensitive systems feet cannot consist of one light syllable.

4.4.3   Foot typology

It will be clear that the addition of the weight-sensitivity parameter means that
we can generate sixteen possible accent systems. However, as we have already
seen, by no means all of these systems actually occur in the languages of the
world, and even the set of possible systems that we have already identified
cannot combine freely with either setting of the weight-sensitivity parameter.
For example, right-headed weight-insensitive feet systems are rare, and left-
headed weight-sensitive systems with left-to-right foot assignment apparently

absent. These facts lead Hayes (1995: ch. 4) to assume a much more restricted inventory of basic metrical units, namely the **syllabic trochee**, the **moraic trochee** and the **iamb**. The inventory is given in (79) (from Hayes 1995: 71):

(79) a. *syllabic trochee*   (×   ·)
                                σ   σ

    b. *moraic trochee*   (×   ·)   *or*   (×)
                            σ̆   σ̆   σ̄

    c. *iamb*   (·   ×)   *or*   (×)
                  σ̆   σ   σ̄

On this analysis, then, weight-insensitive systems are normally left-headed, i.e. trochaic. Syllabic trochees are left-headed weight-insensitive feet, as shown in (80):

(80) a. (×   ·)   b. (×   ·)
          σ   σ   σ   σ   σ

Syllables are gathered into left-headed binary feet, with any leftover syllables, as in (80b), remaining unparsed. A monosyllabic word may form a foot of its own, depending on the language in question (see §4.4.4 below). Hayes (1995: 188ff.), drawing his data from the analysis of Árnason (1985), cites Icelandic as an example of a syllabic trochaic system which allows monosyllabic words to form feet. Relevant forms are given in (81):[22]

(81) ˈJón   'John'
     ˈtaska   'briefcase'
     ˈhöfðingˌja   'chieftain (GEN PL)'
     ˈakvaˌrella   'aquarelle'
     ˈbíóˌgrafíˌa   'biography'

However, Hayes believes that the final secondary accent in, for example, *ˈhöfðingˌja* and *ˈbíóˌgrafíˌa* should be assigned to phonetic lengthening rather than to metrical structure, and should therefore be disregarded in constructing the appropriate foot patterns, given in (82):

(82) a. (×)   b. (×   ·)   c. (×   ·)
          σ   σ   σ   σ   σ   σ
         Jón   tas ka   höf ðing ja

    d. (×   ·)(×   ·)   e. (×   ·)(×   ·)
        σ   σ   σ   σ   σ   σ   σ   σ   σ
       ak va rel la   bí ó gra fí a

[22] The accents on the vowels denote different vowel qualities in Icelandic orthography; they do not indicate tone or accent.

The foot types in (79b) are found in the analysis of weight-sensitive systems. In systems employing the **moraic trochee**, a foot may be formed either by a heavy syllable on its own or by two light syllables. As anticipated in our discussion of mora theory in §3.5, one heavy syllable is equivalent to two light syllables, in that both contain two moras, so that the two types in (79b) share the moraic structure in (83):

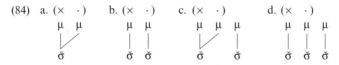

Thus a system such as (83) builds feet on the basis of moraic, rather than syllabic, structure. In moraic trochaic systems, feet consist of exactly two moras, as shown in (84):

(84) a. (× ·)   b. (× ·)   c. (× ·)   d. (× ·)
         μ μ   μ μ   μ μ μ   μ μ μ
          \/ | | \/ | | | |
          ŏ   ŏ ŏ   ŏ   ŏ   ŏ ŏ ŏ

As in the case of the syllabic trochee, systems may allow a final light syllable, as in (84c, d), to remain unparsed; in moraic trochaic systems, however, a heavy syllable always forms a foot.

Hayes (1995: §6.1.4) analyses Wargamay, an Australian language spoken in North Queensland, as having a moraic trochaic system, assigned from right to left. In this language, syllables with a long vowel are heavy; all others are light. Relevant forms are given in (85):

(85) 'maːl   'man'
      'bada   'dog'
      'muːba   'stone fish'
      'giːbaṛa   'fig tree'
      ga'gara   'dilly bag'
      'giɟa,wulu   'freshwater jewfish'

The appropriate patterns are given in (86):

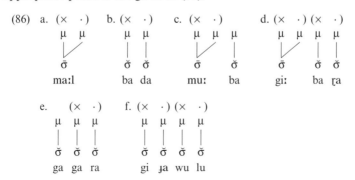

Initial light syllables, as in (86e), remain unparsed (degenerate feet are not permitted in Wargamay).[23] Notice that the analysis apparently generates an incorrect representation for (86d); we find *['giː₁baɽa], with secondary accent on the second syllable, rather than the correct form, ['giːbaɽa]. Hayes attributes this to a destressing rule which has the effect of resolving a clash between two successive stressed syllables in Wargamay.

Like moraic trochaic systems, iambic systems distinguish between heavy and light syllables. In such systems, any syllable following a *light* syllable forms a foot with that syllable, and is its head. Any remaining heavy syllables form feet on their own; remaining light syllables are unparsed.

(87) a. (×)   b. (·   ×)   c. (·   ×)   d. (·   ×)
         ō   ŏ   ŏ   ŏ   ō   ŏ   σ   ŏ

Cayuga, a Lake Iroquoian language, is analysed by Hayes as having an iambic system. He cites the data in (88):

(88)   hēna'toːwas   'they are hunting'
       ēhēna'toːwat   'they will hunt'
       teweka'tawĕnye?   'I'm moving about'
       ka'nesta?   'board'

These have the patterns in (89):

(89)   a. (·   ×) (×)   b. (·   ×) (·   ×)
          ŏ   ŏ   ō   ŏ   ŏ   ŏ   ŏ   ŏ   ŏ
          hē na toː was   ē   hē na toː wat

       c. (·   ×) (·   ×) (·   ×)   d. (·   ×)
          ŏ   ŏ   ŏ   ŏ   ŏ   ŏ   ŏ   ŏ   ŏ
          te we ka ta wĕnye?   ka ne sta?

4.4.4 *Degenerate feet*

We have seen that the footing procedures developed in the previous section often leave a syllable unparsed, or **stray**. In a syllabic trochaic system, any odd-numbered word will contain one such syllable, as shown in (80b) above, while in moraic trochaic and iambic systems, a light syllable may be stray ((84c) and (87d)). In these representations, we simply left the syllable unparsed, as in Icelandic *höfðingja* (82c), Wargamay *muːba* (86c) and *gagara* (86e) and Cayuga *kanesta?* (89d) (the stray syllable is underlined). However, in at least one case, in the syllabic trochaic system of Icelandic, we have assigned a single syllable, *Jón* (82a), to a foot, rather than leaving it unparsed.

---

[23] See §4.4.4 for further discussion of degenerate feet.

Feet formed in this way are referred to as **degenerate**, and are defined by Hayes (1995: 86) as the 'logically smallest possible foot' within each of the types of system defined above. He formalises the notion as in (90):

(90) *Degenerate feet*

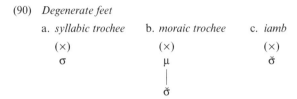

a. *syllabic trochee*   b. *moraic trochee*   c. *iamb*

How do we know whether an otherwise unparsed syllable should form a degenerate foot or not? In the case of a monosyllabic word like Icelandic *Jón*, we might think that any monosyllabic content word must be able to form a foot on its own, and for many languages this is indeed the case, for all three types of system. Hayes provides an extensive list of such languages. However, he also provides a list of languages which do *not* allow degenerate feet. For example, Cairene Arabic, which has a moraic trochaic system, does not allow monosyllabic words consisting of a single light syllable. Languages which have such restrictions are said to display a **minimal word constraint**, such that each phonological word must consist of at least one non-degenerate foot.

We can also demonstrate that stray syllables in polysyllabic words do not form degenerate feet in these languages. Hayes discusses two forms in Cairene Arabic, '*kataba* 'he wrote' and *qat'tala* 'he killed'. The first syllable of *qat'tala* is heavy (CVC); all other syllables in the two forms are light. The footing and accenting of the two forms are shown in (91) (Hayes 1995: 90):

(91) a. (×   )   b. (·   ×   )
         (×   ·)   (×)(×   ·)
         ŏ   ŏ   ŏ   ō   ŏ   ŏ
         ka ta ba   qat ta la

The final syllable of *kataba* remains unparsed, and fails to form a degenerate foot. This is evidenced by the fact that it does not attract primary accent; compare this with *qattala*, containing two full moraic feet, where primary accent falls on the strong syllable of the foot *tala*.

Cairene Arabic, then, does not allow degenerate feet under any circumstances. Languages with a minimal word requirement, however, permit them in monosyllabic words. Even these languages, though, typically only display degenerate feet in what Hayes calls strong positions, i.e. 'when dominated by another grid mark', for example because an unparsed final syllable is subject to a rule assigning primary accent to the last syllable in a word. This leads Hayes to treat the presence or absence of degenerate feet as being due to a parameter, which prohibits degenerate feet either completely (e.g. Cairene Arabic) or in weak positions (e.g. Icelandic).

4.4.5 Ternary feet

There are a number of languages which at first sight appear to be analysable as involving ternary feet, rather than binary feet of the sort we have been considering up to now. Key (1961: 149), for example, analyses the system of Cayuvava, a language spoken in Bolivia, as having the following rule:

> (92) Stress occurs on the antepenultimate syllable and every third syllable preceding it.

The application of this rule is illustrated by the forms in (93), which exemplify the accentual patterns from two up to nine syllables (from Hayes 1995: 309):

> (93) 'eɲe   'tail'
>   'ʃakahe   'stomach'
>   ki'hibere   'I ran'
>   ari'uuʧa   'he came already'
>   ˌʤihira'riama   'I must do'
>   maˌrahaha'eiki   'their blankets'
>   ikiˌtapare'repeha   'the water is clean'
>   ˌʃaadiˌroboβu'ruruʧe   'ninety-nine'

The most appropriate way to incorporate such ternary patterns into our foot inventory would at first sight appear to be to add a new foot type to the inventory given in (79), viz. the **syllabic dactyl**, which would have the structure in (94):

> (94) *syllabic dactyl*   (×   ·   ·)
>   σ   σ   σ

The incorporation of this foot type into our inventory would allow us to represent some of the forms in (93) as in (95), assuming right-to-left foot assignment:

> (95) a.   (×   ·   ·)   b.   (×   ·   ·)(×   ·   ·)
>   σ   σ   σ   σ   σ   σ   σ   σ   σ   σ   σ   σ
>   ki hi be re   i   ki ta pa re re pe ha
>
>   c. (×   ·   ·)(×   ·   ·)(×   ·   ·)
>   σ   σ   σ   σ   σ   σ   σ   σ   σ
>   ʧa a   di ro bo βu ru ru ʧe

Dresher and Lahiri (1991) argue for the introduction of a rather different type of foot, which they call the 'Germanic foot', in order to account for the phenomenon of High Vowel Deletion in Old English which we examined briefly in §3.7.4. There we saw that the vowels /i/ and /u/ delete when they follow a heavy syllable (VC, VV) but not a light syllable (V). However, they also delete when they follow *two* light syllables, as shown in (96):

(96) a. *singular   plural*
       scip   scipu   'ship'
       lim   limu   'limb'
       word   word   'word'
       bān   bān   'bone'

    b. we(o)rod < Early West Saxon */wered-u/ 'troops'
       færeld < *færeldu 'journey'

Dresher and Lahiri suggest that these facts can be accounted for by postulating a **moraic dactyl** (their 'Germanic foot'), with the structure in (97):

(97) *moraic dactyl*   (×   ·)
                     μ μ μ

Thus the strong branch of the foot must contain two moras. High Vowel Deletion, then, can only take place when the high vowel occupies an open syllable in the weak position of the foot. A word such as *scipu* contains two light syllables and therefore only two moras, so that the high vowel 'is required to form the strong branch' of the foot, and is not subject to deletion, as shown in (98a). Forms which do allow deletion, such as those in (98b, c), already have two moras in the strong branch, and so High Vowel Deletion is free to apply:

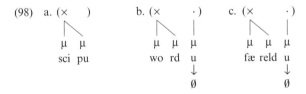

(98) a. (×   )   b. (×   ·)   c. (×   ·)
      μ μ   μ μ μ   μ μ μ
     sci pu   wo rd u   fæ reld u
                     ↓   ↓
                     Ø   Ø

However, Hayes (1995: 307) observes: 'Much recent theorizing in generative grammar focuses on the idea of locality: we obtain interesting and valid predictions by constraining rules to apply within bounded domains. In phonology, the principle of locality often takes the form of limiting what can be counted: a reasonable conjecture is that phonological rules can count only to two.' In other words, it seems preferable to attempt to analyse systems such as that of Cayuvava in terms of the binary foot inventory already established, rather than introducing dactylic feet, in which the principle of locality is necessarily violated, and whose presence in our inventory would lead to an enormous expansion in the generative capacity of the model.

Hayes reanalyses the apparently ternary system of Cayuvava in terms of syllabic trochees by appealing to the notion of **weak local parsing**. Whereas unmarked systems parse sequences into feet by simply moving from a parsed sequence to the immediately adjacent syllable, weak local parsing skips over a syllable after a foot is assigned. This means that in Cayuvava we assign syllabic trochaic feet, with an intervening unparsed syllable between each foot (final syllables are unparsed for reasons of extrametricality; see §4.4.7 below):

(99) a. $(\times \quad \cdot)$
      σ   σ   σ   σ
      ki   hi   be   re

      b. $(\times \quad \cdot) \quad (\times \quad \cdot)$
         σ   σ   σ   σ   σ   σ   σ   σ
         i   ki   ta   pa   re   re   pe   ha

      c. $(\times \quad \cdot) \quad (\times \quad \cdot) \quad (\times \quad \cdot)$
       σ   σ   σ   σ   σ   σ   σ   σ   σ
       ʧa   a   di   ro   bo   βu   ru   ru   ʧe

On this analysis, then, ternary feet do not form part of the inventory of possible feet types.

4.4.6 Unbounded feet

In all the systems which we have considered so far, we have found evidence for dividing up the syllables of a word into bounded feet. Such systems typically display an alternating accentual pattern. However, there exist systems in which it seems we can provide a more appropriate analysis in terms of **unbounded feet**. These are systems in which 'stress can fall an unlimited distance from a boundary or another stress, provided the appropriate conditions are met' (Hayes 1995: 32). Unlike bounded systems, then, accents do not tend to be equidistant from each other throughout the word; rather, we find systems such as that of Classical Arabic in (100) (from McCarthy 1979: 460):

(100) a.   kiˈtaabun   'book (NOM SG)'
           manaaˈdiilu   'kerchiefs (NOM)'
           juˈʃaariku   'he participates'
      b.   ˈmamlakatun   'kingdom (NOM SG)'
           ˈkataba   'he wrote'
           ˈbalaħatun   'date (NOM SG)'

Accentuation in this system is determined by two rules, given by McCarthy as (101):[24]

(101) a. Stress the rightmost non-final heavy syllable.

        b. Otherwise stress the first syllable.

Such a pattern is typical of unbounded systems. Two principles are involved; one which assigns the accent to a heavy syllable at a word-edge, and another which operates in the absence of a heavy syllable, which assigns the accent to some other word-edge syllable. The two principles may or may not target the same word-edge. In the Classical Arabic example in (100), opposite word-edges are selected, but Hayes (1995: §7.2) shows that all combinations are found. Thus Aguacatec, a Mayan language spoken in Guatemala, has the system in (102):

(102) a. Stress the rightmost heavy syllable.

        b. Otherwise stress the final syllable.

This is illustrated by the forms in (103) (from McArthur and McArthur 1956); heavy syllables are those with a long vowel:

(103) a. 'haːluʔ   'today'

             'ʔeːq'um 'carrier'

        b. q'us'q'uh 'delicious'

             k'olč'bil   'seat'

Amele, a Gum language spoken in Papua New Guinea, shows the same pattern as Aguacatec, but selects the opposite word-edge for both parameters, as shown by the data in (104) (from Roberts 1987: 358); heavy syllables are closed:

(104) a. du'æn   'cold'

             gædo'loh 'edge'

             'æn.se   'left hand'

        b. 'mælə   'chicken'

             'nɪfulə   'species of beetle'

Hayes (1995: 297) cites Kwakwala as an example of a language with the fourth possibility; i.e. accent on the first heavy syllable, otherwise on the final syllable.

Instead of approaching the systems discussed here in terms of unbounded foot structure, we might adopt the point of view that these languages have no foot structure at all, thereby allowing us to claim that feet are maximally binary. In such languages, word accent must be derived solely from weight,

---

[24] We ignore here 'superheavy' final syllables, which attract accent.

such that the leftmost or rightmost heavy syllable is assigned the word accent. In a word which has no heavy syllables, accent is assigned by default, usually to the first or last syllable within the word. There are four possible patterns: (i) rightmost heavy, default left (i.e. the final heavy syllable is accented, but if there is no heavy syllable in the word, accent falls on the initial syllable); (ii) rightmost heavy, default right; (iii) leftmost heavy, default left; (iv) leftmost heavy, default right (see Hayes 1995: 296–297; Goldsmith 1990: 180ff.). There are also languages with unbounded feet in which accent is assigned lexically, rather than by, for example, syllable weight. When two accented morphemes combine, factors such as the above also come into play, so that either the rightmost or the leftmost lexical accent is selected as the word accent. If neither morpheme is lexically accented, then a default rule will assign word accent to the leftmost or rightmost syllable, so that four patterns are again possible (see van der Hulst 1997, and cf. our discussion of Russian in §4.3).

4.4.7 Extrametricality

In §4.4.5 we examined evidence which showed that apparently ternary feet could be reanalysed by what Hayes terms 'weak local parsing'. In effect, in languages in which accent falls on every third syllable, a polysyllabic sequence was analysed as ('σ σ) σ ('σ σ) σ ('σ σ) σ, so that between each binary trochaic foot a syllable was left unparsed. However, the final syllable in such sequences is not subject to weak local parsing, as it is not intermediate between two accents. If we are to maintain the claim that there are no dactylic, i.e. ternary, feet, we must provide an account of the status of such final syllables.

At first sight, there appear to be many languages which have a simple rule which assigns primary accent to the antepenultimate syllable. We might therefore argue that in these cases accent location is the result of assigning a ternary foot at the right edge of the word, as in (105):

(105) ...   (×   ·   ·)
       σ   σ   σ   σ   σ   σ

However, a closer look at such systems suggests that, as before, it is not appropriate to postulate such dactylic feet. Accent assignment patterns such as that in (106) are frequently encountered:

(106) Primary accent falls on the penultimate syllable if it is heavy; otherwise it falls on the antepenultimate.

This is largely the system of Classical Latin, in which main stress *never* falls on the final syllable, whether it is heavy or light. In other words, it is simply ignored, so that syllables which 'do not count' in the assignment of stress are considered to be **extrametrical**. This is illustrated in (107), for the words *amicus* /a'miːkus/ 'friend', *tenebrae* /'tɛnɛbreː/ 'darkness', *domesticus* /do'mɛstikus/ 'domestic' (adapted from Hayes 1995: 92); heavy rhymes are VC and VV. Like extrasyllabicity in §3.4.4 (see also below), extrametricality is indicated by angle brackets:

(107) a.   (×)   b. (× ·)   c.   (×)
          σ̆ σ̄ <σ̆>   σ̆ σ̆ <σ̄>   σ̆ σ̄ σ̆ <σ̄>
          a miː kus   tɛ nɛ breː   do mɛs ti kus

The final syllable plays no part in accent assignment, which creates trochees from right to left.

In the examples in (107), the final syllable is made extrametrical. There is ample evidence that other types of units can be ignored in the application of rules, and therefore must be made extrametrical. Thus we saw in §3.8 that a consonant in the rhyme of a word-final syllable is often ignored for the purposes of computing syllable weight. In general, for a word-final syllable to count as heavy in a particular language, it often has to be heavier than a non-final syllable. For example, in a language in which a VC rhyme is heavy, a word-final VC rhyme may count as light. In this respect, consider the English nouns in (108):

(108)   a.   ... V<σ>   b.   ... VC<σ>   c.   ... VV<σ>
             algebra   agenda   arena

Accent placement in these nouns is subject to the extrametricality parameter in (109), so that accent falls on the penultimate syllable if it is heavy (i.e. in English VC or VV), and otherwise on the antepenult:

(109)   *Extrametricality parameter*
        Ignore the final syllable (nouns)

Observe now that the rule governing accent placement in these nouns appears to be similar to that for the verbs considered in §3.8, and repeated as (110):

(110)   a.   ... VC   b.   ... VCC   c.   ... VVC
             astonish   collapse   maintain

Here the final syllable is *not* declared extrametrical, and is therefore available for accentuation. This means that in (110) accent should fall on the final syllable if its rhyme is heavy, and on the penultimate otherwise. At first sight, though, all the verbs in (110) appear to have final syllables in which the rhyme is heavy or indeed superheavy. However, as we saw briefly in §3.8, the generalisation can be maintained if the final consonant of the verbs is considered extrasyllabic (or indeed to be the onset of a following syllable), as in (111):

(111) a. ... V<C>   b. ... VC<C>   c. ... VV<C>
           astonish   collapse   maintain

Now we have the familiar distinction between V (light) and VC/VV (heavy), and the rule applies as expected.

Consonant extrasyllabicity and syllable extrametricality are instantiations of the more general phenomenon of **constituent extrametricality**, which Hayes (1995: 57) suggests may be extended to other constituents, such as the foot or the phonological word. As Vergnaud and Halle (1978) point out, extrametricality is a parametric option in accentual patterns. Furthermore, it is generally restricted to peripheral constituents, i.e. those which occur at the edge of some domain; Hayes claims that the 'unmarked edge for extrametricality is the right edge', as in the cases we have examined so far.

The accentual system of English shows a number of parallels with that of Latin. Consider again some of the English data introduced in §3.8. The appropriate settings for the parameters in (71) will yield the word trees in (112) for *astonish*, *collapse* and *maintain*, respectively:

(112) a. (× ·)   b. (×)   c. (×) (×)
           ŏ ŏ ŏ   ŏ ŏ   ŏ ŏ
           ə stɒ nɪ <ʃ>   kə læp<s>   meɪn teɪ <n>

Exactly the same parameter settings apply to generate the stress patterns of nouns such as *algebra*, *agenda* and *arena*, provided that we ignore the final syllable, rather than just the final consonant:

(113) a. (× ·)   b. (×)   c. (×)
          ŏ̄ ŏ <ŏ>   ŏ ŏ̄ <ŏ>   ŏ ŏ̄ <ŏ>
          æl dʒə brə   ə dʒen də   ə riː nə

The final syllable in the examples in (113), then, is extrametrical, and is ignored by virtue of the appropriate setting of the **extrametricality** parameter. Extrametricality, then, applied to word accentual patterns, offers a means of placing an accent three syllables away from the edge, while maintaining an analysis in terms of binary feet. Thus (105), the characterisation of antepenultimate accent, can better be represented as (114):

(114) ...   (× ·)
          σ σ σ σ σ <σ>

Notice finally that under certain circumstances, only particular *types* of syllable may be considered extrametrical for some process. In Dutch, for example, trisyllabic words with a final heavy syllable have regular antepenultimate accent (van der Hulst 1984; Kager *et al.* 1985): *'albatros* 'albatross', *'horizon* 'horizon', *'hospita* 'landlady', *'pagina* 'page'. In these cases, then, it might be argued that the final syllable is extrametrical (but see the discussion in the next section). However, other trisyllabic words do not regularly have antepenultimate stress, e.g. *bal'lade* 'ballad', with a final light syllable, and *kapi'tein* 'captain', with a final superheavy syllable. Thus, the light syllable in (115b) and the superheavy syllable in (115c) are not extrametrical, unlike the heavy one in (115a):

(115) a. $(\times \quad \cdot)$ b. $(\times \quad \cdot)$ c. $(\times \quad \cdot)(\times)$

 σ̄ σ̄ <σ̄>   σ̄ σ̄ σ̄   σ̄ σ̄ σ̋

 paː ɣiː naː   baː laː də   kaː pi: tɛın

(where σ̋ represents a superheavy syllable).

4.5 English and Dutch compared

We conclude this chapter with a brief examination of two systems of word accentuation which can be shown to be very similar in terms of the parameter settings which they select, even though the patterns which we encounter appear superficially to be very different. We base this on Trommelen and Zonneveld (1999: §§8.1.1–2), which is part of the general account of accentual systems in van der Hulst (1999), but we do not follow their analysis in all aspects.

Trommelen and Zonneveld give the following list of English and Dutch cognates:

(116) | | *English* | | *Dutch* | |
|---|---|---|---|---|
| a. | family | ['fæməlɪ] | familie | [faːˈmiːliː] |
| | Goliath | [gəʊˈlaɪəθ] | Goliath | [ˈɣoːliːɑt] |
| | balance | ['bæləns] | balans | [baːˈlɑns] |
| | president | ['prɛzədənt] | president | [preːziːˈdɛnt] |
| | antecedent | [æntəˈsiːdənt] | antecedent | [ɑntəsəˈdɛnt] |
| b. | libido | [lɪˈbiːdəʊ] | libido | [ˈliːbiːdoː] |
| | violet | ['vaɪələt] | violet | [viːoːˈlɛt] |

In each of these pairs, the primary accent falls on different syllables in the two languages. Nevertheless, Trommelen and Zonneveld argue, the set of parameters assigning accent is identical, although, as we shall see, there are many differences of detail:

(117) a. *final extrametricality:* yes
 b. *foot structure:* bounded, LH, R→L, weight-sensitive
 c. *word structure:* RH

Given these parameter settings, accent assignment to the English forms in (116) is straightforward, and proceeds in the same way as the forms considered in §4.4.6. In all cases, the final syllable is ignored (by (117a)). Weight-sensitive feet are constructed, starting from the right; the left branch of a binary foot is the head. The rightmost foot-head is selected as the head of the word, as shown in (118) for *ante'cedent*:

(118) (·   ×)
       (×   ·) (×)
        σ̆   σ̆   σ̆ <σ̆>
        æn tə siːdənt

The two systems differ in two important respects. The first concerns the definition of syllable weight. For English, VV and VC rhymes are heavy and V rhymes are light; Dutch is similar, but, as we saw in §3.4.1, differs in treating VV rhymes as light, as is evidenced by the accentual patterns in (119), from Trommelen and Zonneveld (1999: §8.1.2.2):

(119) a. elektron   [eːˈlɛktrɔn]   'electron'
           Agamemnon   [aːɣaːˈmɛmnɔn]   'Agamemnon'
           rododendron   [roːdoːˈdɛndrɔn]   'rhododendron'
       b. alfabet   [ˈɑlfaːbɛt]   'alphabet'
           Pythagoras   [piːˈtaːɣoːrɑs]   'Pythagoras'
           Jeruzalem   [jeːˈruːzaːlɛm]   'Jerusalem'

In (119a) the penultimate rhyme is VC, and therefore heavy; in (119b) it is VV, and behaves as light in rejecting accent.

In all the cases in (119), it looks as if the final VC syllable is extrametrical, as we suggested in the previous section. This is supported by the forms in (120), with a VC penult and a VV final syllable, with penultimate accent:

(120) Toronto   [toːˈrɔntoː]   'Toronto'
       Casablanca   [kaːsaːˈblɑŋkaː]   'Casablanca'
       influenza   [ɪnfluːˈɛnzaː]   'influenza'

However, the forms in (120) are in fact neutral between an analysis in which the final syllable is treated as extrametrical and one in which the final two syllables are considered to form a binary left-headed foot, on the assumption that VV syllables are light. That this is not a trivial point is demonstrated by the two sets of words in (121), both of which end in two open syllables. Those in (121a), with penultimate accent, represent the regular pattern for Dutch words of this type; those in (121b), with antepenultimate accent, the irregular, but quite common, pattern:

(121) a. familie   [faːˈmiːliː]   'family'
           pijama   [piːˈjaːmaː]   'pyjamas'
           macaroni   [maːkaːˈroːniː]   'macaroni'
           hypotenusa   [hiːpoːteːˈnuːzaː]   'hypotenuse'
       b. libido   [ˈliːbiːdoː]   'libido'
           tombola   [ˈtɔmboːlaː]   'tombola'
           Amerika   [aːˈmeːriːkaː]   'America'
           Paramaribo   [paːraːˈmaːriːboː]   'Paramaribo'

Given that (121a) represents the regular pattern, and that the forms in (119) appear to provide evidence that VV is light in Dutch, an analysis in terms of final extrametricality would seem inappropriate. Such an analysis would give the following structure for *familie*:

(122) (×   ·)
       ŏ ŏ <ŏ>
       faː miː liː

This would incorrectly yield accent on the antepenultimate, which is the *irregular* pattern instantiated in (121b). Rather, a footing algorithm which treats the final two syllables of *familie* as a foot, as in (123), seems preferable:

(123)   (×   ·)
       ŏ ŏ ŏ
       faː miː liː

How can we arrive at the structure in (123)? Let us assume that the regular patterns of Dutch do *not* display extrametricality. Rather, a final VC syllable, which, recall, is heavy, will form a foot, while a light VV syllable does not. This gives the footing in (124):

(124) a. ...VV.VV   b. ...VC.VV   c. ...VC.VC   d. ...VV.VC
           (×   ·)   (×   ·)   (×)(×)   (×   ·)(×)
       ŏ ŏ ŏ   ŏ ō ŏ   ŏ ō ō   ō ŏ ŏ
       faː miː liː   toː rɔn toː   eː lɛktrɔn   ɑl faː bɛt

On this analysis, final heavy syllables form feet, while final light syllables do not. This in turn means that the parameter in (117c) (word structure: RH) must be modified. Following the ideas outlined in van der Hulst (1984: ch. 5), we assume the following formulation:

(125) *word structure:* RH iff the final foot branches; otherwise LH

This modification is required to prevent forms such as *elektron* and *alfabet* from being assigned final accent, while still allowing the final foot of e.g. *karboˈnade* 'chop' to take accent:

(126) a.   (×   )   b.   (×   )   c.   (× ·)   d. (×   ·)
       (× ·)   (× ·)   (×)(×)   (× ·)(×)
       ŏ   ŏ   ŏ   ŏ   ō   ŏ   ŏ   ō   ŏ   ō   ŏ   ŏ
       faː miː liː   toː rɔn toː   eː lɛktrɔn   ɑl faː bɛt

    e.   (·   ×   )
       (× ·)(× ·)
       ō   ŏ   ŏ   ŏ
       kɑr boː naː də

Because the final foot of *karbonade* contains two syllables, and is therefore branching, it takes primary accent.

There are two other circumstances under which primary accent falls on the final foot. The first involves final superheavy syllables, already discussed in §4.4.7. These are invariably accented, as shown in (127):

(127) kapitein   [kaːpiːˈtɛin]   'captain'
      abrikoos   [aːbriːˈkoːs]   'apricot'
      ledikant   [leːdiːˈkɑnt]   'bedstead'

Clearly, (125) would fail to assign accent to the final foot, which is non-branching. We could generate the correct accentual pattern simply by stipulating that a final foot formed by a superheavy syllable is accented, but this would be unfortunate; it seems reasonable to assume that their ability to be accented is a product of the fact that they are inherently heavier than other syllables. In a mora-based analysis (cf. the discussion in §3.5), a superheavy syllable would contain more moras than a heavy syllable, and might therefore be interpretable as equivalent to a sequence of two 'normal' syllables. Here we follow the proposals of Langeweg (1988) and Zonneveld (1993), who suggest that superheavy syllables are underlyingly disyllabic, with the second syllable containing an empty nucleus. Thus a foot containing a superheavy syllable is branching, as shown in (128):

(128) a. (·   ×   )   b. (·   ×   )
      (× ·)(× ·)   (× ·)(× ·)
      ŏ   ŏ   ŏ   ŏ   ŏ   ŏ   ō   ŏ
      aː briː koː sØ   leː diː kɑn tØ

This account, reminiscent of aspects of the theory of government phonology discussed in §3.8, thus treats words with final superheavies as having the same structure as, for example, *karbonade*, with the only difference lying in whether the final nucleus is realised or not.

This account, as we have noted, is to be preferred to one in which final superheavies are simply stipulated as being accented, in that it attributes their behaviour to their structure. However, no such account seems available for the other category of words which take final accent, illustrated in (116b):

(129) violet   [viːoːˈlɛt]   'violet'
       parasol [paːraːˈsɔl] 'sunshade'
       maniak   [maːniːˈɑk]   'maniac'

The structure of the final syllable is no different from regular cases such as *alfabet*, with antepenultimate accent, and so it seems that the forms in (129) must simply be lexically marked as taking primary accent on the final syllable.

We return now to the irregular forms in (121b), such as *libido* and *tombola*, with antepenultimate instead of the expected penultimate accent. In these cases it seems that an appeal to extrametricality *is* appropriate; the final syllable must be lexically specified as being extrametrical, so that the penultimate light syllable will be footed with the antepenult:

(130) a. $(\times \quad \cdot)$ b. $(\times \quad \cdot)$
          σ̆ σ̆ <σ̆>   σ̆ σ̆ σ̆ <σ̆>
          liː biː doː   aː meː riː kaː

The analysis of Dutch which we have given, then, involves the following parameter setting (cf. the setting for English in (117)):

(131) a. *final extrametricality:* no (except lexically)
       b. *foot structure:*   bounded, LH, R→L, weight-sensitive
       c. *word structure:*   RH iff the final foot branches; otherwise LH

4.6 Summary

In this final chapter we have examined the prosodic structure of the 'word' above the level of the syllable, and we have shown that syllables can be grouped into feet, which, in turn, form the (phonological) word. The chief exponent of the prosodic organisation of syllables into feet and words is accent or stress. In §4.1 we discussed the concept of word accent and its relation to intonation, while §4.2 introduced the notion of the foot. In §4.3 we considered the ways in which accent systems can vary, in particular in terms of the predictability of accent location, both primary and non-primary. §4.4 was concerned with the typology of feet found in the languages of the world, couched within the approach to phonological structure known as metrical phonology. The development of this typology allowed us to provide a comparative analysis of word accent in English and Dutch in §4.5.

4.7   Epilogue: levels and derivations

In this book we have been concerned with theories of phonological representation. As we noted in the preface, this is only one aspect of phonological theory in general. A theory of phonology can be seen as comprising three parts (cf. Goldsmith 1993): a theory of levels (e.g. lexical, phonological, phonetic), a theory of representations (for each level) and a theory of the relationship or mapping between levels.

In *SPE*, there was a clear distinction between what was often called the lexical and the phonological levels. The former contained unspecified features, as well as features marked with 'm' and 'u' or with '+' and '−'. Features at the phonological level had to be fully specified, in terms of '+' and '−' values only (cf. Kaye 1995). In this book we have assumed that there is no real distinction between the lexical and the phonological levels, and have made no distinction between rules that fill in feature-values or unary features and rules that modify the representation. Thus we assume that there is a single phonological input level, which reflects the consequences of setting parameters on units and on the ways in which they can combine at each phonological layer in the hierarchy. This level is affected by a set of rules that fill in, spread and remove feature-values. The phonological operations are sometimes stated as language-specific rules, while in other cases they follow from universal conventions, possibly in response to parameter settings. This view creates a distinction between an initial or phonological **input** level and a final or **output** level. The need for performing phonological operations that create this distinction comes from the idea that the initial phonological level abstracts away from redundancy (properties that are predictable, such as the scope or presence of a feature) and from productive allomorphic alternations (positing an invariant input that loses or acquires certain features in certain contexts).

In *SPE*, the operations (phonological rules) were extrinsically ordered. Extrinsic rule ordering creates *intermediate* levels between the input and output levels. Furthermore, this theory claims that the input and the intermediate levels differ *in kind* from the output level referring to the former as phonological and the latter as phonetic. In fact, it is claimed that the phonetic representations are different in kind, in that they allow the scalar specification of certain features (cf. Kaye 1995).

In our exposition we have not mentioned cases of extrinsic ordering of phonological rules or operations. Although the issue has not been addressed explicitly, we believe, in common with most current theorists, that extrinsic ordering is not necessary in phonology. Thus we do not envisage intermediate levels. Furthermore, we have not adopted the point of view that the final or output level is in any sense less phonological than the initial or input level. Rather, we have assumed that the output level of phonology is not different in kind from the input level.

In fact, since there is no difference in kind between input and output, we prefer to refer to the input and output 'levels' as 'representations characterising a *single* level', i.e. the phonological level. We prefer to reserve the term 'level' for representations (or sets of representations) which differ in their representational vocabulary. Thus we might identify the phonological level, the phonetic level, the morphological (or morpho-syntactic) level and other possible levels outside the domain of phonology.

The phonological output representation should contain all information necessary to derive a phonetic interpretation, but the nature of the resulting phonetic level (however it is represented in a particular model) has not been our consideration, nor has been the mapping between the phonological and the phonetic levels. This mapping is not a trivial matter, however, because the phonological level *is* qualitatively distinct from the phonetic level, in the sense that the latter is a direct representation of articulatory or acoustic events. With this understanding of the relationship between the phonological and the phonetic levels, we have in this book been considering the nature of representations at the phonological level, and have drawn a distinction between an input and output representation, the latter resulting from the application of an unordered set of phonological operations or rules.

The relation between input and output representation at the phonological level can be seen as a function F, which maps one representation onto the other. If we disregard the fact that in *SPE* the input and output levels were assumed to be different in kind (cf. above), we can say that in this model the mapping function F was an ordered set of rules. In our book the content of this function F is an *unordered* set of rules and conventions. Other views are possible, and one, developed in Optimality Theory (OT; see for an introduction Kager 1999) has become very influential in recent times. Instead of rules which modify an input representation, OT proposes that the correct output for any input is selected from an infinite set of possible outputs, by an extrinsically ordered set of universal constraints.

In our view, the central claim of OT is largely orthogonal to the issues of levels and representations which we have discussed in this book. However, some optimality theorists would disagree, claiming that OT does not need a theory of representations or parameters to account for cross-linguistic differences. Rather, to exclude output 'candidates' with representations that contain combinations of phonological entities which are never found in languages, OT postulates a set of universally highly ranked constraints, which in effect characterise the set of possible phonological representations. Generally, though, these constraints are not spelled out. In practice, it seems to us that OT analyses make implicit assumptions about the structure of phonological representations which are drawn from the repertoire of views such as those that we have discussed in this book. What remains as a more crucial difference between the view taken in this book and OT lies in the treatment of the kind of cross-linguistic differences that we have called parametric. OT replaces parameter setting by constraint ranking. The typical OT constraint in some sense functions as a 'unary parameter', which cannot be turned off, but instead must be dominated by another unary constraint, whose effect is to make the original constraint inapplicable.

We believe, then, that any phonological theory must have a coherent view of phonological representation. We hope that we have persuaded the reader of this book that this is indeed so, and that we have succeeded in showing that the phonological structure of the word remains a fertile area for the formulation of theories of phonological representation.

4.8 Further reading

On accent systems (§4.1), see Bolinger (1972), Hyman (1977), Schane (1979), Goldsmith (1982) and Beckman (1986). The relation between accent and its exponents is discussed by Lehiste (1970), van Heuven and Sluijter (1996) and Dogil (1999). Accounts of Japanese accentuation are given by Haraguchi (1977), Beckman and Pierrehumbert (1986), Pierrehumbert and Beckman (1988). On pitch-accent systems, see the papers in van der Hulst and Smith (1988b), as well as Bruce and Hermans (1999), Dogil (1999), Hualde (1999). Intonation is dealt with in Pierrehumbert (1980), Bolinger (1986), Ladd (1996), Cruttenden (1997) and Gussenhoven and Bruce (1999). On clitics, see Anderson (1996) and Nespor (1999).

On the foot as a unit of timing (§4.2), see Abercrombie (1964) and Catford (1977). Kiparsky and Youmans (1989) contains papers on metre; see for example Hayes (1989b). See also Hanson and Kiparsky (1996). The distinction between stress-timed and syllable-timed languages is due to Pike (1943). See also Dauer (1983), Selkirk (1984a) and Nespor and Vogel (1989). General works on the foot include C. Rice (1992), Kager (1993), Hayes (1995) and van der Hulst (1997).

For work on the typology of stress and accent systems (§4.3), see Haraguchi (1977), Hyman (1977), Halle and Vergnaud (1987a), Hayes (1995). The relationship between primary and non-primary accent is dealt with by van der Hulst (1984), Roca (1986), Hurch (1996) and van de Vijver (1998). On the cycle in phonology, see Kean (1974), Kiparsky (1979), Halle and Vergnaud (1987b) and Cole (1995).

For the principles and history of metrical theory, and its notation (§§4.4, 4.4.1), see Liberman (1975), Liberman and Prince (1977), Halle and Vergnaud (1978), Kiparsky (1979), Prince (1980, 1983), Hayes (1981), Giegerich (1985), Levin (1985), Hogg and McCully (1987), Goldsmith (1990), Halle (1990), Halle and Idsardi (1995) and Kager (1995).

On foot typology and related matters (§§4.4.3–4.4.7), see many of the above references, as well as Hayes (1982), Archangeli (1988b), Lahiri and van der Hulst (1988), Halle *et al.* (1993) and Mester (1994).

Accent in English and/or Dutch (§4.5) is discussed by, for example Halle and Keyser (1971), Selkirk (1980), van der Hulst (1984), Langeweg (1988), Kager (1989), Zonneveld (1993), Burzio (1994) and Trommelen and Zonneveld (1999).

For an account of accent within a historical context, see Salmons (1992). See also Lahiri *et al.* (1999). Some of the papers in Archibald (1997) deal with the acquisition of accent. See also Fikkert (1994), and, for a general account of acquisition, Jusczyk (1997).

Appendix

THE INTERNATIONAL PHONETIC ALPHABET (revised to 1993, updated 1996)

CONSONANTS (PULMONIC)

	Bilabial	Labiodental	Dental	Alveolar	Postalveolar	Retroflex	Palatal	Velar	Uvular	Pharyngeal	Glottal
Plosive	p b			t d		ʈ ɖ	c ɟ	k ɡ	q ɢ		ʔ
Nasal	m	ɱ		n		ɳ	ɲ	ŋ	N		
Trill	B			r					R		
Tap or Flap				ɾ		ɽ					
Fricative	ɸ β	f v	θ ð	s z	ʃ ʒ	ʂ ʐ	ç ʝ	x ɣ	χ ʁ	ħ ʕ	h ɦ
Lateral fricative				ɬ ɮ							
Approximant		ʋ		ɹ		ɻ	j	ɰ			
Lateral approximant				l		ɭ	ʎ	L			

Where symbols appear in pairs, the one to the right represents a voiced consonant. Shaded areas denote articulations judged impossible.

CONSONANTS (NON-PULMONIC)

Clicks		Voiced implosives		Ejectives	
ʘ	Bilabial	ɓ	Bilabial	ʼ	Examples:
ǀ	Dental	ɗ	Dental/alveolar	pʼ	Bilabial
ǃ	(Post)alveolar	ʄ	Palatal	tʼ	Dental/alveolar
ǂ	Palatoalveolar	ɠ	Velar	kʼ	Velar
ǁ	Alveolar lateral	ʛ	Uvular	sʼ	Alveolar fricative

OTHER SYMBOLS

ʍ	Voiceless labial-velar fricative	ɕ ʑ	Alveolo-palatal fricatives
w	Voiced labial-velar approximant	ɺ	Alveolar lateral flap
ɥ	Voiced labial-palatal approximant	ɧ	Simultaneous ʃ and x
ʜ	Voiceless epiglottal fricative		
ʢ	Voiced epiglottal fricative	Affricates and double articulations can be represented by two symbols joined by a tie bar if necessary.	k͡p t͡s
ʡ	Epiglottal plosive		

VOWELS

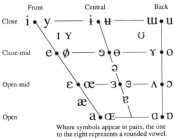

Where symbols appear in pairs, the one to the right represents a rounded vowel.

SUPRASEGMENTALS

ˈ	Primary stress	ˌfoʊnəˈtɪʃən
ˌ	Secondary stress	
ː	Long	eː
ˑ	Half-long	eˑ
̆	Extra-short	ĕ
ǀ	Minor (foot) group	
‖	Major (intonation) group	
.	Syllable break	ɹi.ækt
‿	Linking (absence of a break)	

DIACRITICS

Diacritics may be placed above a symbol with a descender, e.g. ŋ̊

̥ Voiceless	n̥ d̥	̤ Breathy voiced	b̤ a̤	̪ Dental	t̪ d̪
̬ Voiced	s̬ t̬	̰ Creaky voiced	b̰ a̰	̺ Apical	t̺ d̺
ʰ Aspirated	tʰ dʰ	̼ Linguolabial	t̼ d̼	̻ Laminal	t̻ d̻
̹ More rounded	ɔ̹	ʷ Labialized	tʷ dʷ	̃ Nasalized	ẽ
̜ Less rounded	ɔ̜	ʲ Palatalized	tʲ dʲ	ⁿ Nasal release	dⁿ
̟ Advanced	u̟	ˠ Velarized	tˠ dˠ	ˡ Lateral release	dˡ
̠ Retracted	e̠	ˤ Pharyngealized	tˤ dˤ	̚ No audible release	d̚
̈ Centralized	ë	̴ Velarized or pharyngealized	ɫ		
̽ Mid-centralized	ě	̝ Raised	e̝	(ɹ̝ = voiced alveolar fricative)	
̩ Syllabic	n̩	̞ Lowered	e̞	(β̞ = voiced bilabial approximant)	
̯ Non-syllabic	e̯	̘ Advanced Tongue Root	e̘		
˞ Rhoticity	ɚ a˞	̙ Retracted Tongue Root	e̙		

TONES AND WORD ACCENTS

LEVEL			CONTOUR		
e̋ or	˥	Extra high	ě or	˩˥	Rising
é	˦	High	ê	˥˩	Falling
ē	˧	Mid	e᷄	˧˥	High rising
è	˨	Low	e᷅	˩˧	Low rising
ȅ	˩	Extra low	e᷈	˧˩˧	Rising-falling
↓		Downstep	↗		Global rise
↑		Upstep	↘		Global fall

246

REFERENCES

Abaglo, P. and D. Archangeli (1989). Language-particular underspecification: Gengbe /e/ and Yoruba /i/. *Linguistic Inquiry* 20. 457–80.

Abercrombie, D. (1964). Syllable quantity and enclitics in English. In D. Abercrombie, D. B. Fry, P. A. D. McCarthy, N. C. Scott and J. L. M. Trim (eds.) *In honour of Daniel Jones*. London: Longman. 216–22.

(1965). A phonetician's view of verse structure. In D. Abercrombie, *Studies in phonetics and linguistics*. London: Oxford University Press. 16–25.

(1967). *Elements of general phonetics*. Edinburgh: Edinburgh University Press.

Allen, W. S. (1973). *Accent and rhythm: prosodic features of Latin and Greek*. Cambridge: Cambridge University Press.

Anderson, J. M. (1969). Syllabic or non-syllabic phonology. *Journal of Linguistics* 5. 136–43.

(1987). The limits of linearity. In J. M. Anderson and J. Durand (eds.) *Explorations in dependency phonology*. Dordrecht: Foris. 199–220.

Anderson, J. M. and J. Durand (1988). Vowel harmony in Nez Perce. In van der Hulst and Smith (1988a: vol. II). 1–17.

Anderson, J. M. and C. J. Ewen (1987). *Principles of dependency phonology*. Cambridge: Cambridge University Press.

Anderson, J. M. and C. Jones (1974). Three theses concerning phonological representations. *Journal of Linguistics* 10. 1–26.

(1977). *Phonological structure and the history of English*. Amsterdam: North-Holland.

Anderson, S. R. (1973). *u*-umlaut and Skaldic verse. In S. R. Anderson and P. Kiparsky (eds.) *A Festschrift for Morris Halle*. New York: Holt, Rinehart and Winston. 3–13.

(1976). Nasal consonants and the internal structure of segments. *Language* 52. 326–44.

(1982). The analysis of French schwa: or, how to get something from nothing. *Language* 58. 534–73.

(1984). A metrical interpretation of some traditional claims about quantity and stress. In Aronoff and Oehrle (1984). 83–106.

(1985). *Phonology in the twentieth century: theories of rules and theories of representations*. Chicago: University of Chicago Press.

References

(1996). How to put your clitics in their place. *The Linguistic Review* 13. 165–91.

Aoki, H. (1968). Towards a typology of vowel harmony. *International Journal of American Linguistics* 34. 142–5.

Archangeli, D. (1984). *Underspecification in Yawelmani phonology and morphology.* Ph.D. dissertation, Massachusetts Institute of Technology.

(1988a). Aspects of underspecification theory. *Phonology* 5. 183–207.

(1988b). Extrametricality in Yawelmani. *The Linguistic Review* 4. 101–20.

(1991). Syllabification and prosodic templates in Yawelmani. *Natural Language and Linguistic Theory* 9. 231–83.

Archangeli, D. and D. Pulleyblank (1989). Yoruba vowel harmony. *Linguistic Inquiry* 20. 173–217.

(1994). *Grounded phonology.* Cambridge, Mass.: MIT Press.

Archibald, J. (ed.) (1997). *Phonological acquisition and phonological theory.* Hillsdale, N.J.: Lawrence Erlbaum.

Árnason, K. (1980). *Quantity in historical phonology: Icelandic and related cases.* Cambridge: Cambridge University Press.

(1985). Icelandic word stress and metrical phonology. *Studia Linguistica* 39. 93–129.

Aronoff, M. and R. T. Oehrle (eds.) (1984). *Language sound structure: studies in phonology presented to Morris Halle by his teacher and students.* Cambridge, Mass.: MIT Press.

Avery, P. and K. D. Rice (1989). Segment structure and coronal underspecification. *Phonology* 6. 179–200.

Awedyk, W. (1975). *The syllable theory and Old English phonology.* Wrocław: Ossolineum.

Baart, J. (1987). *Focus, syntax, and accent placement: towards a rule system for the derivation of pitch accent patterns in Dutch as spoken by humans and machines.* Ph.D. dissertation, University of Leiden.

Baltaxe, C. A. M. (1978). *Foundations of distinctive feature theory.* Baltimore: University Park Press.

Bao, Z. (1990). *On the nature of tone.* Ph.D. dissertation, Massachusetts Institute of Technology.

Basbøll, H. (1999). Syllables in Danish. In van der Hulst and Ritter (1999). 69–92.

Beckman, M. E. (1986). *Stress and non-stress accent.* Dordrecht: Foris.

Beckman, M. E. and J. B. Pierrehumbert (1986). Intonational structure in English and Japanese. *Phonology Yearbook* 3. 255–310.

Bell, A. and J. B. Hooper (eds.) (1978). *Syllables and segments.* Amsterdam: North Holland.

Bendor-Samuel, John T. (1960). Some problems of segmentation in the phonological analysis of Tereno. *Word* 16. 348–55.

Benediktsson, H. (1963). Some aspects of Nordic umlaut and breaking. *Language* 39. 409–31.

Bickmore, L. S. (1995). Accounting for compensatory lengthening in the CV and moraic frameworks. In Durand and Katamba (1995). 119–48.

Bird, S. (1995). *Computational phonology: a constraint-based approach.* Cambridge: Cambridge University Press.

Blevins, J. (1995). The syllable in phonological theory. In Goldsmith (1995). 206–44.

Boas, F. (1947). *Kwakiutl grammar with a glossary of the suffixes.* Transactions of the American Philosophical Society. New Series, Vol. 37, Part 3.

Bolinger, D. L. (1972). Accent is predictable (if you're a mind-reader). *Language* 48. 633–44.

(1978). Intonation across languages. In Greenberg (1978). 471–524.

(1986). *Intonation and its parts: the melody of language.* Stanford: Stanford University Press.

Booij, G. E. (1995). *The phonology of Dutch.* Oxford: Clarendon Press.

Borowsky, T. J. (1986). *Topics in the lexical phonology of English.* Ph.D. dissertation, University of Massachusetts, Amherst. Published 1990, New York: Garland.

(1993). On the Word level. In S. Hargus and E. M. Kaisse (eds.) *Studies in Lexical Phonology.* San Diego: Academic Press. 199–234.

Boxwell, H. and M. Boxwell (1966). Weri phonemes. In S. A. Wurm (ed.) *Papers in New Guinea linguistics.* Vol. V. Canberra: Australian National University. 77–93.

Brentari, D. (1995). Sign language phonology: ASL. In Goldsmith (1995). 615–39.

(1999). *A prosodic model of sign language phonology.* Cambridge, Mass.: MIT Press.

Brockhaus, W. (1995). Skeletal and suprasegmental structure within Government Phonology. In Durand and Katamba (1995). 180–221.

Brockhaus, W. (1999). The syllable in German: exploring an alternative. In van der Hulst and Ritter (1999). 169–218.

Broselow, E. (1995). Skeletal positions and moras. In Goldsmith (1995). 175–205.

Broselow, E., S.-I. Chen and M. Huffman (1997). Syllable weight: convergence of phonology and phonetics. *Phonology* 14. 47–82.

Browman, C. P. and L. Goldstein (1986). Towards an articulatory phonology. *Phonology Yearbook* 3. 219–52.

(1989). Articulatory gestures as phonological units. *Phonology* 6. 201–51.

(1992). Articulatory Phonology: an overview. *Phonetica* 49. 155–80.

Bruce, G. and B. Hermans (1999). Word tone in Germanic languages. In van der Hulst (1999). 605–58.

Burzio, L. (1994). *Principles of English stress.* Cambridge: Cambridge University Press.

Cairns, C. E. (1988). Phonotactics, markedness and lexical representation. *Phonology* 5. 209–36.

Cairns, C. E. and M. H. Feinstein (1982). Markedness and the theory of syllable structure. *Linguistic Inquiry* 13. 193–226.

Catford, J. C. (1977). *Fundamental problems in phonetics.* Edinburgh: Edinburgh University Press.

Charette, M. (1990). Licence to govern. *Phonology* 7. 233–53.

(1991). *Conditions on phonological government.* Cambridge: Cambridge University Press.

References

Chomsky, N. and M. Halle (1968). *The sound pattern of English*. New York: Harper and Row.

Churchward, C. M. (1940). *Rotuman grammar and dictionary*. Sydney: Australasian Medical Publishing Company.

Clements, G. N. (1977). The autosegmental treatment of vowel harmony. In W. U. Dressler and O. E. Pfeiffer (eds.) *Phonologica 1976*. Innsbruck: Innsbrucker Beiträge zur Sprachwissenschaft. 111–19.

(1981). Akan vowel harmony: a nonlinear analysis. *Harvard Studies in Phonology* 2. 108–77.

(1985). The geometry of phonological features. *Phonology Yearbook* 2. 225–52.

(1988). Toward a substantive theory of feature specification. *Papers from the Annual Meeting of the North East Linguistic Society* 18. 79–93.

(1989). A unified set of features for consonants and vowels. Ms., Cornell University.

(1990). The role of the sonority cycle in core syllabification. In J. Kingston and M. Beckman (eds.) *Papers in laboratory phonology I: between the grammar and physics of speech*. Cambridge: Cambridge University Press. 283–333.

(1991). Vowel height assimilation in Bantu languages. *Proceedings of the Annual Meeting, Berkeley Linguistics Society* 17. 25–64.

(1992). Phonological primes: gestures or features? *Phonetica* 49. 181–93.

Clements, G. N. and J. A. Goldsmith (eds.) (1984). *Autosegmental studies in Bantu tone*. Dordrecht: Foris.

Clements, G. N. and E. V. Hume (1995). The internal organization of speech sounds. In Goldsmith (1995). 245–306.

Clements, G. N. and S. Keyser (1983). *CV phonology: a generative theory of the syllable*. Cambridge, Mass.: MIT Press.

Clements, G. N. and E. Sezer (1982). Vowel and consonant disharmony in Turkish. In van der Hulst and Smith (1982b: part 2). 213–55.

Cohn, A. (1990). *Phonetic and phonological rules of nasalization*. Ph.D. dissertation, University of California at Los Angeles.

(1993). Nasalisation in English: phonology or phonetics. *Phonology* 10. 43–81.

Cole, J. (1995). The cycle in phonology. In Goldsmith (1995). 70–113.

Coleman, J. (1998). *Phonological representations: their names, forms and powers*. Cambridge: Cambridge University Press.

Collins, B. S. and I. M. Mees (1996). *The phonetics of English and Dutch*. Leiden: E. J. Brill.

Corrigan, R., F. Eckman and M. Noonan (eds.) (1989). *Linguistic categorization*. Amsterdam: John Benjamins.

Crothers, J. (1978). Typology and universals of vowel systems. In Greenberg (1978). 93–152.

Cruttenden, A. (1997). *Intonation*. 2nd edn. Cambridge: Cambridge University Press.

Cyran, E. (1997). *Resonance elements in phonology: a study in Munster Irish*. Lublin: Wydawnictwo Folium.

Dauer, R. (1983). Stress-timing and syllable-timing reanalyzed. *Journal of Phonetics* 11. 51–62.

Davenport, M. and J. Staun (1986). Sequence, segment and configuration: two problems for dependency phonology. In Durand (1986a). 135–59.

Davis, S. (1985). *Topics in syllable phonology.* Ph.D. dissertation, University of Arizona. Published 1988, New York: Garland.

(1989). Location of the feature [continuant] in feature geometry. *Lingua* 78. 1–22.

(1990). The onset as a constituent of the syllable: evidence from Italian. *Papers from the Annual Regional Meeting, Chicago Linguistic Society* 26:2. 71–9.

(1994). Geminate consonants in moraic phonology. *Proceedings of the West Coast Conference on Formal Linguistics* 13. 32–45.

De Chene, B. and S. R. Anderson (1979). Compensatory lengthening. *Language* 55. 505–35.

Dell, F. (1995). Consonant clusters and phonological syllables in French. *Lingua* 95. 5–26.

Dell, F. and M. Elmedlaoui (1985). Syllabic consonants and syllabification in Imdlawn Tashlhiyt Berber. *Journal of African Languages and Linguistics* 7. 105–30.

Dikken, M. den and H. G. van der Hulst (1988). Segmental hierarchitecture. In van der Hulst and Smith (1988a: vol. I). 1–78.

Dixon, R. M. W. (1980). *The languages of Australia.* Cambridge: Cambridge University Press.

Dogil, G. (1988). Phonological configurations: natural classes, sonority and syllabicity. In van der Hulst and Smith (1988a: vol. I). 79–103.

(1999). The phonetic manifestation of word stress in Lithuanian, Polish, German and Spanish. In van der Hulst (1999). 273–311.

Donegan, P. J. (1973). Bleaching and coloring. *Papers from the Annual Regional Meeting, Chicago Linguistic Society* 9. 386–97.

Dresher, B. E. and H. G. van der Hulst (1995). Head–dependent asymmetries in phonology. In H. G. van der Hulst and J. M. van de Weijer (eds.) *Leiden in last.* The Hague: Holland Academic Graphics. 401–31.

(1998). Head–dependent asymmetries in phonology: complexity and visibility. *Phonology* 15. 317–52.

Dresher, B. E. and A. Lahiri (1991). The Germanic foot: metrical coherence in Old English. *Linguistic Inquiry* 22. 251–86.

Dressler, W. U., O. E. Pfeiffer and J. R. Rennison (eds.) (1981). *Phonologica 1980.* Innsbruck: Innsbrucker Beiträge zur Sprachwissenschaft.

Duanmu, S. (1990). *A formal study of syllable, tone, stress and domain in Chinese languages.* Ph.D. dissertation, Massachusetts Institute of Technology.

Durand, J. (ed.) (1986a). *Dependency and non-linear phonology.* London: Croom Helm.

Durand, J. (1986b). French liaison, floating segments and other matters in a dependency framework. In Durand (1986a). 161–201.

Durand, J. and F. Katamba (eds.) (1995). *Frontiers of phonology: atoms, structures, derivations.* London: Longman.

References

Ebeling, C. L. (1966). The grammar of literary Avar. *Studia Caucasica* 2. 58–100.

Echeverría, M. S. and H. Contreras (1965). Araucanian phonemics. *International Journal of American Linguistics* 31. 132–5.

Ewen, C. J. (1978). The phonology of the diminutive in Dutch: a dependency account. *Lingua* 45. 141–73.

(1980a). *Aspects of phonological structure, with particular reference to English and Dutch.* Ph.D. dissertation, University of Edinburgh.

(1980b). The characterisation of glottal stricture in dependency phonology. *York Papers in Linguistics* 8. 35–47.

(1995). Dependency relations in phonology. In Goldsmith (1995). 570–85.

Ewen, C. J. and H. G. van der Hulst (1985). Single-valued features and the non-linear analysis of vowel harmony. In H. Bennis and F. H. Beukema (eds.) *Linguistics in the Netherlands 1985.* Dordrecht: Foris. 39–48.

Farmer, A. L. (1979). Phonological markedness and the sonority hierarchy. *MIT Working Papers in Linguistics* 1. 172–7.

Ferguson, C. A., L. M. Hyman and J. J. Ohala (eds.) (1975). *Nasálfest: papers from a symposium on nasals and nasalization.* Stanford: Language Universals Project, Stanford University.

Fikkert, P. (1994). *On the acquisition of prosodic structure.* Ph.D. dissertation, University of Leiden.

Firth, J. R. (1948). Sounds and prosodies. In Palmer (1970). 1–26.

Fischer-Jørgensen, E. (1985). Some basic vowel features. In Fromkin (1985). 79–99.

Foley, J. (1977). *Foundations of theoretical phonology.* Cambridge: Cambridge University Press.

Fromkin, V. A. (ed.) (1978). *Tone: a linguistic survey.* New York: Academic Press.

(1985). *Phonetic linguistics: essays in honor of Peter Ladefoged.* Orlando: Academic Press.

Fuchs, A. (1976). 'Normaler' und 'kontrastiver' Akzent. *Lingua* 38. 293–312.

Fudge, E. (1969). Syllables. *Journal of Linguistics* 5. 253–86.

(1987). Branching structure within the syllable. *Journal of Linguistics* 23. 359–77.

Giegerich, H. J. (1981). Zero syllables in metrical theory. In Dressler *et al.* (1981). 153–60.

(1985). *Metrical phonology and phonological structure.* Cambridge: Cambridge University Press.

Goad, H. (1993). *On the configuration of height features.* Ph.D. dissertation, University of Southern California.

Goldsmith, J. A. (1976). *Autosegmental phonology.* Ph.D. dissertation, Massachusetts Institute of Technology.

(1982). Accent systems. In van der Hulst and Smith (1982b: vol. I). 47–63.

(1985). Vowel harmony in Khalkha Mongolian, Yaka, Finnish and Hungarian. *Phonology Yearbook* 2. 253–75.

(1989). Licensing, inalterability, and harmonic rule application. *Papers from the Annual Regional Meeting, Chicago Linguistic Society* 25:1. 145–56.

252

(1990). *Autosegmental and metrical phonology*. Oxford: Blackwell.

(1992). A note on the genealogy of research traditions in modern phonology. *Journal of Linguistics* 28. 149–63.

(1993). Harmonic phonology. In J. A. Goldsmith (ed.) *The last phonological rule*. Chicago: University of Chicago Press. 21–60.

(1994). Disentangling autosegments: a response. *Journal of Linguistics* 30. 499–507.

(ed.) (1995). *The handbook of phonological theory*. Cambridge, Mass. and Oxford: Blackwell.

(1997). Review of Bird (1995). *Phonology* 14. 133–41.

Gordon, E. V. (1957). *An introduction to Old Norse*. 2nd edn. Oxford: Clarendon Press.

Greenberg, J. (ed.) (1978). *Universals of human language*. Vol. II: *Phonology*. Stanford: Stanford University Press.

Griffen, T. D. (1976). Toward a nonsegmental phonology. *Lingua* 40. 1–20.

Gussenhoven, C. (1984). *On the grammar and semantics of sentence accents*. Dordrecht: Foris.

Gussenhoven, C. and G. Bruce (1999). Word prosody and intonation. In van der Hulst (1999). 233–71.

Hall, T. A. (1997). *The phonology of coronals*. Amsterdam: John Benjamins.

Halle, M. (1959). *The sound pattern of Russian*. The Hague: Mouton.

(1983). On distinctive features and their articulatory implementation. *Natural Language and Linguistic Theory* 1. 91–107.

(1990). Respecting metrical structure. *Natural Language and Linguistic Theory* 8. 149–76.

(1995). Feature geometry and feature spreading. *Linguistic Inquiry* 26. 1–46.

Halle, M. and G. N. Clements (1983). *Problem book in phonology*. Cambridge, Mass.: MIT Press.

Halle, M. and W. J. Idsardi (1995). General properties of stress and metrical structure. In Goldsmith (1995). 403–43.

Halle, M. and S. J. Keyser (1971). *English stress: its growth and its role in verse*. New York: Harper and Row.

Halle, M., W. O'Neil and J.-R. Vergnaud (1993). Metrical coherence in Old English without the Germanic foot. *Linguistic Inquiry* 24. 529–38.

Halle, M. and K. N. Stevens (1971). A note on laryngeal features. *MIT Quarterly Progress Report* 101. 198–213.

(1979). Some reflections on the theoretical bases of phonetics. In B. Lindblom and S. Öhman (eds.) *Frontiers of speech communication*. London: Academic Press. 335–49.

Halle, M. and J.-R. Vergnaud (1978). Metrical structures in phonology. Ms., Massachusetts Institute of Technology.

(1981). Harmony processes. In W. Klein and W. Levelt (eds.) *Crossing the boundaries in linguistics*. Dordrecht: Reidel. 1–22.

(1987a). *An essay on stress*. Cambridge, Mass.: MIT Press.

(1987b). Stress and the cycle. *Linguistic Inquiry* 18. 45–84.

References

Hammond, M. (1988). On deriving the well-formedness condition. *Linguistic Inquiry* 19. 319–25.

Hankamer, J. and J. Aissen (1974). The sonority hierarchy. In A. Bruck, R. A. Fox and M. W. La Galy (eds.) *Papers from the parasession on natural phonology.* Chicago: Chicago Linguistic Society. 131–45.

Hanson, K. and P. Kiparsky (1996). A parametric theory of poetic meter. *Language* 72. 287–335.

Haraguchi, S. (1977). *The tone pattern of Japanese.* Tokyo: Kaitaku-sya.

Harris, J. (1990). Segmental complexity and phonological government. *Phonology* 7. 255–300.

(1994). *English sound structure.* Oxford and Cambridge, Mass.: Blackwell.

(1997). Licensing Inheritance: an integrated theory of neutralisation. *Phonology* 14. 315–70.

Harris, J. and J. Kaye (1990). A tale of two cities: London glottalling and New York tapping. *The Linguistic Review* 7. 251–74.

Harris, J. and G. Lindsey (1995). The elements of phonological representation. In Durand and Katamba (1995). 34–79.

Harris, J. W. (1983). *Syllable structure and stress in Spanish.* Cambridge, Mass.: MIT Press.

Hayes, B. (1981). *A metrical theory of stress rules.* Ph.D. dissertation, Massachusetts Institute of Technology. Revised version distributed by Indiana University Linguistics Club. Published 1985, New York: Garland.

(1982). Extrametricality and English stress. *Linguistic Inquiry* 13. 227–76.

(1983). A grid-based theory of English meter. *Linguistic Inquiry* 14. 357–93.

(1984a). The phonology of rhythm in English. *Linguistic Inquiry* 15. 33–74.

(1984b). The phonetics and phonology of Russian voicing assimilation. In Aronoff and Oehrle (1984). 318–28.

(1987). A revised parametric metrical theory. *Papers from the Annual Meeting of the North East Linguistic Society* 17. 274–89.

(1989a). Compensatory lengthening in moraic phonology. *Linguistic Inquiry* 20. 253–306.

(1989b). The prosodic hierarchy in meter. In Kiparsky and Youmans (1989). 253–306.

(1994). Weight of CVC can be determined by context. In J. Cole and C. Kisseberth (eds.) *Perspectives in phonology.* Stanford: CSLI. 61–79.

(1995). *Metrical stress theory: principles and case studies.* Chicago: University of Chicago Press.

Hayward, K. M. and R. J. Hayward (1989). Guttural: arguments for a new distinctive feature. *Transactions of the Philological Society* 87. 179–93.

Hayward, R. J. (1988). In defense of the skeletal tier. *Studies in African Linguistics* 19. 131–72.

Herbert, R. K. (1986). *Language universals, markedness theory, and natural phonetic processes.* Berlin: Mouton de Gruyter.

Heuven, V. van and A. Sluijter (1996). Notes on the phonetics of word prosody. In R. Goedemans, H. G. van der Hulst and E. Visch (eds.) *Stress patterns of the world*. Part 1: *Background*. The Hague: Holland Academic Graphics. 233–69.

Hoard, J. E. (1978). Remarks on the nature of syllabic stops and affricates. In Bell and Hooper (1978). 59–72.

Hock, H. H. (1986). Compensatory lengthening: in defense of the concept 'mora'. *Folia Linguistica* 20. 431–60.

Hogg, R. M. (1992a). Phonology and morphology. In R. M. Hogg (ed.) *The Cambridge history of the English language*. Vol. I: *The beginnings to 1066*. Cambridge: Cambridge University Press. 67–167.

(1992b). *A grammar of Old English*. Vol. I: *Phonology*. Oxford: Blackwell.

Hogg, R. M. and C. B. McCully (1987). *Metrical phonology: a coursebook*. Cambridge: Cambridge University Press.

Hooper, J. B. (1976). *An introduction to natural generative phonology*. New York: Academic Press.

Hualde, J. I. (1999). Basque accentuation. In van der Hulst (1999). 947–93.

Huffman, M. and R. Krakow (eds.) (1993). *Nasals, nasalization, and the velum*. Orlando: Academic Press.

Hulst, H. G. van der (1984). *Syllable structure and stress in Dutch*. Dordrecht: Foris.

(1985). Ambisyllabicity in Dutch. In H. Bennis and F. Beukema (eds.) *Linguistics in the Netherlands 1985*. Dordrecht: Foris. 57–66.

(1988). The geometry of vocalic features. In van der Hulst and Smith (1988a: vol. II). 77–125.

(1989). Atoms of segmental structure: components, gestures and dependency. *Phonology* 6. 253–84.

(1993). Units in the analysis of signs. *Phonology* 10. 209–41.

(1995). Radical CV phonology: the categorial gesture. In Durand and Katamba (1995). 80–116.

(1997). Issues in foot typology. *Toronto Working Papers in Linguistics* 16. 77–101.

(ed.) (1999). *Word prosodic systems in the languages of Europe*. Berlin: Mouton de Gruyter.

Hulst, H. G. van der and C. J. Ewen (1991). Major class and manner features. In P. M. Bertinetto, M. Kenstowicz and M. Loporcaro (eds.) *Certamen phonologicum II: papers from the 1990 Cortona Phonology Meeting*. Turin: Rosenberg and Sellier. 19–41.

Hulst, H. G. van der and N. A. Ritter (eds.) (1999). *The syllable: views and facts*. Berlin: Mouton de Gruyter.

Hulst, H. G. van der and N. S. H. Smith (1982a). An overview of autosegmental and metrical phonology. In van der Hulst and Smith (1982b: part 1). 1–45.

(eds.) (1982b). *The structure of phonological representations*. 2 parts. Dordrecht: Foris.

(1985). The framework of nonlinear generative phonology. In H. G. van der Hulst and N. S. H. Smith (eds.) *Advances in nonlinear phonology*. Dordrecht: Foris. 3–55.

References

(eds.) (1988a). *Features, segmental structure and harmony processes.* 2 vols. Dordrecht: Foris.

(eds.) (1988b). *Autosegmental studies on pitch accent.* Dordrecht: Foris.

Hulst, H. G. van der and K. L. Snider (eds.) (1993). *The phonology of tone: the representation of tonal register.* Berlin: Mouton de Gruyter.

Hulst, H. G. van der and J. M. van de Weijer (1991). Topics in Turkish phonology. In H. Boeschoten and L. Verhoeven (eds.) *Turkish linguistics today.* Leiden: E. J. Brill. 11–59.

(1995). Vowel harmony. In Goldsmith (1995). 495–534.

Hume, E. V. (1990). Front vowels, palatal consonants and the rule of umlaut in Korean. *Papers from the Annual Meeting of the North East Linguistic Society* 20. 230–43.

(1992). *Front vowels, coronal consonants and their interaction in non-linear phonology.* Ph.D. dissertation, Cornell University.

Hume, E. V. and D. Odden (1995). The superfluity of [consonantal]. *Papers from the Annual Meeting of the North East Linguistic Society* 25. 245–61.

Hurch, B. (1996). Accentuations. In B. Hurch and R. Rhodes (eds.) *Natural Phonology: the state of the art.* Berlin: Mouton de Gruyter. 73–96.

Hyman, L. M. (1973). The feature [grave] in phonological theory. *Journal of Phonetics* 1. 329–37.

(1975). *Phonology: theory and analysis.* New York: Holt, Rinehart and Winston.

(1977). On the nature of linguistic stress. In L. M. Hyman (ed.) *Studies in stress and accent.* Los Angeles: Department of Linguistics, University of Southern California. 37–82.

(1985). *A theory of phonological weight.* Dordrecht: Foris.

(1992). Moraic mismatches in Bantu. *Phonology* 9. 255–65.

Ingram, D. (1978). The role of the syllable in phonological development. In Bell and Hooper (1978). 143–55.

Inkelas, S. and D. Zec (eds.) (1990). *The phonology–syntax connection.* Chicago: University of Chicago Press.

(1995). Syntax–phonology interface. In Goldsmith (1995). 535–49.

Itô, J. (1986). *Syllable theory in prosodic phonology.* Ph.D. dissertation, University of Massachusetts. Published 1988, New York: Garland.

Itô, J. and R. A. Mester (1992). Weak layering and word binarity. Report LRC-93-08, Linguistic Research Center, University of California, Santa Cruz.

Itô, J., R. A. Mester and J. Padgett (1995). Licensing and redundancy: underspecification in Optimality Theory. *Linguistic Inquiry* 26. 571–613.

Iverson, G. K. (1983). On glottal width features. *Lingua* 60. 331–9.

Jackendoff, R. (1977). *X̄-syntax: a study of phrase structure.* Cambridge, Mass.: MIT Press.

Jacobs, H. (1989). *Nonlinear studies in the historical phonology of French.* Ph.D. dissertation, Catholic University of Brabant.

Jakobson, R., C. G. M. Fant and M. Halle (1951). *Preliminaries to speech analysis.* Cambridge, Mass.: MIT Press.

Jakobson, R. and M. Halle (1956). *Fundamentals of language*. The Hague: Mouton.

Jakobson, R. and L. R. Waugh (1979). *The sound shape of language*. Brighton: Harvester Press.

Jones, C. (1976). Some constraints on medial consonant clusters. *Language* 52. 121–30.

(1989). *A history of English phonology*. London: Longman.

Jones, D. (1977). *English pronouncing dictionary*. 14th edn, ed. A. C. Gimson. Cambridge: Cambridge University Press.

Jusczyk, P. W. (1997). *The discovery of spoken language*. Cambridge, Mass.: MIT Press.

Kager, R. (1989). *A metrical theory of stress and destressing in English and Dutch*. Dordrecht: Foris.

(1993). Alternatives to the iambic–trochaic law. *Natural Language and Linguistic Theory* 11. 381–432.

(1995). The metrical theory of word stress. In Goldsmith (1995). 367–402.

(1999). *Optimality Theory: a textbook*. Cambridge: Cambridge University Press.

Kager, R., M. Trommelen and E. Visch (1985). Over Nederlandse lettergreep- en klemtoonstruktuur. (Review of van der Hulst 1984.) *Spektator* 15. 123–38.

Kahn, D. (1976). *Syllable-based generalizations in English phonology*. Ph.D. dissertation, Massachusetts Institute of Technology. Published 1980, New York: Garland.

Kaisse, E. M. (1985). *Connected speech: the interaction of syntax and phonology*. New York: Academic Press.

(1992). Can [consonantal] spread? *Language* 68. 313–32.

Kaisse, E. and P. A. Shaw (1985). On the theory of Lexical Phonology. *Phonology Yearbook* 2. 1–30.

Kaye, J. (1989). *Phonology: a cognitive view*. Hillsdale, N.J.: Lawrence Erlbaum.

(1990). 'Coda' licensing. *Phonology* 7. 301–30.

(1995). Derivations and interfaces. In Durand and Katamba (1995). 289–332.

(1996). Do you believe in magic? In H. Kardela and B. Szymanek (eds.) *A Festschrift for Edmund Gussmann from his friends and colleagues*. Lublin: The University Press of the Catholic University of Lublin. 155–76.

Kaye, J. D. and J. Lowenstamm (1984). De la syllabicité. In F. Dell, D. Hirst and J.-R. Vergnaud (eds.) *Forme sonore du langage*. Paris: Hermann. 123–59.

Kaye, J., J. Lowenstamm and J.-R. Vergnaud (1985). The internal structure of phonological elements: a theory of charm and government. *Phonology Yearbook* 2. 305–28.

(1990). Constituent structure and government in phonology. *Phonology* 7. 193–231.

Kean, M.-L. (1974). The strict cycle in phonology. *Linguistic Inquiry* 5. 179–203.

(1980). *The theory of markedness in generative grammar*. Indiana University Linguistics Club.

Keating, P. A. (1988a). Survey of phonological features. Indiana University Linguistics Club.

(1988b). Underspecification in phonetics. *Phonology* 5. 275–92.

(1991). Coronal places of articulation. In Paradis and Prunet (1991). 29–48.

References

Kenstowicz, M. (1994). *Phonology in generative grammar*. Oxford: Blackwell.

Kenstowicz, M. and C. Kisseberth (1979). *Generative phonology*. New York: Academic Press.

Kerek, A. (1971). *Hungarian metrics: some linguistic aspects of iambic verse*. Bloomington: Indiana University.

Key, H. (1961). Phonotactics of Cayuvava. *International Journal of American Linguistics* 27. 143–50.

Kiparsky, P. (1977). The rhythmic structure of English verse. *Linguistic Inquiry* 8. 189–247.

(1979). Metrical structure assignment is cyclic. *Linguistic Inquiry* 10. 421–42.

(1981). Remarks on the metrical structure of the syllable. In Dressler *et al.* (1981). 245–56.

(1982). From cyclic phonology to lexical phonology. In van der Hulst and Smith (1982b: part 1). 131–75.

(1985). Some consequences of Lexical Phonology. *Phonology Yearbook* 2. 85–138.

(1995). The phonological basis of sound change. In Goldsmith (1995). 640–70.

Kiparsky, P. and G. Youmans (eds.) (1989). *Rhythm and meter*. Orlando: Academic Press.

Klausenburger, J. (1977). A non-rule of French: h-aspiré. *Linguistics* 192. 45–52.

(1978). French linking phenomena: a natural generative analysis. *Language* 54. 21–40.

Kornai, A. (1995). *Formal phonology*. New York: Garland.

Kubozono, H. (1989). The mora and syllable structure in Japanese. *Language and Speech* 32. 249–78.

Kuroda, S.-Y. (1967). *Yawelmani phonology*. Cambridge, Mass.: MIT Press.

Ladd, D. R. (1996). *Intonational phonology*. Cambridge: Cambridge University Press.

Ladefoged, P. (1971). *Preliminaries to linguistic phonetics*. Chicago: Chicago University Press.

(1973). The features of the larynx. *Journal of Phonetics* 1. 73–83.

(1975). *A course in phonetics*. New York: Harcourt Brace Jovanovich.

(1980). What are linguistic sounds made of? *Language* 56. 485–502.

Ladefoged, P. and I. Maddieson (1989). Phonological features for places of articulation. In L. M. Hyman and C. Li (eds.) *Language, speech and mind*. London: Routledge. 49–61.

(1996). *The sounds of the world's languages*. Oxford: Blackwell.

Ladefoged, P. and A. Traill (1994). Clicks and their accompaniments. *Journal of Phonetics* 22. 33–64.

Lahiri, A. and S. E. Blumstein (1984). A re-evaluation of the feature coronal. *Journal of Phonetics* 12. 133–45.

Lahiri, A. and B. E. Dresher (ms). OSL in West Germanic. University of Konstanz and University of Toronto.

Lahiri, A. and H. G. van der Hulst (1988). On foot typology. *Papers from the Annual Meeting of the North East Linguistic Society* 18. 286–309.

Lahiri, A. and J. Koreman (1988). Syllable weight and quantity in Dutch. *Proceedings of the West Coast Conference on Formal Linguistics* 7. 217–28.

Lahiri, A., T. Riad and H. Jacobs (1999). Diachronic prosody. In van der Hulst (1999). 355–422.

Langendoen, D. T. (1968). *The London school of linguistics*. Cambridge, Mass.: MIT Press.

Langeweg, S. J. (1988). *The stress system of Dutch*. Ph.D. dissertation, University of Leiden.

Lapointe, S. G. and M. H. Feinstein (1982). The role of vowel deletion and epenthesis in the assignment of syllable structure. In van der Hulst and Smith (1982b: part 2). 69–120.

Lass, R. (1971). Boundaries as obstruents: Old English voicing assimilation and universal strength hierarchies. *Journal of Linguistics* 7. 15–30.

(1975). How intrinsic is content? Markedness, sound change and 'family universals'. In D. Goyvaerts and G. K. Pullum (eds.) *Essays on the sound pattern of English.* Ghent: Story-Scientia. 475–504.

(1976). *English phonology and phonological theory: synchronic and diachronic studies.* Cambridge: Cambridge University Press.

(1984a). *Phonology: an introduction to basic concepts.* Cambridge: Cambridge University Press.

(1984b). Vowel system universals and typology: prologue to theory. *Phonology Yearbook* 1. 75–111.

(1987). *The shape of English.* London: J. M. Dent.

(1992). Phonology and morphology. In N. Blake (ed.) *The Cambridge history of the English language*. Vol. II: *1066–1476.* Cambridge: Cambridge University Press. 23–155.

Lass, R. and J. M. Anderson (1975). *Old English phonology.* Cambridge: Cambridge University Press.

Lehiste, I. (1970). *Suprasegmentals.* Cambridge, Mass.: MIT Press.

Levelt, C. C. (1994). *On the acquisition of place.* Ph.D. dissertation, University of Leiden.

Levin, J. (1985). *A metrical theory of syllabicity.* Ph.D. dissertation, Massachusetts Institute of Technology.

Liberman, M. (1975). *The intonational system of English.* Ph.D. dissertation, Massachusetts Institute of Technology.

Liberman, M. and A. S. Prince (1977). On stress and linguistic rhythm. *Linguistic Inquiry* 8. 249–336.

Liddell, S. and R. Johnson (1989). American Sign Language: the phonological base. *Sign Language Studies* 64. 197–277.

Lindau, M. (1978). Vowel features. *Language* 54. 541–63.

(1985). The story of /r/. In Fromkin (1985). 157–68.

Lombardi, L. (1991). *Laryngeal features and laryngeal neutralization.* Ph.D. dissertation, University of Massachusetts, Amherst.

References

(1996). Postlexical rules and the status of privative features. *Phonology* 13. 1–38.

Loporcaro, M. (1996). Lengthening and raddoppiamento fonosintattico. In M. Maiden and M. Parry (eds.) *The dialects of Italy*. London: Routledge. 41–51.

Lowenstamm, J. and J. Kaye (1986). Compensatory lengthening in Tiberian Hebrew. In Wetzels and Sezer (1986). 97–132.

McArthur, H. and L. McArthur (1956). Aguacatec (Mayan) phonemes within the stress group. *International Journal of American Linguistics* 22. 72–6.

McCarthy, J. J. (1979). On stress and syllabification. *Linguistic Inquiry* 10. 443–65.

(1988). Feature geometry and dependency: a review. *Phonetica* 43. 84–108.

(1994). The phonetics and phonology of Semitic pharyngeals. In P. Keating (ed.) *Papers in laboratory phonology 3: phonological structure and phonetic form*. Cambridge: Cambridge University Press. 191–233.

McCarthy, J. J. and A. S. Prince (1993). *Prosodic Morphology I: constraint interaction and satisfaction*. Ms., University of Massachusetts, Amherst and Rutgers University.

McCarthy, J. J. and A. Taub (1992). Review of Paradis and Prunet (1991). *Phonology* 9. 363–70.

McCawley, J. D. (1968). *The phonological component of a grammar of Japanese*. The Hague: Mouton.

McMahon, A., P. Foulkes and L. Tollfree (1994). Gestural representations and Lexical Phonology. *Phonology* 11. 277–316.

Macken, M. A. (1995). Phonological acquisition. In Goldsmith (1995). 671–96.

Maddieson, I. (1978). Universals of tone. In Greenberg (1978). 335–65.

(1984). *Patterns of sounds*. Cambridge: Cambridge University Press.

Malsch, D. L. and R. Fulcher (1989). Categorizing phonological segments: the inadequacy of the sonority hierarchy. In Corrigan *et al.* (1989). 69–80.

Merrifield, W. R. (1963). Palantla Chinantec syllable types. *Anthropological Linguistics* 5. 1–16.

Mester, R. A. (1988). Dependent tier ordering and the OCP. In van der Hulst and Smith (1988a: vol. II). 127–44.

(1994). The quantitative trochee in Latin. *Natural Language and Linguistic Theory* 12. 1–61.

Mester, R. A. and J. Itô (1989). Feature predictability and underspecification: palatal prosody in Japanese mimetics. *Language* 65. 258–93.

Minkova, D. (1991). *The history of final vowels in English: the sound of muting*. Berlin: Mouton de Gruyter.

Mohanan, K. P. (1991). On the bases of underspecification. *Natural Language and Linguistic Theory* 9. 285–325.

Murray, R. and T. Vennemann (1983). Sound change and syllable structure in Germanic phonology. *Language* 59. 514–28.

Napoli, D. J. and M. Nespor (1979). The syntax of word-initial consonant gemination in Italian. *Language* 55. 812–42.

Nathan, G. S. (1989). Preliminaries to a theory of phonological substance: the substance of sonority. In Corrigan *et al.* (1989). 55–67.

Nespor, M. (1999). Stress domains. In van der Hulst (1999). 117–59.

Nespor, M. and I. Vogel (1982). Prosodic domains of external sandhi rules. In van der Hulst and Smith (1982b: part 1). 225–55.

    (1986). *Prosodic phonology.* Dordrecht: Foris.

    (1989). On clashes and lapses. *Phonology* 6. 69–116.

Newman, P. (1972). Syllable weight as a phonological variable. *Studies in African Linguistics* 3. 301–24.

Ní Chiosáin, M. (1994). Irish palatalisation and the representation of place features. *Phonology* 11. 89–106.

Noske, R. (1992). *A theory of syllabification and segmental alternation, with studies on the phonology of French, German, Tonkawa and Yawelmani.* Ph.D. dissertation, Catholic University of Brabant.

Ó Dochartaigh, C. (1978). Lenition and dependency phonology. *Éigse* 17. 457–94.

Odden, D. (1978). Further evidence for the feature [grave]. *Linguistic Inquiry* 9. 141–44.

    (1988). Anti antigemination and the OCP. *Linguistic Inquiry* 19. 451–75.

    (1991). Vowel geometry. *Phonology* 8. 261–89.

    (1995). Tone: African languages. In Goldsmith (1995). 444–75.

Ogden, R. (1999). Non-terminal phonological features in Finnish. In van der Hulst and Ritter (1999). 651–72.

Ogden, R. and J. K. Local (1994). Disentangling autosegments from prosodies: a note on the misrepresentation of a research tradition in phonology. *Journal of Linguistics* 30. 477–98.

Ohala, J. (1992). Alternatives to the sonority hierarchy for explaining segmental sequential constraints. *Papers from the Annual Regional Meeting, Chicago Linguistic Society* 28:2. 319–38.

Oostendorp, M. van (1995). Vowel quality and syllable projection. Ph.D. dissertation, Catholic University of Brabant.

Osborne, H. A., Jr (1966). Warao I: phonology and morphophonemics. *International Journal of American Linguistics* 32. 108–23.

Padgett, J. (1995). *Stricture in feature geometry.* Stanford: CSLI.

Palmer, F. R. (ed.) (1970). *Prosodic analysis.* Oxford: Oxford University Press.

Paradis, C. and J.-F. Prunet (eds.) (1991). *The special status of coronals: internal and external evidence.* New York: Academic Press.

Peperkamp, S. (1995). On the prosodic incorporation of clitics. Paper presented at the Conference on Interfaces in Phonology, Berlin.

Perlmutter, D. M. (1992). Sonority and syllable structure in American Sign Language. *Linguistic Inquiry* 23. 407–42.

Pierrehumbert, J. B. (1980). *The phonetics and phonology of English intonation.* Ph.D. dissertation, Massachusetts Institute of Technology.

Pierrehumbert, J. B. and M. E. Beckman (1988). *Japanese tone structure.* Cambridge, Mass.: MIT Press.

References

Piggott, G. L. (1988). A parametric approach to nasal harmony. In van der Hulst and Smith (1988a: vol. I). 131–67.

(1992). Variability in feature dependency: the case of nasality. *Natural Language and Linguistic Theory* 10. 33–77.

(1995). Epenthesis and syllable weight. *Natural Language and Linguistic Theory* 13. 283–326.

(1997). Licensing alignment: an integrated theory of neutralisation. *Phonology* 14. 437–77.

Piggott, G. L. and H. G. van der Hulst (1997). Locality and the nature of nasal harmony. *Lingua* 103. 85–112.

Piggott, G. L. and R. Singh (1985). The phonology of epenthetic segments. *Canadian Journal of Linguistics* 30. 415–53.

Pike, K. L. (1943). *Phonetics*. Ann Arbor: University of Michigan Press.

Polgárdi, K. (1998). Vowel harmony: an account in terms of government and optimality. Ph.D. dissertation, University of Leiden.

Prince, A. S. (1980). A metrical theory for Estonian quantity. *Linguistic Inquiry* 11. 511–62.

(1983). Relating to the grid. *Linguistic Inquiry* 14. 19–100.

Prince, A. S. and P. Smolensky (1993). *Optimality Theory: constraint interaction in generative grammar*. Ms., Rutgers University and University of Colorado, Boulder.

Pulgram, E. (1970). *Syllable, word, nexus, cursus*. The Hague: Mouton.

Pulleyblank, D. (1988a). Vocalic underspecification in Yoruba. *Linguistic Inquiry* 19. 233–70.

(1988b). Underspecification, the feature hierarchy and Tiv vowels. *Phonology* 5. 299–326.

(1994). Underlying mora structure. *Linguistic Inquiry* 25. 344–53.

(1995). Feature geometry and underspecification. In Durand and Katamba (1995). 3–33.

Pulleyblank, E. G. (1989). The role of coronal in articulator based features. *Papers from the Annual Regional Meeting, Chicago Linguistic Society* 25:1. 379–93.

Rennison, J. R. (1986). On tridirectional feature systems for vowels. In Durand (1986a). 281–304.

(1990). On the elements of phonological representations: the evidence from vowel systems and vowel processes. *Folia Linguistica* 24. 175–244.

Revithiadou, A. (1999). *The prosody–morphology interface*. Ph.D. dissertation, University of Leiden.

Rice, C. (1992). *Binarity and ternarity in metrical theory: parametric extensions*. Ph.D. dissertation, University of Texas, Austin.

Rice, K. D. (1992). On deriving sonority: a structural account of sonority relationships. *Phonology* 9. 61–99.

(1995). Peripheral in consonants. *Canadian Journal of Linguistics* 39. 191–282.

Rice, K. D. and P. Avery (1997). Variability in a deterministic model of language acquisition: a theory of segmental elaboration. In Archibald (1997). 23–42.

Ringen, C. O. (1975). *Vowel harmony: theoretical implications.* Ph.D. dissertation, Indiana University.

(1988). Transparency in Hungarian vowel harmony. *Phonology* 5. 327–42.

Ritt, N. (1994). *Quantity adjustment: vowel lengthening and shortening in Early Middle English.* Cambridge: Cambridge University Press.

Ritter, N. A. (1995). *The role of universal grammar in phonology: a Government Phonology approach to Hungarian.* Ph.D. dissertation, New York University.

Roberts, J. R. (1987). *Amele.* London: Croom Helm.

Roca, I. (1986). Secondary stress and metrical rhythm. *Phonology Yearbook* 3. 341–70.

Rosenthall, S. and H. G. van der Hulst (1999). Weight-by-position by position. *Natural Language and Linguistic Theory* 17. 499–540.

Rowicka, G. (1999). *On ghost vowels: a strict CV approach.* Ph.D. dissertation, University of Leiden.

Rubach, J. (1996). Shortening and ambisyllabicity in English. *Phonology* 13. 197–237.

Rubach, J. and G. Booij (1990). Syllable structure assignment in Polish. *Phonology* 7. 121–58.

Sagey, E. (1986). *The representation of features and relations in nonlinear phonology.* Ph.D. dissertation, Massachusetts Institute of Technology.

(1988). Degree of closure in complex segments. In van der Hulst and Smith (1988a: vol. I). 169–208.

Salmons, J. (1992). *Accentual change and language contact: comparative survey and a case study of early Northern Europe.* London: Routledge.

Sanders, G. (1972). *The simplex-feature hypothesis.* Indiana University Linguistics Club.

Sandler, W. (1989). *Phonological representation of the sign: linearity and non-linearity in American Sign Language.* Dordrecht: Foris.

Schane, S. A. (1973). [back] and [round]. In S. R. Anderson and P. Kiparsky (eds.) *A Festschrift for Morris Halle.* New York: Holt, Rinehart and Winston. 174–84.

(1979). Rhythm, accent, and stress in English. *Linguistic Inquiry* 10. 483–502.

(1984). The fundamentals of particle phonology. *Phonology Yearbook* 1. 129–55.

Schein, B. and D. Steriade (1986). On geminates. *Linguistic Inquiry* 17. 691–744.

Schmidt, D. (1992). Compensatory lengthening in a segmental moraic theory of representation. *Linguistics* 30. 513–34.

Scobbie, J. M. (1997). *Autosegmental representation in a declarative constraint-based framework.* New York: Garland.

Selkirk, E. O. (1972). *The phrase phonology of English and French.* Ph.D. dissertation, Massachusetts Institute of Technology.

(1978). The French foot: on the status of 'mute' e. *Studies in French Linguistics* 1. 141–150.

(1980). The role of prosodic categories in English word stress. *Linguistic Inquiry* 11. 563–605.

(1982). The syllable. In van der Hulst and Smith (1982b: part 2). 337–83.

(1984a). *Phonology and syntax: the relation between sound and structure.* Cambridge, Mass.: MIT Press.

References

(1984b). On the major class features and syllable theory. In Aronoff and Oehrle (1984). 107–36.

(1995). Sentence prosody: intonation, stress, and phrasing. In Goldsmith (1995). 550–69.

Sluijter, A. (1995). *Phonetic correlates of stress and accent.* Ph.D. dissertation, University of Leiden.

Smith, N. S. H. (1988). Consonant place features. In van der Hulst and Smith (1988a: vol. I). 209–35.

Spencer, A. (1985). Eliminating the feature [lateral]. *Journal of Linguistics* 20. 23–43.

(1996). *Phonology: theory and description.* Oxford: Blackwell.

Stanley, R. (1967). Redundancy rules in phonology. *Language* 43. 393–436.

Steriade, D. (1982). *Greek prosodies and the nature of syllabification.* Ph.D. dissertation, Massachusetts Institute of Technology. Published 1990, New York: Garland.

(1987). Redundant values. *Papers from the Annual Regional Meeting, Chicago Linguistic Society* 23:2. 339–62.

(1995). Underspecification and markedness. In Goldsmith (1995). 114–74.

(1996). *Licensing laryngeal features. UCLA Working Papers in Phonology* 1.

Stevens, K. N. (1972). The quantal nature of speech. In E. E. David and P. B. Denes (eds.) *Human communication: a unified view.* New York: McGraw Hill. 51–66.

(1989). On the quantal nature of speech. *Journal of Phonetics* 17. 3–45.

Stevens, K. N. and S. J. Keyser (1989). Primary features and their enhancement in consonants. *Language* 65. 81–106.

Stevens, K. N., S. J. Keyser and H. Kawasaki (1986). Toward a phonetic and phonological theory of redundant features. In J. S. Perkell and D. H. Klatt (eds.) *Invariance and variability in speech processes.* Hillsdale, N.J.: Lawrence Erlbaum. 426–49.

Stewart, J. M. (1967). Tongue root position in Akan vowel harmony. *Phonetica* 16. 185–204.

(1983). Akan vowel harmony: the word structure conditions and the floating vowels. *Studies in African Linguistics* 14. 111–39.

Stoel-Gammon, C. and J. P. Stemberger (1994). Consonant harmony and phonological underspecification in child speech. In M. Yavas (ed.) *First and second language phonology.* San Diego: Singular Publishing Group. 63–80.

Svantesson, J. O. (1985). Vowel harmony shift in Mongolian. *Lingua* 67. 283–329.

Tranel, B. (1987). *The sounds of French.* Cambridge: Cambridge University Press.

(1991). CVC light syllables, geminates and Moraic Theory. *Phonology* 8. 291–302.

(1995). French final consonants and nonlinear phonology. *Lingua* 95. 131–67.

Trigo, L. (1991). On pharynx–larynx interactions. *Phonology* 8. 113–36.

Trommelen, M. (1983). *The syllable in Dutch, with special reference to diminutive formation.* Dordrecht: Foris.

Trommelen, M. and W. Zonneveld (1999). Word-stress in West-Germanic languages: English. In van der Hulst (1999). 478–515.

Trubetzkoy, N. S. (1939). *Grundzüge der Phonologie*. Göttingen: Vandenhoek and Ruprecht. Translated 1969 by C. A. M. Baltaxe as *Principles of phonology*. Berkeley and Los Angeles: University of California Press.

Ultan, R. (1973). Some reflections on vowel harmony. *Working Papers on Language Universals* 12. 37–67.

Vago, R. (1973). Abstract vowel harmony systems in Uralic and Altaic languages. *Language* 49. 579–605.

(1976). More evidence for the feature [grave]. *Linguistic Inquiry* 7. 671–4.

(ed.) (1980). *Issues in vowel harmony*. Amsterdam: John Benjamins.

Vennemann, T. (1972). On the theory of syllabic phonology. *Linguistische Berichte* 18. 1–18.

(1988). *Preference laws for syllable structure and the explanation of sound change*. Berlin: Mouton de Gruyter.

Vennemann, T. and P. Ladefoged (1973). Phonetic features and phonological features. *Lingua* 32. 61–74.

Vergnaud, J.-R. and M. Halle (1978). Metrical structures in phonology. Ms., Massachusetts Institute of Technology.

Vihman, M. (1978). Consonant harmony: its scope and function in child language. In Greenberg (1978). 281–334.

Vijver, R. van de (1998). *The iambic issue: iambs as a result of constraint interaction*. Ph.D. dissertation, University of Leiden.

Visch, E. A. M. (1989). *A metrical theory of rhythmic stress phenomena*. Ph.D. dissertation, University of Utrecht.

Walsh Dickey, L. (1997). *The phonology of liquids*. Ph.D. dissertation, University of Massachusetts, Amherst.

Wang, W. S.-Y. (1968). Vowel features, paired variables, and the English vowel shift. *Language* 44. 695–708.

Weijer, J. van de (1994). *Segmental structure and complex segments*. Ph.D. dissertation, University of Leiden.

Wells, J. (1982). *Accents of English*. Vol. II: *The British Isles*. Cambridge: Cambridge University Press.

Wetzels, L. (1986). Phonological timing in Ancient Greek. In Wetzels and Sezer (1986). 297–344.

Wetzels, L. and E. Sezer (eds.) (1986). *Studies in compensatory lengthening*. Dordrecht: Foris.

Wilbur, R. B. (1990). Why syllables? What the notion means for ASL research. In S. Fischer and P. Siple (eds.) *Theoretical issues in sign language research*. Vol. I. Chicago: University of Chicago Press. 81–108.

(1993). Syllables and segments: hold the movement and move the holds! In G. Coulter (ed.) *Current issues in ASL phonology*. New York: Academic Press. 135–68.

Williamson, K. (1977). Multivalued features for consonants. *Language* 53. 843–71.

References

Wood, S. (1982). *X-ray and model studies of vowel articulation. Lund Working Papers in Linguistics* 23.

Yip, M. (1988). The OCP and phonological rules: a loss of identity. *Linguistic Inquiry* 19. 65–100.

(1989). Feature geometry and cooccurrence restrictions. *Phonology* 6. 349–74.

(1995). Tone in East Asian languages. In Goldsmith (1995). 476–94.

Zec, D. (1994). *Sonority constraints on prosodic structure.* New York: Garland.

(1995a). Sonority constraints on syllable structure. *Phonology* 12. 85–129.

(1995b). The role of moraic structure in the distribution of segments within syllables. In Durand and Katamba (1995). 149–79.

Zonneveld, W. (1993). Schwa, superheavies, stress and syllables in Dutch. *The Linguistic Review* 10. 59–110.

INDEX

Abercrombie D. 205, 205 n10
accent 196–7
  affixation 197–8, 209–10, 212
  bracketed metrical grid 203
  clashes 215, 218
  compounding 212–13
  culminativity 197 n2, 203
  cyclicity 216 n20
  demarcative function 197
  domains 197, 202
  English–Dutch comparison 237–41
  feet 202, 203, 207, 219
  focus 199–201
  lapses 218
  lexical accent languages 198, 211
  minimal pairs 213
  morphology 209–11, 214, 215–16, 216 n20
  non-primary 201–2, 204 n9, 213–16, 218
  phrasal accent 200, 202, 213, 214–15
  pitch peaks 199–200, 201
  primary 201–2, 207–13, 216–18, 222, 223
  quantity-sensitivity 223
  secondary (*see* accent: non-primary)
  stress shift 215, 218
  systems 221–8
    English–Dutch comparison 237–41
    fixed accent 197–8, 207–10
    free accent 198, 207, 208, 210–11
    unaccented syllables 197, 199, 200–1
  weight-sensitivity 133–5
  words 197–202, 207–13, 220–1
    grammatical 199, 200–1, 202
    monosyllabic 198
  see also metrical theory
adjacency 40
affixation 197–8, 209–10
  accent-attracting 212
  accent-bearing 212

accent-neutral 210, 212
  integrating 212
affricates 1–3, 10, 155, 155 n29
Aguacatec 233
Akan 19–20, 41
Allen, W. S. 19
Amele 233
Ancient Greek 171
Anderson, J. M. 13–14, 27, 45, 65 n12, 104 n30, 143 n24
Anderson, S. R. 34, 208
Apinayé 34–5
appendices (syllable structure) 136–7, 138–9
Arabic
  Cairene 229–30
  Classical 232–3
  Moroccan 189
Araucanian 222
Archangeli, D. 75, 77, 89, 91, 93, 94–6, 99–100
archiphonemes 43 n32
archisegments 43 n32
Árnason, K. 226
articulation
  articulator theory 22–3, 24, 60–3
  /h/ 27
  laterals 31–3
  manner 12
  place of articulation theory 22, 23, 26–7
  see also assimilation processes
articulatory phonology 51
aspiration 125–6
assimilation processes
  lateral 31–3
  nasal 3–6, 26–7, 30–1, 40, 43–4
  spreading 31, 33, 36, 40–2, 69–72
Australian languages 25

267

- 14th ICES
- HEC Kaye
- SAL
- Armbr
- Census
- 4th Cash-Om
- Bybu rev.

The Eth.
Originated
the Semites